Open Subjects

Edinburgh Critical Studies in Renaissance Culture

Series Editor: Lorna Hutson

Titles available in the series:

*Open Subjects: English Renaissance Republicans, Modern Selfhoods
and the Virtue of Vulnerability*
James Kuzner
978 0 7486 4253 3 Hbk

*The Phantom of Chance: From Fortune to Randomness in Seventeenth-
Century French Literature*
John D. Lyons
978 0 7486 4515 2 Hbk

Visit the Edinburgh Critical Studies in Renaissance Culture website at
www.euppublishing.com/series/ecsrc

Open Subjects

English Renaissance Republicans,
Modern Selfhoods, and the Virtue
of Vulnerability

James Kuzner

Edinburgh University Press

Edinburgh University Press Ltd
22 George Square, Edinburgh

www.euppublishing.com

Typeset in 10.5/13 Adobe Sabon
by Servis Filmsetting Ltd, Stockport, Cheshire, and
printed and bound in Great Britain by
CPI Antony Rowe, Chippenham and Eastbourne

A CIP record for this book is available from the British Library

ISBN 978 0 7486 4253 3 (hardback)

Contents

Acknowledgements

Many of the ideas in this book began to form during my years as a graduate student in the English department at Johns Hopkins University, where I had the good fortune of a superlative group of classmates and friends, including Matthew Taylor, Tara Bynum, Bryan Conn, Rachael Hoff, Claire Jarvis, Jason Hoppe, Andrew Sisson and Mark Noble. Among faculty at Hopkins, I would like to thank Amanda Anderson, Simon During, Frances Ferguson, Stephen Campbell, Gabrielle Spiegel and Paola Marrati; special thanks to Sharon Cameron, for teaching me how to read, and to two advisors, Richard Halpern and Jonathan Goldberg. I do not relish thinking of the form that this book might have assumed without their preternaturally generous help.

In their existence after Hopkins, the ideas of *Open Subjects* have taken shape in response to many perceptive audiences, among them ones at Wayne State, Alabama, Harvard and McGill, as well as ones at meetings of the Modern Language Association, the Shakespeare Association of America, the Group for Early Modern Cultural Studies and the Renaissance Society of America. Thanks to my former colleagues at Pomona College, for giving me a start, and to my current colleagues at Case Western Reserve University, who have supported my research and given me the sense of having made a good choice of vocation. I am grateful, too, to the journal editors who chose helpful readers and who have granted permission to reprint portions of this book. Part of Chapter 2 appeared as 'Unbuilding the City: *Coriolanus* and the Birth of Republican Rome', in *Shakespeare Quarterly*, vol. 58, issue 2, pages 174–99. Copyright 2007 Folger Shakespeare Library. Another part of that chapter, in very different form, will appear as '"And here's thy hand": *Titus Andronicus* in a Time of Terror', in *Shakespeare Yearbook* (as part of a 'Shakespeare after 9/11' critical roundtable, ed. Julia Lupton, 2010), forthcoming from the Edwin Mellen Press, Lewiston, NY. Part of Chapter 5 appeared as 'Habermas Goes to Hell: Pleasure,

Public Reason, and the Republicanism of *Paradise Lost*', in *Criticism: A Quarterly for Literature and the Arts*, vol. 51, issue 1, pages 105–45. Copyright 2009 Wayne State University Press.

For reading and responding to drafts of chapters (and, in some cases, to every chapter of the manuscript), I would like to thank J. K. Barrett, Sean Keilen, Marshall Brown, Victoria Kahn, Philip Lorenz, Rayna Kalas, Judith Anderson, Jonathan Crewe, Daniel Juan Gil, Lynn Enterline, Kathryn Schwarz, Bryan Lowrance, Curtis Perry, Lori Humphrey Newcomb, Sharon O'Dair, Julia Reinhard Lupton and Laurel Flinn. Aaron Kunin and Barbara Correll deserve a special mention here, not just as exemplary intellectuals but as exemplary friends; Bill Sherman, who has overseen my efforts since my days as an undergraduate, deserves the same. With respect to Edinburgh University Press, I am especially indebted to Lorna Hutson, whose enthusiastic support for and insight into the project helped bring it to completion; to two anonymous readers, whose thoughtful and encouraging reports came at an excellent moment; and to the Press's editors, whose timely, scrupulous attention has made publishing a pleasure.

In closing, I want to thank the members of my families in hemispheres both north and south, for their love and support. This book is for Jonathan and for Laurel; it would not have come to be without his refining fire or her kindly flame.

Series Editor's Preface

Edinburgh Critical Studies in Renaissance Culture may, as a series title, provoke some surprise. On the one hand, the choice of the word 'culture' (rather than, say, 'literature') suggests that writers in this series subscribe to the now widespread assumption that the 'literary' is not isolable, as a mode of signifying, from other signifying practices that make up what we call 'culture'. On the other hand, most of the critical work in English literary studies of the period 1500–1700 which endorses this idea has rejected the older identification of the period as 'the Renaissance', with its implicit homage to the myth of essential and universal Man coming to stand (in all his sovereign individuality) at the centre of a new world picture. In other words, the term 'culture' in the place of 'literature' leads us to expect the words 'early modern' in the place of 'Renaissance'. Why, then, 'Edinburgh Critical Studies in *Renaissance Culture*'?

The answer to that question lies at the heart of what distinguishes this critical series and defines its parameters. As Terence Cave has argued, the term 'early modern', though admirably egalitarian in conception, has had the unfortunate effect of essentialising the modern, that is, of positing 'the advent of a once-and-for-all modernity' which is the deictic 'here and now' from which we look back.[1] The phrase 'early modern', that is to say, forecloses the possibility of other modernities, other futures that might have arisen, narrowing the scope of what we may learn from the past by construing it as a narrative leading inevitably to Western modernity, to 'us'. *Edinburgh Critical Studies in Renaissance Culture* aims rather to shift the emphasis from a story of progress – early modern to modern – to series of critical encounters and conversations with the past, which may reveal to us some surprising alternatives buried within texts familiarly construed as episodes on the way to certain identifying features of our endlessly fascinating modernity. In keeping with one aspect of the etymology of 'Renaissance' or 'Rinascimento' as 'rebirth', moreover, this series features books that explore and interpret anew elements of the critical encounter between writers of the period 1500–1700 and texts of Greco-Roman literature, rhetoric, politics, law, oeconomics, *eros* and friendship.

The term 'culture', then, indicates a license to study and scrutinise objects other than literary ones, and to be more inclusive about both the forms and the material and political stakes of making meaning both in the past and in the present. 'Culture' permits a realisation of the benefits to be reaped after two decades of interdisciplinary enrichment in the arts. No longer are historians naïve about textual criticism, about rhetoric, literary theory or about readerships; likewise, literary critics trained in close reading now also turn easily to court archives, to legal texts, and to the historians' debates about the languages of political and religious thought. Social historians look at printed pamphlets with an eye for narrative structure; literary critics look at court records with awareness of the problems of authority, mediation and institutional procedure. Within these developments, modes of research that became unfashionable and discredited in the 1980s – for example, studies in classical or vernacular 'source texts', or studies of literary 'influence' across linguistic, confessional and geographical boundaries – have acquired a new critical edge and relevance as the convergence of the disciplines enables the unfolding of new cultural histories (that is to say, what was once studied merely as 'literary influence' may now be studied as a fraught cultural encounter). The term 'Renaissance' thus retains the relevance of the idea of consciousness and critique within these textual engagements of past and present, and, while it foregrounds the Western European experience, is intended to provoke comparativist study of wider global perspectives rather than to promote the 'universality' of a local, if far-reaching, historical phenomenon. Finally, as traditional pedagogic boundaries between 'Medieval' and 'Renaissance' are being called into question by cross disciplinary work emphasising the 'reformation' of social and cultural forms, so this series, while foregrounding the encounter with the classical past, is self-conscious about the ways in which that past is assimilated to the projects of Reformation and Counter-Reformation, spiritual, political and domestic, that finally transformed Christendom into Europe.

Individual books in this series vary in methodology and approach, sometimes blending the sensitivity of close literary analysis with incisive, informed and urgent theoretical argument, at other times offering critiques of grand narratives of the period by their work in manuscript transmission, or in the archives of legal, social and architectural history, or by social histories of gender and childhood. What all these books have in common, however, is the capacity to offer compelling, well-documented and lucidly written critical accounts of how writers and thinkers in the period 1500–1700 reshaped, transformed and critiqued the texts and practices of their world, prompting new perspectives on what we think we have learned from them.

Lorna Hutson

Note

1. Terence Cave, 'Locating the Early Modern', *Paragraph*, 29:1 (2006) 12–26, 14.

Introduction: Vulnerable Crests of Renaissance Selves

One of the first recorded English uses of 'vulnerable' comes from the mouth of Macbeth, in a famously erroneous claim to be *in*vulnerable: 'Let fall thy blade on vulnerable crests,' he tells Macduff, 'I bear a charmed life, which must not yield / To one of woman born' (V, vii, 40–2).[1] Here we see the culmination of Macbeth's extreme, alterable and now fatal reactions to his status as a mortal being. We have seen him strive to eliminate competitors for the throne, a striving that, after Duncan's death, gives rise to overpowering paranoia – a sense of utter exposure, of fatal trespass threatened upon his person. Macbeth enters a state in which 'every noise appalls' him; he becomes a being plunged into 'restless ecstasy', undone by the living and the dead, believing that 'every minute' of Banquo's very existence 'thrusts / Against my near'st of life' (II, ii, 56; III, ii, 22; III, i, 18–19). The whole of Macbeth's world – every image, every word, the mere fact that he occupies the same social field as Banquo – seems to expose him and to send him headlong toward his demise. Later in the play, Macbeth is mistakenly assured of his invincibility by an apparition (to whose mollifying words he, as with so much else, proves unhealthily susceptible). Suddenly, Macbeth becomes indifferent to the dangers that had overwhelmed him just moments before. Convinced that the boundaries shielding him cannot be pierced, he acts as though he is not of woman born – as though he is exempt from exposure to others, from the precarious quality that the play suggests is characteristic of human life.

Macbeth seeks to compensate for his vulnerability with self-defensive, self-aggrandising violence; in the end he gives himself over to death when he believes he can only give death to others. He never appreciates a telling ambivalence about vulnerability, one familiar to early modernity but supposedly obsolete now (or so states the *Oxford English Dictionary* (*OED*)): namely, that 'vulnerable' initially indicates not just what it does for Macbeth, 'susceptible of receiving wounds', but also 'wounding' or 'having power to wound'.[2] For Macbeth the question of vulnerability is either/or, absolute. Either he can wound or he can be wounded; he can either have total control over himself and his enemies or be controlled totally, obliterated by those enemies. He never imagines that he could inhabit a position at once exposed and liveable, nor, more crucially, that an acknowledgement and embrace of vulnerability as other than sheer weakness could serve as the path to a 'charmed life' other than the one he wishes to live.

Open Subjects explores the portrayal, in Renaissance texts as well as in classical and current political theory, of what Shakespeare seems to long for in *Macbeth* – a life far more open than the one that Macbeth himself seeks to make. The exploration finds its ground and its limits by placing these texts between two languages, one republican and the other radical, that are concerned with the self and with how we are oriented – how we can be averse but also attached – to our vulnerability. Studies of the republican legacy have proliferated in recent years,[3] always to advocate a republican self that grows increasingly invulnerable. This book, which focuses on works by Spenser, Shakespeare, Marvell and Milton, is the first to present a genealogy for the modern self in which its republican origins can be understood far more radically. In doing so, my study is also the first to draw radical and republican thought into sustained conversation, and to locate a republic for which shared vulnerability is essential. At a time when the drive to safeguard citizens has gathered enough momentum to justify almost any state action, *Open Subjects* asks whether vulnerability is the evil that we so often – less insanely than Macbeth but nevertheless deeply – believe it to be; and my position, which republican, radical and Renaissance texts have led me to adopt, is that it is not. For the balance of this Introduction I would like to specify the coordinates of the position and explain why I believe we ought to give it our regard.

Despite the complex, often contradictory nature of republican thought, it has been brought to bear on the present political moment mostly in order to illuminate and augment strains of thought that are either liberal or 'communitarian'. Both, I show in my first chapter, emphasise the potential of community to minimise vulnerability – usually through the provision of negative freedoms and positive liberties – and thus to foster selves who are bounded, discrete and delineated. This is true of work across various disciplines over the last several decades – in, for instance, the literary criticism of Annabel Patterson, David Norbrook and Andrew Hadfield; the historical work of J. G. A. Pocock, Quentin Skinner and Blair Worden; and political theory ranging from that of

Philip Pettit to that of Michael Sandel. When Norbrook approaches a play like *Macbeth*, to take our opening example, he thus focuses on a reinforced selfhood that would guard against vulnerability in a manner less lunatic than Macbeth's. Specifically, Norbrook finds in *Macbeth* a buried, ambivalent, yet recoverable investment in regicide and in a constitution that, providing individual protections and entitlements, recognises and safeguards selves as discrete entities.[4] From this perspective, the political interest of the play – and of other texts in the republican tradition – abides in this investment.

Such scholarship is not simply or straightforwardly mistaken. For instance, republican thinkers regularly invoke a 'mixed' constitution as a device that would protect citizens against arbitrary monarchical will and provide them with a role in a self-governing polity. Cicero does so in the classical period, as do early modern political thinkers ranging from Thomas Smith and George Buchanan to Marchamont Nedham and James Harrington. The oversight of recent work resides in the equation of republicans' opposition to political tyranny with their opposition to vulnerability as such – as if, say, defending rights against unwanted violence requires the complete rejection of susceptible forms of life. Contrary to recent studies of republicanism, I show how having a high estimate of vulnerability – so much so as to see virtue in it – is not opposed to, but rather is an important aspect of, the republican outlooks of several Romans who are critical to the English Renaissance, including Livy, Lucan and, most especially, Cicero himself.

For Cicero, as for many Renaissance figures, shared vulnerability is central to community's existence, as much what being together offers as what it rules out. From this perspective, the problem of vulnerability is not absolute; the problem, instead, is to distinguish when it is salutary from when it is genuinely pernicious. Spenser, Shakespeare, Marvell and Milton make a number of striking assumptions along these lines, most of which are recognisably republican. For many of us, the insertion of the self into social space ought to be innocuous; for them it is at once a dangerous and a potentially therapeutic exposure. We often assume that words cannot act like things, they that words can have direct, even magical bodily effects. If we tend to value speech that can disclose the self, they tend to value speech that transforms the self; and if we commonly think that friendship should fortify individual will, they commonly think that friendship tampers with it. The imaginative worlds in which such vulnerabilities accumulate, I show, are ones where what is inside and what is outside individual boundaries become inseparably, dynamically and sometimes even indistinguishably tied to each other, where individuals do not make connections so much as they become those connections. In these worlds, selves are opened up to a broad spectrum of the experience of vulnerability, from more mild forms – such as being captivated by another's seductive arguments, or sharing another's suffering – to more intense ones, such as draining the self of agency or allowing personal boundaries to be violated and changed.

In the eyes of most republican critics, historians and political philosophers, such a picture of selfhood may appear distinctly non-modern and even retrograde. Republican readings contrary to mine reinforce the commonplace notion, discussed in my first chapter, that the subject becomes modern by embracing possibilities, new in early modernity, for cultivating a deeper, well-protected interior. Historians of selfhood as disparate as Charles Taylor, Jerrold Seigel and Timothy Reiss, likewise, present pictures of a modern self whose boundaries become increasingly well fortified. These historians also share with 'republican' scholars in their counters to Stephen Greenblatt's famous argument in *Renaissance Self-Fashioning*, where becoming more bounded is indeed how we become modern but where personal boundaries look more like social impositions than achievements that secure individual autonomy.[5]

For all their differences, these accounts all regard bounded selfhood and modern selfhood as synonymous. In this, they narrow the field of possibilities within which early modern and modern selves move. Literary critics such as Margreta de Grazia, Gail Kern Paster and Cynthia Marshall have shown how constructs of bounded selfhood were far from pervasive within the early modern imagination,[6] and in *Open Subjects*, I show how this was also, differently and strikingly, true of English republicans. I show not only how possibilities for unguarded existence belong to the classical and Renaissance worlds, but also how, in altered forms, such possibilities are very much still with us – for instance, in the work of Jacques Derrida, Michel Foucault, Leo Bersani, Judith Butler, Jean-Luc Nancy, Georges Bataille and Giorgio Agamben. All are radical in a particular way, one derived from post-structural theory and to be distinguished, to greater or lesser degrees, from other radicalisms – such as, say, the left radical tradition in England and 'liberal' nineteenth-century radicalism. Derrida, Foucault and others adopt radical positions of particular interest here in that they argue for the impossibility of bounded selfhood and identify dangers that come from insisting – as a liberal, a communitarian, or otherwise – on bounded existence. All also find therapeutic and political value in being unbounded, whether by embracing human existence as one defined by a deep vulnerability to words, by taking on the (at times terrifying) openness of pure hospitality, or by seeking to become so exposed and so undone by being with others as to become utterly incapable of possessiveness. Strikingly, radical positions often share – and can always be placed in conversation – with republican ones.

To those for whom modern selves are bounded ones, unbounded selves belong to pre-modernity; but the binary does not hold. The extent to which I endorse Bruno Latour's notion that we have never been modern, in other words, is also the extent to which I advance Renaissance republican texts as opening routes to alternative modernities. *Open Subjects* argues that these texts speak to projects of modernity by belonging to what some would consign to the dark past of pre-modernity, and that grasping their political significance – not to mention the legacy of English republicanism – requires further appraisal of and appreciation for precisely this. With this in mind, allow me to explain how the chapters on Spenser, Shakespeare, Marvell and Milton pursue these trains of thought.

After a chapter that dilates on the above-mentioned contexts, I lay out a general theory of vulnerability by examining book IV of *The Faerie Queene* in dialogue with friendship discourse from the classical period to the present. I chart the capacity of friendship in Spenser's epic to shape selfhood – its ability both to respect and to strengthen the boundaries that are necessary for self-concern, as well as to ignore and erode those boundaries. Spenser puzzles over two rival views. The first follows a basic structure evident both in stories of friendship in the Renaissance and in contemporary politics of friendship, ranging from those of John Rawls to those of Hannah Arendt; here, initial acts of self-sacrifice, accompanied by renunciations of utility, lead to reinforced selfhood and satisfied self-interest. Spenser does at times endorse this structure, but he is also critical of what friendships that fit the structure so often require: an instrumental approach to the world and to others in it. Moreover, Spenser fully endorses relations wherein uselessness is truly assumed, relations – and republican life – wherein self-sufficiency allows for undoing. The strongest examples here can be found in Britomart's bed scene with Amoret in canto i and in her surrender to an already surrendered Artegall in canto vi. In the first scene, interior existence is emptied out in disorienting affective ecstasy; in the second, Spenser portrays the founding of the English nation itself to depend not on aggrandised subjects but on ones subject to a shared surrender that nullifies will entirely. In both scenes, Spenser constructs a politics of friendship founded not on disciplined self-fashioning but on the unfashioning of selves plunged into overpowering interaction – on a 'between' that is seen as salutary even as it can be incapacitating. Doing so, Spenser's thinking can be put beside friendship theory as old as that of Cicero and as new as that of Georges Bataille, Maurice Blanchot and Judith Butler. In radical and republican thought alike, to form the bonds of friendship – bonds that sustain community – means to give oneself over to susceptibility and to loss. The selves of greatest interest to both are those devoid of self-interest.

In my third chapter, I shift from Spenserian pastoral epic to the public square of Shakespeare's *Coriolanus* – where there are no happy endings, the notion of an integral self is drained of its utopian potential almost entirely, and the traditional notion of a bounded republican self is rejected utterly. In this chapter, I offer an alternative to those who have recuperated *Coriolanus* as a progressive document that charts the passage from models of absolute sovereignty to those that advocate self-sovereignty. Radical theory, I point out, has identified potential dangers in the notion of bounded selfhood central to republican arguments about the play; and in *Coriolanus*, Shakespeare builds many such dangers – for instance, those detailed in Agamben's accounts of the state of exception – into the very structure of the Roman republic. The play is not, I argue, a pro-republican or proto-liberal document. But we can still read it as a politically viable one, particularly if we look to Coriolanus himself, a figure for extreme practices of self-undoing that could point the way out of the state of exception and into a 'world elsewhere', one that is specifically sexual and that lends itself to the work of Leo Bersani. *Coriolanus* is, thus, flagrantly anti-republican in its radicalism – in its attitude to the liberating potential of republican government and in its advocacy of sexual undoing wholly other to republican theory. While the Spenser chapter attends to the intersection between the republican and the radical, then, Shakespeare's last Roman play suggests a disjunction between the two. *Titus Andronicus*, however, complicates Shakespeare's attitude toward republicanism and toward forms of open selfhood. In *Titus*, Shakespeare advocates an intersubjective openness which resembles that advocated in Cicero and Livy in the classical period and, more recently, in Habermas's later work – openness that is not as total as that of Coriolanus but that might well have saved him. Taken together, *Titus* and *Coriolanus* help us to conceive of theorists such as Bersani and Habermas as supplements to each other. While we tend to think of the two as irreconcilable, *Titus* and *Coriolanus* prompt us to abandon this idea, on the grounds that, until we do, the embrace of open selfhood cannot last.

My chapters on Spenser and Shakespeare describe the fundamentally precarious nature of social being – and suggest a politics of friendship that acknowledges and even embraces that nature. Implicit but mostly unexplored in these chapters is how susceptibility is often specifically linguistic, underwritten by assumptions about what words can and should be used to do. If Chapters 2 and 3 focus on how far vulnerability can be taken without leading to ruin, my last two chapters focus on how we can use language to keep vulnerability salutary. Chapter 4, which focuses on Andrew Marvell, begins by noting that most republican criticism, mistakenly, advances his Protestantism as a way to progress beyond atavistic, harmful forms of open being and linguistic naiveté understood as Catholic. When republican critics read Marvell, Catholicism functions mainly as a figure for tyrannical government and unclear, coercive language, for societies in which subjects are, lamentably, accorded only the most flimsy of fortifications against dangerous words. I argue against this critical tendency, locating moments in Marvell's poetry, primarily his 'Upon Appleton House', that offer positive figurations of Catholic or 'transubstantial' speech – which, in the seventeenth century, could refer to any language that failed to distinguish between word and world, and so displayed a heightened sense as to how words affect things. Much of 'Appleton House', I argue, embraces this vulnerability – in its depiction of the force of the nuns' smooth tongues, of the speaker's world-creating, mosaic language, and of the words that transubstantiate him into the objects of Nunappleton. Marvell's poem loses its sense of sovereign selfhood in favour of being open to an incredible, even magical shaping power of language, a power that – as Butler points out in the domain of theory – continues to occupy a prominent cultural position and that in Lucan's *Pharsalia* is critical to the survival of republican culture. One aspect of this linguistic magic, I show, is to change boundaries from structures that separate things into structures that bind them together, and I end by showing how, in questioning the very ontology of boundaries, Marvell questions temporal separations as well. He thus suggests an accommodating view of the speaking subject's development, a history of selfhood which would not insist that the presence of personal frontiers depends on the eradication of transubstantiality, one which would not assume that being modern – or republican – means being invulnerable to words.

If the Marvell chapter suggests limits in the view that attaches critical distance to modernity and linguistic vulnerability to an atavistic past, my final chapter shows how *Paradise Lost* imagines spaces for critical, yet susceptible subjects. I show this through the lens of public sphere theory, especially that of Cicero, Milton, Habermas and Foucault. Milton has often been considered in early Habermasian terms that are then labelled republican; in such readings, if Miltonic subjects develop a public comportment defined by strict, uncompromising critical discipline, they make themselves essentially unsusceptible to passion and can participate in ideal, coercion-free debate. But such readings, if not unfounded, are also not exhaustive. I argue that Milton's portrayals of Paradise and Pandemonium find value in coupling rational argument and sensual embrace, in the pleasures of public argument, and in the enjoyable, transitory world made by vulnerable subjects within conversation's space. For this reason, I discuss *Paradise Lost* in late Foucaultian terms, ones that mingle pleasure with critique and that aim first not at uncoerced consensus but at immediate enjoyment. In his representations of the fallen angels and of the fall of Adam and Eve, Milton explores what can constitute a 'public', and in doing so he attends to interactions defined by a blending of ostensibly public and private spaces and behaviours – gardens and coffeehouses, the giving of reasons and the taking of pleasures – whose separation allows for the emergence of the modern, public self in the early Habermasian framework. By instead emphasising the hybridity of rational delight, Milton not only anticipates Foucault but also follows Ciceronian thought about the public subject. And since to be republican – for Milton and Cicero alike – was often to lack a republic, being republican often meant being taken in by visions of the transitory worlds that are made, and exist, in conversation and nowhere else. So while my first chapter shows how republics depend on shared vulnerability for their advent, my last looks at the forms that vulnerability can assume in the absence of those republics.

At the threshold of the Enlightenment in which the bounded self supposedly emerges, Milton's epic displays how the paths we make to modernity – the histories of modern, republican selfhood – are multiple; one attractive path, *Paradise Lost* suggests, leads not to the elimination but to the recovery of hybrid, vulnerable spaces and ways of being in the world. In an epilogue to the book, I end with an observation which stems from this: that the path to any desirable future for open selfhood must mirror the fleeting, precarious and contingent joys so far offered by vulnerable experience. This fact is not to be regretted, since the very existence of such a future for vulnerability demands that it – and we – remain precarious.

Notes

1. All references are to Eugene M. Waith (ed.), *The Tragedy of Macbeth* (New Haven, CT: Yale University Press, 1954).
2. Below are the first two entries from the *OED Online* (Oxford University Press, 2007):

    1. Having power to wound; wounding. Obs.1
    1609 Ambassy Sir R. Sherley 13 The male children practise to ride greate horses, to throw the Vulnerable and Ineuitable darte.

      2. a. That may be wounded; susceptible of receiving wounds or physical injury.

3. This fact will be made evident throughout this book, often with reference to work published within the last few years. For an exhaustive list that details just how fascinated early modernists have become with republicanism in recent decades, see Reid Barbour's bibliographical essay, 'Recent Studies in Seventeenth-Century Literary Republicanism', *English Literary Renaissance* 34 (2004), 387–417.

4. See Norbrook's '*Macbeth* and the Politics of Historiography', 78–116, in Kevin Sharpe and Steven N. Zwicker (eds), *Politics of Discourse* (Berkeley, CA: University of California Press, 1987).

5. *Renaissance Self-Fashioning: From More to Shakespeare* (Chicago: University of Chicago Press, 1980). Greenblatt emphasises how, for each emergent possibility that seems to offer autonomy, there exists a counter-movement that impinges on the self, a potential for negative experiences of susceptibility to social structures (1–2).

6. See Paster, *Humoring the Body: Emotions and the Shakespearean Stage* (Chicago: University of Chicago Press, 2004); Marshall, *The Shattering of the Self: Violence Subjectivity, and Early Modern Texts* (Baltimore: Johns Hopkins University Press, 2002), 20, 53; and de Grazia, 'The Ideology of Superfluous Things: *King Lear* as Period Piece', in de Grazia, Maureen Quilligan and Peter Stallybrass (eds), *Subject and Object in Renaissance Culture* (Cambridge: Cambridge University Press, 1996), 17–42. For a critique of Paster's position, one that focuses on the practices of the self that emphasise the careful, disciplined calibration of processes of ingestion and excretion, see Michael Schoenfeldt, *Bodies and Selves in Early Modern England: Physiology and Inwardness in Spenser, Shakespeare, Herbert, and Milton* (Cambridge: Cambridge University Press, 1999). For a fascinating dialogue about psychoanalysis and early modern structures of selfhood, see Lynn Enterline and David Hillman, 'Other Selves, Other Bodies', *Shakespeare Studies* 33 (2005), 62–72.

Chapter 1

Legacies of Republicanism, Histories of the Self

This chapter gives the background against which the ideas of *Open Subjects* come into focus. I look at how we presently view two connected topics: the legacy of early modern republicanism and the history of modern selfhood. The view established, I then explore how we might begin to re-orient our perspectives, and describe the forms of life that appear when we do so.

Open Subjects and the English Republican Legacy

I have said that one critical tradition to which *Open Subjects* offers an alternative could be called 'republican'. I have also said that the alternative that I present is itself republican. The question of Spenser, Shakespeare, Marvell and Milton's republicanism – its facets as well as its legacy – arises time and again in this book, and I want to be up front in explaining this ostensible paradox. Many dimensions of republican thought emerge over the course of my analysis, but I can also put my point about such thought fairly simply: whereas republican figures are usually understood to regard vulnerability as that which community ought to minimise, I show how these figures also embrace vulnerability as that which community has to offer.

The question of what qualifies as 'republican' is a difficult one. Of republicanism, John Adams writes that '[t]here is not a more unintelligible word in the English language.'[1] Hyperbolic as that statement might be, Jonathan Scott rightly points out that republicans, especially of the English variety, struggled to develop a shared sense as to whether republican thought entailed a specific constitutional prescription, a way of life or a general attitude toward the world, or whether it might instead be no more than 'a series of rhetorical or polemical postures'.[2] As J. G. A. Pocock puts it, with some exceptions 'republicanism in England was a language, not a programme.' And the language itself was exceedingly complex.[3] A major pitfall, David Wootton claims, is thus of taking 'this unintelligible word too much for granted'.[4] Wootton does not actually regard the word as unintelligible, but rather believes it to be incredibly complex. The study of republicanism remains incomplete unless and until we examine the complexity in its entirety, and for Wootton, this undertaking is without discernible end.

Nevertheless, recent studies of republicanism have advanced the undertaking, expanding the temporal and substantive dimensions of the 'republican'. For example, whereas some studies claim that in England, republican thought is of minimal visibility prior to the 1640s, Markku Peltonen has shown how many sixteenth- and early seventeenth-century thinkers advocated crucial components of later republican theory, such as freedom from tyranny, civic duty and the *vita activa* more generally.[5] Within literary studies, Annabel Patterson, Andrew Hadfield and Patrick Cheney have tracked the re-formulation of these classical ideals in the work of figures writing prior to 1640, including Spenser, Marlowe and Shakespeare.[6]

If such studies have expanded our sense of when republicanism becomes thinkable in England, recent research has also expanded our sense of what counts as 'republican'. While many studies have assumed that what counts must, if nothing else, emanate from a resolutely anti-monarchical frame of mind,[7] works by Patrick Collinson, Alan Cromartie and Victoria Kahn have offered compelling arguments that in early modernity the terms 'republic' and 'monarchy' – and all that we attach to both – are hardly mutually exclusive. For Collinson, this has meant thinking through the coexistence of, say, Elizabeth's reign and places such as Swallowfield; for Swallowfield, Collinson points out, was effectively a self-governing republic.[8] Cromartie, in a similar vein, has argued that even as emphasis in England shifted from personal to rule-bound monarchy – even as popular consent gained momentum as the criterion of legitimacy, much as it would from the 1640s onward – monarchy itself grew increasingly revered in the English imagination.[9] Collinson and Cromartie demonstrate the complementarity of monarchy and republican concepts of consent and self-government, and if they have shown how concepts thought incompatible with monarchy are not so, Kahn, for her part, has done the reverse, showing how republicanism is compatible with concepts typically linked not just to monarchy but even to tyranny. Kahn has, for instance, detailed how Machiavelli invokes Roman figures such as Brutus to demonstrate unlikely affinities between self-government and the use of force and fraud.[10]

In suggesting that English republicanism does not coincide with the mid-seventeenth-century monarchical collapse, the studies just mentioned have drawn attention to what can be gained by a broadening of scope. One might object at this point that the net effect of this tendency in recent studies has been to render the republican so expansive as to drain the term of meaning, or to make of 'republicanism' for us what it once was for John Adams. One could argue that republicanism in these accounts becomes indistinguishable from classical humanism, or, ultimately, that it comes to seem like a synonym for 'early modern politics'.

But to do so would be to overstate the case. It will be clear that I agree that republican thought is not always anti-monarchical, for example, but it is always anti-absolutist; it may, similarly, not be altogether opposed to force and fraud, but it is opposed to the unfettered, arbitrary will of the sovereign. 'Republicanism', in England, is not meaningless or unintelligible. Nor is it hopelessly capacious. Indeed, the term's capaciousness is one of its great virtues, for the depth and complexity of republican writing derives precisely from this openness, from its many attempts to think through the quintessentially republican concern of how we might form political communities – and cultivate individual attitudes – so as to minimise the evils of tyranny and arbitrary violence. All figures discussed here add richness to the body of republican thought in their efforts to further this conversation. The fact that not all those labelled republican are staunchly against monarchy thus seems less important than the possibilities that they open for political thought.

Open Subjects explores one such possibility: that of how we think about vulnerability. I make no pretence to having the last word on English republicanism, let alone on republican thought as such. Simply but not unimportantly, I call into question the aspect of republican thought that I mentioned above and that has, I believe, been taken too much for granted: that when it comes to our susceptibility as mortal creatures, republics exist only as bulwarks against such susceptibility. Most of those interested in republicanism assume this to be so, not just literary critics – who I cover elsewhere in this book – but also most prominent historians and political theorists. For most, English republicanism comes into being for the reason supplied by Pocock, because 'Englishmen were neither willing nor necessitated to define themselves as naked before *fortuna*' – and because they, 'in a moment from which only *virtu* could save them', refused to remain vulnerable to fortune's 'mindless force', wishing instead to reconstitute a stable polity.[11] The notion that vulnerability is only an enemy to the polity has proven so powerful as to have been adopted by scholars writing from both sides of what Scott takes to be the great divide in work on republicanism: the divide that separates those for whom republican thought is an 'analysis of liberty' and those for whom it is a more civic-minded 'politics of virtue'.[12]

When scholars see liberty at the core of republican thought, they tend to focus on what Quentin Skinner has called the 'neo-Roman' theory of freedom as non-domination. Skinner explains that while most political thinkers believe that the state should 'respect and preserve the liberty of its individual citizens', this liberty is conceived in radically different ways.[13] In one conception, which Skinner ascribes to Isaiah Berlin and which he believes is now dominant, government should merely ensure 'that its citizens do not suffer any unjust or unnecessary interference in the pursuit of their chosen goals' (119). Liberty thus conceived, Skinner points out, is compatible not only with monarchy but even with absolutism; for a monarch might retain the power to interfere in his subjects' lives, but as long as he refrains from doing so, liberty in this framework still exists.

For classical and early modern republicans, by contrast, such liberty is insufficiently robust. Rather than merely being free from 'unjust or unnecessary interference', to enjoy republican liberty individuals must be freed from the very threat of arbitrary interference. Skinner shows how, from Cicero and Sallust into the English Civil War and beyond, republicans insist that simply to be subject to the arbitrary will of another is to be in a state of subjection.[14] The subjection exists whether or not the will is exercised.

To be so dominated enervates and drains both subjects and, by extension, their republics. As Skinner puts it, 'servitude breeds servility,'[15] for 'if you live at the mercy of someone else',

> you will always have the strongest motives for playing safe. There will be many choices, in other words, that you will be disposed to avoid, and many others that you will be disposed to make, and the cumulative effect will be to place extensive restraints on your freedom of action. (213–14)

By weakening its people, rendering them passive and fearful, the republic is itself weakened. Skinner writes that 'no deeds of manly courage or great heartedness can be expected from such abject peoples . . . Nor can they be expected to benefit themselves and their country by winning great fortunes.'[16] At the heart of republican thinking, Skinner argues in a recent two-volume study of its European forms, are thus antimonarchism, freedom from the possibility of arbitrary interference – or freedom as 'non-domination' – and governmental structures most likely to limit such interference.[17]

When the theory of freedom as non-domination is approached from the perspective of explicit political advocacy,[18] vulnerability's status becomes very clear. Philip Pettit, for example, argues that individuals have a serious grievance when they are free from actual unjust interference but not from the threat of it. Such a grievance is that

> expressed by the wife who finds herself in a position where her husband can beat her at will, and without any possibility of redress; by the employee who dare not raise a complaint against an employer, and who is vulnerable to any of a range of abuses, some petty, some serious, that the employer may choose to perpetrate . . . and by the welfare dependant who finds that they are vulnerable to the caprice of a counter clerk for whether or not their children will receive meal vouchers.[19]

Drawing on the neo-Roman framework, Pettit believes that although '[c]ontemporary thought suggests that individuals in these positions retain their freedom to the extent that they are not actively coerced or obstructed,' they are not fully free: '[t]hey live in the shadow of the other's presence, even if no arm is raised against them.' They are, as Pettit puts it, 'demeaned by their vulnerability' (5). As for the 'servile' subject described by Skinner, vulnerability humiliates and disables the self. Only by securing a state of non-domination can demeaned subjects renovate their self-images; self-image improves as republican autonomy takes root. In a similar account, John W. Maynor writes that the health of civil society itself depends on non-domination: 'agents who experience a decrease in their vulnerability to arbitrary interference from others' will 'feel confident of their status', and only then will they be 'able to extend a degree of trust and civility toward other nondominating agents' and, thus, help maintain a well-functioning social world.[20]

For Skinner, Pettit and Maynor, the great insight of republican thought resides in its defence of robust and fundamental individual freedom. They describe the benefits that arrive when we believe ourselves to be bounded centres of freely willed decision. They also specify negative effects that can come from being susceptible to the arbitrary will of someone else. In attending almost solely to vulnerability's negative aspects, however – how it can be exploited to humiliate, demean and so on – neo-Romans, like Macbeth in the example with which this book began, regard the question of vulnerability as all or nothing. Skinner, Pettit and Maynor assume that whenever you are vulnerable, the threat of a hand raised against you is present – cripplingly, unforgettably so; and society, for them, crumbles accordingly. Thinking in this fashion, all three neglect how for many republicans – including Cicero himself – republican protection against unwanted vulnerability coexists with, opens the possibility for, and even depends on the exposure of vulnerability's more positive, desirable and useful forms.

'Neo-Romans' attend most to how republican thought yields a deeper, more comprehensive, or at least more fundamental freedom – how it might allow us to feel and to be self-directed in the ways that count. But historians and political theorists of other stripes direct their attention elsewhere. They hone in on how republican forms of life demand the subordination of the self that is driven by discrete, private interests to the self that is devoted to civic virtue and to the public good. From this perspective, the pre-eminent freedom is not freedom from the threat of arbitrary interference – the freedom which John Stuart Mill would later call 'pursuing our own good in our own way' and the only freedom deserving of the name[21] – but rather the freedom to participate in government, to exercise political liberty.

This freedom might in fact curb personal liberty and leave individuals open to arbitrary interference. As Charles Taylor puts it, such freedom merely yields the 'sense of having a say in decisions in the political domain, which would shape everyone's lives'.[22] Numerous historians have located a tendency in English republicans to emphasise civic virtue that trumps the right to self-propriety. Among them are Scott (who sees republicans opposing private interest politics 'on behalf of the publicly interested virtues of a self-governing civic community');[23] Gordon Wood (for whom, in Wootton's phrase, 'the essence of republicanism is virtue,' its antithesis being self-interest);[24] and Blair Worden (who argues that all republicans 'connected both liberty and virtue with the subordination of private interest to the public good').[25]

Finding as much or more value in what is public and shared as in what is private and individual – in 'freedom to' rather than 'freedom from' – these historians share with political philosophers who take recourse to republican theory and have affinities with the programme known as 'communitarianism', a strand of thinking about the republican legacy that has been developed by figures such as Taylor, Michael Sandel, Michael Walzer and Alasdair MacIntyre. Communitarians, like the historians just mentioned, employ republican thought very differently than do neo-Romans, and the chief difference is this: if neo-Romans critique liberal conceptions for offering autonomy that is not robust enough, communitarians critique such conceptions from the opposite direction, claiming that liberals aspire toward freedom that is unreasonably thoroughgoing.

Sandel, for instance, writes that 'the liberal conception of citizens as freely choosing, independent selves, unencumbered by moral or civic ties antecedent to choice' is untenable because it 'cannot account for a wide range of moral and political obligations that we commonly recognize'.[26] Our lives, put in terms used by neo-Romans, are full of interference, some of which is unnecessary and possibly even arbitrary. But for Sandel this is not always only a bad thing. If we insist 'that we are bound only by ends and roles that we choose for ourselves', we must deny 'that we can ever be claimed by ends we have not chosen – ends given by nature or God, for example, or by our identities as members of families, peoples, cultures, or traditions' (27). To deny bonds antecedent to choice is to act contrary to life as it is – and ought to be – lived; in a flourishing republic of interdependent individuals, we are chosen as much as we choose, claimed as much as we claim.

Taylor, similarly, shows how the claims of republican community are tolerable only for selves who reject the atomism at times presupposed by both liberals and neo-Romans. For republican ideals of civic virtue to flourish, we must attribute deep value to shared existence – to will that is overlapping rather than discrete and delineated, to 'we-identities' rather than merely 'I' identities, and to common goods irreducible to an aggregate of our interests as individuals. Only then can Sandel's vision of an ideal republic have genuine appeal.[27]

Like *Open Subjects*, these studies of the republican legacy de-emphasise notions of selfhood as bounded, discrete and delineated. The present study might even be said to develop the communitarian premise that 'sharing itself is of value.'[28] Where I differ from Sandel and Taylor resides, partly, in how we justify the value of sharing and the abandonment of resolutely bounded selfhood. Taylor's thought I return to below. As for Sandel, he makes the case for civic engagement largely on the grounds that liberty depends on it: '[t]he public philosophy by which we live', Sandel avers, 'cannot secure the liberty it promises, because it cannot inspire the sense of community and civic engagement that liberty requires.'[29] The problem with atomistic thinking that Sandel identifies, in other words, is that such thinking misses the fact that liberty needs civic virtue in order to exist, not that it misses out on experiences of being-with that are of intrinsic value (which is very much the claim of *Open Subjects*). For Sandel, atomism falls short by failing to make good on its promise of autonomy: '[l]iberated though we may be from the burden of identities we have not chosen, entitled though we may be to the range of rights', Sandel writes, 'we find ourselves overwhelmed as we turn to face the world on our resources' (29). Atomistic selves of the contemporary liberal state wish to be protected and free but find that they are isolated, overwhelmed, utterly susceptible to the outside of self.

Sandel justifies the need for communitarian thinking, then, not simply or even primarily on the grounds that 'sharing itself is of value,' as Taylor believes, but through a claim for the liberty that civic engagement might secure.[30] The difference between the neo-Roman Pettit and the communitarian Sandel is not primarily about whether the claims and pull of community – and the openness that this entails – should supersede the claims of the individual. The difference between the two is primarily about identifying a feasible degree of autonomy and discerning how to obtain it, about whether we should proliferate rights so as to secure legal freedom from arbitrary interference, or should focus instead on the freedoms of civic engagement. In either case, the ultimate end is being invested with some measure of individual autonomy; the ultimate evil is being demeaned by vulnerability, feeling overwhelmed by the world.

In this study, I focus on how classical and English Renaissance republicans often espouse a very different set of values and priorities than those laid out by neo-Romans and communitarians. But neither school of thought, I want to emphasise, is wrong to see – or to value – the idea that certain vulnerabilities are precisely what republican structures ought to eliminate.

Many English republicans do, for instance, sometimes regard citizen safety as the republic's primary reason for being. This is true of sixteenth-century figures like Thomas Smith, for whom people come together into a commonwealth 'for the conservation of themselves aswell in peace as in warre';[31] Interregnum personalities such as Marchamont Nedham, who writes that the first end 'of all civic communion' is 'public safety';[32] and Restoration republicans like Algernon Sidney, who imagines community as a kind of protective social clothing.[33] There are, as well, moments when English republicans write of vulnerability in nightmarish terms that resemble those employed by Pettit. Shortly after the execution of Charles I, Nedham argues against the return of monarchy on the grounds that '[i]f now we have burdens, we must then look to have furrows made upon our backs. If now we are through necessity put to endure a few whips, we shall then of set purpose be chastised with scorpions.'[34]

Further support for neo-Roman and communitarian visions of republicanism can be found in the fact that republics often are, from this perspective, designed to protect citizens by way of a mixed constitution, one that would ensure balance between the interests of the one, the few and the many. Such a constitution would supply some measure of both 'communitarian' freedom to participate (or at least to be represented) in a self-governing polity, as well as 'neo-Roman' freedom from arbitrary will – freedom that, in Sidney's words, protects selves from 'subjection to the fluctuating and irregular will of a man'.[35] When Nedham invokes Sallust, similarly, it is to support the idea that 'though there may sometimes happen a good king that will not make use of it [arbitrary power] to their prejudice, yet even then the people are not safe because . . . it is in his power to be wicked if he please.'[36] Viewed from this perspective, the threat of having our vulnerability exposed is ever-present – and republican checks against it are all-important. Absolute monarchies are politically unpalatable because they offer no safeguards; they leave the citizenry open to a king's potential or realised wickedness.

According to many sixteenth- and seventeenth-century republicans, people are vulnerable to the king because the king, being but a man, is himself vulnerable, especially to his own passions. This fact, unfortunate but undeniable, leads to a tyranny that begins within the person of the king and that, if unchecked, spreads through his kingdom. An early Scottish republican, George Buchanan, believes that any monarch's affective vulnerability renders him unfit for absolute rule: 'because we fear he be not firme enough against inordinat affections, which may, and for the most part use to decline men from truth', Buchanan writes, 'we shall adjoyn to him the Law, as it were a Colleague, or rather a bridler of his lusts.'[37] Kings must be attached to and bolstered by bodies of law that exceed them and that they cannot alter according to whim. Otherwise, as Sidney would point out a century later, the fluctuations of a single self will be mirrored in commonwealths themselves: kingdoms headed by an absolute monarch 'may have their ebbings and flowings according the virtues or vices of princes or their favourites; but can never have any stability, because there is, and can be none in them'.[38]

Selves are vulnerable in constitution, incapable, on their own, of fully mastering either the passions threatening to undo them from within or the violence threatening from without. One republican response to this fact is to say that selves must be inserted into, and protected by, structures that offer stability, that neutralise unruly passions and the pernicious, tyrannical actions to which they lead. Thus James Harrington dreamt of men who, 'infused' into a body politic, would be 'refined or made incapable of passion'.[39] Harrington famously concludes that a just polity can only be ensured by the proper constitution:

> 'Give us good men and they will make us good laws' is the maxim of a demagogue, and (through the alteration which is commonly perceivable in men, when they have power to work their own wills) exceeding fallible. But 'give us good orders, and they will make us good men' is the maxim of a legislator and the most infallible in politics.[40]

From this perspective, vulnerability seems inimical to, perhaps even appears as the other of, republican community. When absolutism – or mob rule, or oligarchy – takes hold, vulnerability is everywhere exposed, every inch of the body politic open to assault.

But republican attitudes – including the attitudes of some of those just mentioned – are not so simple. That republicans uniformly oppose the exposure of subjects to a tyrant's arbitrary will, for example, does not entail their opposition to the vulnerability of subjects as such. In fact, much republican thinking regards certain vulnerabilities as of inestimable personal and political value. As will become clear, this point is most evident when we focus not only on republican constitutions but also on how republicans are constituted, not only on stances toward law – toward negative freedoms and positive liberties aimed at minimising vulnerability – but also on republican outlooks, the attitudes toward social existence that define republican selves in an everyday sense. Individual chapters show that this is so for Spenser, Shakespeare, Milton and Marvell, all of whom have been labelled republican; and it is certainly so for a classical republican who is prominent in the following chapters, who had a serious influence on early modern political thought,[41] and who all of the figures treated here would have known well:[42] the Roman Marcus Tullius Cicero.

Skinner rightly sees Cicero valuing non-domination in the *Philippics*. But if Cicero was concerned about what might be done to him in the absence of legal protection, the project of his political writings is not to eliminate vulnerability from the polis. As Cicero understands them, republics both must make peace with, and even recognise their dependence on, vulnerability of various kinds.

First of all, Cicero points out that susceptibility – to change, decay and transformation that one does not will – cannot be eliminated, whatever we might wish. Developing the Polybian theory of anacyclosis, Cicero details its pertinence to governmental structures as to selves. In *On the Commonwealth*, Cicero writes that '[a]nything that is too successful – in weather, or harvests, or human bodies – generally turns into its opposite, and that is particularly true of commonwealths . . . No form of government is maintained for very long.'[43] In the English republican context, too, the mutability of states is often – if not always – understood to be intractable – for example, when Thomas Smith writes of man's body and the body politic as coequals, the nature of both being 'never to stand still in one maner of estate, but to grow from the lesse to the more, and decay from the more againe to the lesse, till it come to the fatall end and destruction';[44] or when Nedham writes that '[n]or are the huge bodies of commonwealths exempted from the same fate with plants, brutes, men, and other petty individuals,' for whom 'the second moment of their perfection [is] the first toward their dissolution.'[45]

For all that Cicero and English republicans who share with him advocate a mixed constitution, the spirit of government is as important as its form, since at any moment the form might mutate. Cicero, like most republicans, endorses a mixed state, but also claims that of the three types of government, 'any one, even though it may not be perfect or in my opinion the best possible, still is tolerable as long as it holds to the bond which first bound men together.'[46] For the government that preserves the bond is bound to change; in fact, the more successful the preserver is – the more immutable it seems – the more likely change becomes.

To discern the animating spirit of the ideal Ciceronian republic, then, we would do well to look elsewhere than to the set of laws and fixed structures that would guarantee specific degrees of negative freedom and positive liberty. We might instead look to 'the bond which first bound men together', the root causes of community. According to Cicero, '[t]he first cause of assembly' is not necessity or fear – fear of having vulnerability exposed, possessions unprotected, or individual interests ignored; community begins, rather, 'as a kind of natural herding together of men' (18). The human race, 'not isolated or prone to wandering alone . . . is so created that not even in an abundance of everything <do men wish to live a solitary existence>' (18). Making a similar point much later, George Buchanan would actually oppose man's desire to protect private interests and his desire for community. Whereas '[u]tility indeed to some seems to be very efficacious, both in begetting and conserving the publick society of mankind', Buchanan argues, 'there is a far more venerable, or ancient cause of mens associating, and a more antecedaneous & sacred bond of their civil community.'[47] The desire to protect private interest cannot be what gives rise to civil association, because 'if every one would have a regard to this own private advantage, then surely that very utility would rather dissolve than unite humane society together' (12). Buchanan does not just posit a tension between the self's pursuit of self-interest and its belonging to community; he regards the two as mutually exclusive. Men flock together, as they do for Cicero, by an instinct outside individual interest, one 'by nature so deeply rooted in man, that if any one had the affluence of all things . . . yet he will think his life unpleasant without humane converse' (12).

Human beings share with animals this impulse to 'herd' together. What separates them, for Cicero, is that the impulse originates in reason. Reason's operation is worth pausing over, as it clarifies the place of vulnerability in the bonds of Ciceronian community:

> The intellect is, as it were, keen-sighted in its ability to grasp the causes and effects of things, to compare similarities, to combine different items together, and to connect the future with the present, comprehending the whole course of a subsequent life. The same power of reason makes people want each

other's company and has produced a natural congruence of language and behaviour. Beginning with the bonds of affection between family and friends, we are prompted to move gradually further out and associate ourselves firstly with our fellow citizens and then with every person on earth. As Plato wrote to Archytas, we bear in mind that we are born not just for ourselves but for our country and our people, so much so that only a small fraction of us remains for ourselves.[48]

Several dimensions of Ciceronian reason stand out here. All stand in contrast to republican reason as described by many of the literary critics and historians of republicanism invoked in these pages. First, reason is not the faculty by which the self separates and distinguishes things – subjects and objects, past and present – from each other, thereby achieving a measure of critical distance. Here Cicero views reason as that which combines, connects and comprehends, as that which draws together. Second, Cicero does not oppose reason to passion or desire but posits reason as the wellspring of both; reason generates the desire for company and for affective ties. In this Cicero is unlike, say, Harrington, and contradicts the Stoic precepts that he elsewhere holds. Third, as reason extends bonds of affection ever outward, rather than fuel self-concern it drains the self of all but a fraction of that concern. Community forms out of a natural, rational impulse, and for Cicero, to be rational is to desire a belonging that depletes our ability to be possessive individuals. (In this, Cicero does share with Harrington, for whom, if 'reason be nothing else but interest,' 'the interest of mankind be the right interest.')[49] Lastly, since selves do not seek community for the sake of protection or entitlement, reason does not prompt them to focus, first and foremost, on securing the kinds of negative freedoms and positive liberties that neo-Romans and communitarians place at the republican core.

Quite the contrary: for Cicero, political belonging often means placing oneself at greater risk. Since reason binds things together instead of separating them, being 'rational' means being bound – and thus opened up – to others. The Ciceronian self, with so little of itself withheld, embraces that openness even when it means being imperilled. 'Nature', Cicero writes, 'has given men such a need for virtue and such a desire to defend the common safety that this force has overcome all the enticements of pleasure and ease';[50] of himself, Cicero writes (truthfully or not) that 'I did not hesitate to subject myself to the greatest tempests, even thunderbolts, of fate for the sake of saving my fellow citizens' (5).

Nedham strikes a similar chord when he writes that what ought to assume primacy for the republican self is not the individual but the 'public safety, in relation whereunto each member of the commonwealth is concerned to have a care of the whole'.[51] Thomas Smith also follows Cicero in this regard, saying that our very humanity resides in the capacity to think beyond the self-preservative impulses that, according to Smith, guide animal life:

> we be not born only to ourselves but partly to the use of our country, of our parents, of our kinfolk, and partly of our friends and neighbors. And therefore all good virtues are grafted in us naturally, whose effects be to do good to others, wherein shows forth the image of God in man whose property is ever to do good to others and to distribute goodness abroad, like no niggard nor envious thing. Other creatures, as they resemble nothing of that godly image, so they study no common utility of the other but only the conservation of themselves and propagation of their own kind.[52]

Even Sidney, more invested in autonomy than Smith, does not stray too far from this sort of thinking. To be sure, Sidney works to reject the idea, which Smith had admired in classical republicans like Cicero, that we are, from birth onwards, bound and indebted to others. Sidney believes this idea to be intrinsic to absolutist thinking. For Sidney, accepting that we are born to others means accepting the tyrant's yoke; refusing to imagine that some are 'born with crowns upon their heads, and all others with saddles upon their backs', Sidney believes 'that every man is a king till he divest himself of his right, in consideration of something he thinks better for him.'[53] Man's sovereignty over himself, in the Sidneyan framework, proceeds from nature – on the grounds that men cannot owe more than they have received, and if man at birth has nothing, he owes nothing.

And yet even as Sidney makes this argument he also registers how, as humans, we are almost immediately drawn into spheres of deep obligation – to family, community and so on. These spheres compromise the unfettered freedom that, Sidney implies, we possess perhaps only at the moment of birth.[54] Even more: without the absolutist context within which subjects are forced to clamour for individual liberty and for the right to pursue their own interests, Sidneyan selves become much more other-concerned and more inclined to self-risk. When 'publick powers are employ'd for the publick benefit', according to Sidney, citizens 'do not spare their persons, purses, or friends' (272). In this, Sidney repeats the Ciceronian idea that no part of life can be free from duty, from ties that draw the self outside itself far more than in communitarian frameworks.[55] In such frameworks, civic-mindedness is valuable as the only real way to fulfil individual liberties and interests. The republicans just discussed sometimes follow this line of thinking, but also, I hope to have suggested, often reverse the order of priority. When they do, the logic runs as such: civic virtue secures freedom from tyranny, but such freedom makes that virtue – practised to the point of self-sacrifice – all the more appealing, and more admirable than the pursuit of individual interest could ever be.

None of this is to say that Ciceronian lines of thought have little investment in liberty. Given that Cicero was killed on the orders of Marcus Antonius, he was well aware of the dangers of arbitrary power and of the need for checks against it. As will be clear, my own aim is not at all to claim that the concept of autonomy has no utility or that bounded selfhood is always without worth. But it remains true that bounded existence recedes into the background when Cicero and those who share with him go about imagining ideal citizens. Such citizens risk themselves without hope of reward, place self-risk at the core of virtue. In this sense, the courage required of us to embrace vulnerable being – more than temperance, wisdom or justice – may be the most crucial republican virtue.

To explain how the virtue of vulnerability might find a place in the present context, I thus focus not on liberal or communitarian strains of thought but on certain radical ones, for which vulnerability is also often virtuous. This is not, of course, to say that the vulnerabilities endorsed by classical and early modern republicans and by contemporary radicals are everywhere the same or even similar. For instance, in the Cicero quoted above, the sacrifice of bounded selfhood assumes a very familiar – often conservative – form, that of the person given over to the ultimate subordination of private interest to the public good, giving himself up for his country. Such is precisely the sort of sacrifice that Coriolanus refuses to perform, and one way that I will claim that radical thought does not just overlap with, but rather illuminates a limitation of, republican thought stems from such claims: that the loss of certain lives is critical to the 'common safety'. But Cicero, as will become clear, also imagines the susceptibility of republican subjects in more subtle and perhaps more usable ways, when the vulnerability imagined is shared – for example, in his theories of friendship and rhetoric, which I examine in detail in Chapters 2 and 5. Such vulnerabilities – ones often embraced by both republicans and radicals – are the objects of this study's attention.

This being so, I should explain why, in exploring the virtues of vulnerability, I discuss republican and radical thought alongside each other. On the simplest level, it is a discovery of hitherto unnoticed connections and the start of a conversation, one whose conclusions are sometimes startling. In my Milton chapter, to cite one example, I read the public sphere theory of *Paradise Lost* next to that of Cicero, Foucault and Michael Warner; and when one considers their respective attitudes toward the role that pleasure might play in critique – what the taking of pleasures might have to do with the giving of reasons – Cicero and Milton appear more radical than the avowedly radical Warner and help round out Foucaultian theories of the public subject.

Second, pointing out connections between the radical and the republican permits me to make more historically plausible some often contested links between radical and English Renaissance thought. The Spenser chapter, among others, exemplifies this. That we can find vulnerability which is central to Cicero's republican friendship theory, I show, helps ground Spenser's affinities with twentieth-century radicals such as Blanchot and thus with forms of self-undoing that we might otherwise assume to be anti-republican and so – or at least – politically unpalatable from a Spenserian point of view.

Third, showing how Renaissance texts can help link republican and radical thought allows me to show how these forms of thought not only illuminate but even depend upon each other – especially if we seek to draw an adequate picture of the vulnerable, 'open' subject. Republican and radical outlooks overlap, but only imperfectly so, and they also reveal each other's shortcomings. This I consider at most length in the Shakespeare chapter. There, I show how the Roman plays allow us to see how more limited, guarded forms of openness present in republican thought (and in, say, *Titus*) require more total, dangerous forms of openness offered by radicals such as Bersani (and plays such as *Coriolanus*), but also vice versa. Out of such discussions, I aim to help render the modern self as flexible as possible.

Open Subjects and the History of the Subject

As subsequent chapters demonstrate, questions of what makes for a republican self often become questions of what makes, and should make, for a modern self. For critics such as Patterson and Norbrook, I will show, 'republican' means 'proto-modern', and 'modern' means 'bounded'; for them, republican structures help individuals delineate and develop themselves along axes easy to recognise, and to value, in the present moment. In this assessment, Patterson and Norbrook are by no means alone, and so to clarify the contribution of *Open Subjects*, as well as to fill in the background against which my project is set, I want to discuss some recent histories not of republican selfhood but of selfhood as such, with special attention to the place of boundedness within those histories.

Here, the boundedness explored is often understood less in terms of the rights that delineate the self, as in republican accounts, and more in terms of the interiority that allows the self to consider itself distinct, make the world an object of critical thought, and so on. Later chapters will show how many accounts of republicanism and modern selfhood connect the two forms of boundedness – to say, for example, either that one's interior, critical faculties depend on rights for their protection, or that to retain rights one must possess the sort of critical faculties that will insist on those rights. Because of this connection, histories of self-hood merit some careful consideration.

In *Sources of the Self*, Charles Taylor presents a thorough articulation of the extent to which the history of the modern self can in fact be construed as the history of its increasing boundedness.[56] For Taylor, modern identity is made up of an ensemble of defining characteristics, including 'the sense of inwardness, freedom, individuality, and being embedded in nature' (ix). His story begins with the earliest seeds of modern self-hood as evident in pre-modernity, particularly with Plato's emphasis on rational self-mastery – mastery which bears the fruits of 'unity with oneself, calm, and collected self-possession' (116). Taylor then details how Augustine develops Plato by understanding self-mastery in terms of the dichotomy between inner and outer, advocating radical reflexivity, and placing heightened emphasis on the human capacity for choice (137).

One can perhaps anticipate where Taylor is headed. The idea of bounded existence comes to fruition, for him, in Descartes' offer of a new form of rational mastery, one presented as 'a matter of instrumental control' (149). Out of the Cartesian framework there develops 'a new understanding of subject and object, where the subject is, as it were, over against the object' (188), and as the early modern shades into the modern, instrumental, disengaged selfhood develops but also often comes under criticism. Disengagement, though it affords the feeling of freedom, has the potential to drain life of meaning and also tends to be self-defeating, since a society of free, atomistic individuals 'saps the will to maintain this freedom' that disengagement was to guarantee (502).

Sources of the Self is remarkable in scope and subtlety. Taylor's greatest insight, perhaps, resides in his call that we not reject any aspect of modern selfhood – whether, say, of disengaged, instrumental reason or expressive self-fulfilment – simply because its 'exclusive pursuit leads to contemptible or disastrous consequences' (511). Such consequences, Taylor remarks, show only that each aspect of the modern identity must be 'part of a "package", to be sought within a life which is also aimed at other goods' (511). While I will occasionally emphasise some 'contempt-ible or disastrous' effects of the coldness and disengaged calculation that can accompany modern selfhood in its bounded form, I find Taylor's counsel sound and do not reject boundedness altogether. Where I will seek to supplement *Sources of the Self* is in the rather small 'package' of modern identity that it presents.

On the one hand, Taylor seems right to point out how, after Descartes and Locke, we tend to see selves in atomistic terms. According to Taylor,

> Atomist views always seem nearer to common sense, more immediately available. Even though they don't stand up very well in argument (at least, so I believe), even though a modicum of explanation is enough to show their inadequacy, nevertheless this explanation is continually necessary. It's as though without a special effort of reflection on this issue we tend to fall back into an atomist/instrument way of seeing. (196)

For Taylor, we ought not to rely solely on detached, atomistic self-conceptions because they deny, among other things, what Taylor calls 'the transcendental condition of interlocution', to which we are all bound and because of which selves can define themselves only with reference to their material and social environments (39). Still, Taylor's supplements to atomism rely rather heavily on constructs of boundedness. Such alternatives include a civic humanist self that, like the communitarian self, values self-sovereignty even as it also values communal involvement, and a self embedded in nature so as to cultivate a kind of expressive individualism. Taylor restricts himself to bounded selfhood partly because in his view such a conception of selfhood is inescapable for us moderns, living as we do in a world of fairly rigid subject/object distinctions. 'What I hope emerges from this lengthy account of the growth of the modern identity', he writes,

> is how all-pervasive it is, how much it envelops us, and how deeply we are implicated in it: in a sense of self defined by the powers of disengaged reason as well as of the creative imagination, in the characteristically modern understandings of freedom and dignity and rights, in the ideal of self-fulfilment and expression. (503)

Here, Taylor perhaps goes too far. He rightly points out how some of the most radical theorists of self (along with what he calls 'anti-moderns') take recourse to the very constructs of boundedness that they claim to reject – how they 'invoke rights, equality, and self-responsible freedom as well as fulfilment in their political and moral life' (511). I sometimes employ these constructs as well; I hope I do not seem to reject them. But the fact that critics of bounded selfhood appeal to facets of that self does not entail what Taylor assumes: that the subject has been set over and against the object irrevocably and that we cannot, except perhaps as a purely conjectural exercise, think outside this binary framework – so captured by the framework that it is now unappealing, and almost impossible, for us to adopt unbounded forms of life which Taylor would label 'pre-modern'. This is not so. For example, to say that we cannot or would not want to do away with individual rights does not mean that we cannot hold vulnerability in esteem. We can; many – including the radicals and republicans discussed here – do.

Taylor believes that 'we are only selves insofar as we move in a certain space of questions, as we seek and find an orientation to the good' (34). I am inclined to agree – finding myself unable to define myself except by my proximity to or distance from what I regard as 'good' – but the space of questions in which we move is not, and need not be, as circumscribed as Taylor claims. Making a final choice or seeing a clean break between bounded and unbounded forms of life, I would argue, is neither necessary nor advisable. Within the framework of this book, a legitimate question will be about which form of life we want to grant relative privilege, to place in the primary position, at any given moment and in our general outlooks, when we focus on what it is right to do as well as when we attend to what it is good to be.[57]

In the decades since *Sources of the Self*, Jerrold Seigel and Timothy Reiss have each written similarly sweeping histories of selfhood and have also charted ways out of purely instrumental, atomistic positions. Seigel does so by attending to the interrelation of what, for him, are selfhood's three dimensions: the bodily, the relational and the reflective.[58] Beginning with Aristotle and continuing through Foucault and Derrida, Seigel generally presents the first two dimensions as compromising the autonomy promised by the third. The bodily self is that 'shaped by the body's needs', and the relational self is 'what our relations with society and with others shape us or allow us to be'; only on the reflective level is the self 'an active agent of its own realization' (5–6). The passage to modernity, in Seigel's view, consists partly in the interrelation of bodily, relational and reflective aspects becoming increasingly fraught; whereas 'writers before the seventeenth century seldom saw the relations between the self's different dimensions as a problem,' for moderns the issue of how the self could, for instance, be reflective, given that it was already relational – how one could secure a measure of autonomy while existing, necessarily, within social constraints – becomes very serious, becomes in a sense the primary issue of modern selfhood (36).

Seigel shows how one attempt to solve the issue is to make of it a non-issue: to posit a one-dimensional view, whereby the self pursues one aspect of selfhood to the complete exclusion of the other two. (Seigel sees Foucault, to cite an example, adopting a pair of one-dimensional perspectives, one that privileges extreme bodily experience, and another that privileges extreme reflectivity.)[59] Seigel prefers multi-dimensional views; he argues for inextricable connections between selfhood's three dimensions – all, for Seigel, limit but also support each other – and thus regards 'multi-dimensionality as the only genuine mode of selfhood'. One-dimensional models, on the other hand, 'are abstract and one-sided' (31). 'We should be grateful', Seigel claims in his critique of Foucault, 'that the history of thinking about selfhood contains . . . more sober and in the end more illuminating alternatives, dedicated to establishing a nourishing and balanced relationship between the varied components of personal existence' (650). One such alternative is that offered by Locke, who 'regarded people as powerfully shaped by the world around them, but also as free in some degree from both animal need and social determination, and thus as capable of determining some of their thoughts and actions as their own' (89).

In this book, I, too, sometimes place emphasis on how early modern figures construct multi-dimensional selves, ones at once bodily, relational and reflective; my chapter on Shakespeare, focusing as it does on the need for both Habermasian intersubjectivity (which combines the relational and reflective modes) and a more total openness (which fuses the relational and the bodily), should suggest as much. But I often view selfhood's dimensions very differently from Seigel, and I take issue with *The Idea of the Self* in that it, like Taylor's history, narrows the horizon of experience for modern selves. It does so in two important respects.

First, Seigel needlessly denigrates one-dimensional perspectives. Seigel knows that such perspectives may have some utility,[60] but in practice tends to dismiss them as simplistic. His material on Foucault – and, for instance, on the 'disgusting contents' of Bataille's works – makes this evident (611). In *Open Subjects*, by contrast, I often describe moments in which one- or two-dimensional experience is, with good reason, accorded the highest regard: for instance, when Aufidius dreams in *Coriolanus* of a wholly bodily existence, or when, in book IV of *The Faerie Queene*, Britomart and Amoret become their relation with each other, and Britomart and Artegall are drawn into somatic relation so powerfully that they are deprived of their reflective capacities, yet in a way that saves them. In early modernity and today, that relational and bodily aspects of self might undermine reflective autonomy is sometimes the best imaginable outcome.

I also depart from Seigel in my conception of how multi-dimensionality can and should operate and thus of what constitutes a 'nourishing' relationship to self. Generally, I do not privilege reflectivity or see the bodily and relational spheres as Seigel often does, in terms of negatively valenced forms of vulnerability – what Seigel refers to as 'animal need' and a 'social determination' not unlike that described by Greenblatt or

Pettit; and so I do not see the self as needing to balance its aspects so that, say, the self's reflective capacities not be too compromised. Instead, I see selves arranging those aspects into flexible, temporary hierarchies that allow for vulnerability to be had in a way that is liveable and even salutary. To demonstrate this, I occasionally take recourse to the figure that Seigel perhaps unfairly critiques as one-dimensional: Foucault. I show in my final chapter, for instance, that a number of Foucault's later works, in a manner akin to Milton's *Paradise Lost*, enlist reflectivity (making the world an object of thought) and relationality (doing so with others) for the end of bodily pleasure. The speaker of 'Appleton House', similarly, reflects on the natural world in a way that mirrors Foucault's reflections on boundaries – not to be separated or bounded from that world but to be better bound to it.

If for Seigel a problem of modernity is how to secure a space of reflective autonomy, in *Mirages of the Selfe* Reiss takes a quite different tack, arguing that a more pressing problem is how to prevent modern notions of autonomous selfhood from eroding communal bonds.[61] To help solve the problem, Reiss argues in contrast to Taylor, claiming that we can turn to texts written well into early modernity. Not until Rousseau, Reiss claims, can we find the notion of a self that is 'private in essence', a self that precedes the community against which it is set (50). Until then, self-conceptions are founded mostly on what Reiss calls 'passibility', 'a sense of being embedded in and acted on' by biological, social and spiritual domains that comprised personhood (2).

Reiss highlights the extent to which the passible self, in both the classical and early modern periods, was far from autonomous in thought and action.[62] If Taylor is right, and I think he is, in believing that we tend to revert to atomistic thinking about the self – to consider the individual prior to and separate from community rather than the community prior to and constitutive of the individual – then *Mirages of the Selfe* is a useful contribution to thinking about selfhood. Reiss believes that 'to define "the ethical" foremost in terms of individual agency is a modern, even post-Kantian, move falsifying any ethics grounded, exactly, in a non-individualist sense of personhood' (135). He believes that if we define the ethical in this way, we do so at our peril. In exploring the ethical value of vulnerability – of not possessing discrete individual agency – *Open Subjects* attempts to help answer Reiss's call to think about ethics outside the frame of the self-determining subject.

For all this, the present study differs from Reiss's significantly. First, Reiss assumes that in order to find alternatives to the atomistic, supposedly autonomous self in the contemporary landscape, one must turn to non-Western cultures.[63] In this, Reiss overstates the extent to which ideas of autonomy now dominate Western thought about selfhood and overlooks some interesting ways that Western texts from distant and more recent periods are in sympathy rather than at odds. Through the lens provided by republican thought, every chapter of *Open Subjects* demonstrates as much, showing how classical, early modern and contemporary texts on selfhood are deeply linked.

Second, Reiss and I operate with markedly different senses of what community can and should offer the self. As implied by his material on Montaigne, for Reiss community supplies many of the 'circles' that compose the self and so grant it stability and consistency. Reiss focuses on the degree to which selves exist because community exists – how selves are defined relationally, through what precedes them, rather than through volitional self-creation. But if Reiss does not see selves as autonomous he, like communitarian thinkers discussed above, none the less sees them as defined – as bounded, discrete and delineated – and sees community's worth in lending selves this definition. *Open Subjects*, as will be clear by now, attends to ways that classical, early modern and contemporary thinkers show how community – the experience of being-with – undoes, unsettles or makes unthinkable well-defined self-conceptions at least as much as it encourages such conceptions.

Conclusion: *Open Subjects* and the History of the Present

One question that arises in Taylor, Seigel and Reiss has to do with how ideas about the self change in the passage from antiquity to early modernity to today. In working through the literary figures who feature prominently in my chapters, and in moving from classical and early modern republicanism to contemporary radicalism in those chapters, I do not present either sequence as part of the meaningful temporal trajectory that, say, Taylor and Reiss see, albeit differently, in the self's deepening interior recesses and increasing autonomy. I have not presented such a meaningful trajectory because I cannot detect one. Nevertheless, a question that might well be asked, one that I would like to answer as I end this book's beginnings, is whether *Open Subjects* offers or subscribes to a history of the subject, and if so, what kind of history that might be.

If I am writing a history of selfhood, it is as much a history seen in terms of intersections and continuities as it is a history of breaks, rupture and difference. If positive valuations of vulnerability do not disappear over the course of the Renaissance, neither do more bounded ways of being in the world suddenly emerge around the turn of the seventeenth century. Just as Markku Peltonen has exposed flaws in the overly periodising view that English republicanism begins with the English Revolution, so are aspects of bounded selfhood – for instance, inwardness and negative freedoms – evident in earlier periods, a point amply demonstrated by medievalists such as Lee Patterson and David Aers.[64] It may be possible to find positive valuations of both bounded and vulnerable aspects of selfhood in any given period; since the 'history' of the subject suggested in these pages is not one of rupture, my claim is far from Greenblatt's suggestion that reading early modern texts is like witnessing the formation of modern identity, and even further from the view that the supposed emergence of a bounded self in early modernity involves rejecting an atavistic, open self belonging to pre-modernity.[65]

My history of the subject instead might be said to resemble the 'history of the present' described by Foucault. For Foucault, writing history means writing not in terms of collapse, disappearance, replacement and emergence, but in terms of accumulation, transformation and reappearance. For Foucault, writing history means giving genuine, not token, attention to both similitude and difference.

Foucault is careful, as I hope to be, to bear in mind that the present moment 'is a time like any other, or rather, a time which is never quite like any other'[66] – that past and present are not the same. While I place as much or more emphasis on continuity than on difference in comparing past and present, I do not proceed as though past and present are equivalent. I posit and depend on important distinctions between thinking about vulnerability in the classical period, in the sixteenth or seventeenth century, and in the twentieth or twenty-first. One attraction of earlier texts, as will become clear, is that they seem somewhat less prone either to succumb to the essentially defensive stance toward vulnerability – as a human quality that ought to be always guarded against – or to place arbitrary limits on exactly how, to what degree and in which circumstances, we are or ought to be vulnerable to others. So while I believe, for instance, that a poem such as Marvell's 'Appleton House' forms part of a coherent counter-tradition that values vulnerable aspects of selfhood – a tradition currently punctuated by figures such as Butler – I also believe that that tradition has by no means developed in a linear or progressive fashion. On this ground, I hope to show how classical and Renaissance texts are not merely reflective of, but are also instructive to, current theorisations of the open subject.

At the same time, I also follow Foucault in his sense that 'the time we live in is not the unique or fundamental or irruptive point in history where everything is completed and begun again', that we ought not conceive of the present as taking place in either a newfound 'abyss of darkness' or a 'triumphant daybreak'.[67] Speaking of rationality's history, for example, Foucault writes that his aim has been to describe not a single bifurcation of reason but an 'abundant ramification' of it, 'different modifications in which rationalities engender one another, oppose and pursue one another'.[68] For Foucault, in other words, past and present are alike even as they are not, and so writing history, rather than simply uncovering what has been lost, instead means attending to 'the accumulated existence of discourses' in hopes of composing the history of the present; it means listening to 'the words that still resonate in our ears' and deciding how we might want to relate to those words – how we might want to reconfigure 'the present field of possible experiences'.[69]

In my history of the open subject I, likewise, focus on how concepts of boundedness and openness are deployed – and on how they have accumulated – in the classical period, early modernity and today. In doing so, I chart those instances and domains in which we ought to insist on boundaries and those instances and domains in which we ought instead to embrace vulnerability – and on how Spenser, Shakespeare, Marvell and Milton help the project along, furnishing us with a vocabulary by which to describe each sort of instance and to distinguish one sort of instance from the other. I thus approach Renaissance texts as part of a useable past, in their relation to the present moment as well as to possible futures.

A final word about those futures, about how they might be composed out of our past and present. The word is not Foucault's but Jürgen Habermas's. Elsewhere in this book I, like others, will emphasise tensions and antagonisms between Foucault and Habermas, arguably the primary theoretical influence on current 'republican' literary criticism with which I take issue. But the history of the present that Foucault writes and the forms of life for which Habermas longs are not always so starkly opposed.

I have mentioned that the history offered here will not be the history of a triumph – of bounded selfhood over its open antecedent, or the reverse – nor of the wish for such a triumph. Becoming modern, in Habermas's work, sometimes involves this wish, a point that Chapter 5 explains in detail. But as Chapter 3 suggests, Habermas is also often attuned to how, in following the route to modernity, we ought not to leave so much behind. He acknowledges that in his advocacy of a shift from what he calls 'mythic' outlooks to modern ones – in asking that we adopt the detached, self-reflective vantage needed to distinguish between subjective, social and objective worlds – we forget much that is of value. Habermas remarks that modern societies can 'learn something from understanding alternative, particularly premodern forms of life'; he believes that we should not forget 'the losses required by our own path to the modern world'; he calls for the construction of a more capacious, accommodating and dynamic way of being in the world.[70] Foucault would not accept the distinction between modernity and pre-modernity as easily as Habermas does, but in his focus on the accumulation (rather than the simple succession) of outlooks and forms of life, he can be used to help answer Habermas's call. To the extent that both are interested in the persistence of bounded and open subjects, Habermas and Foucault are in real sympathy.[71]

In such moments, Habermas – like, say, Reiss – suggests that we moderns err when we reject mythic worldviews, a point borne out in my texts of focus. We will see, for instance, how the assumption of critical distance cuts us off from the immediacy and presence offered by experiences of exposure; such is the fate of Brutus and Sicinius in *Coriolanus* and of Satan in *Paradise Lost*. Reserved about the promise of modernity, Habermas (like theorists with whom I share more obvious affinities) implies that the ideal subject would be one in whom the 'modern' and the mythic, the bounded and the vulnerable, play important parts – that part of the project of modernity consists in finding a balance between the two. Habermasian theories of intersubjectivity, which I cover in Chapter 3, bear this out.

To be sure, there are tensions – some of them inescapable – between the outlook of a discrete, rights-bearing self and the outlook that, acceding to vulnerability, potentially undoes the self. I do not seek to deny such tensions. But like many of the thinkers discussed in this book – and like virtually all who are of a republican cast – I also do not treat them as absolute. A balance between these outlooks can be struck in part because they can be adopted in separate contexts rather than contest with each other within a single context. In the face of unwanted threat or coercion, it makes sense to emphasise boundedness, whereas in other spheres of life – for example, in friendship or in public life – insisting on personal borders can, among other things, block pleasure's progress or lead to self-defensive aggression. Besides, the bounded and unbounded need each other. They must be balanced. As I will explain, we need bounded forms of life to preserve and even intensify the experience of undoing, and the stark solitude of a perfectly enclosed life would be intolerable. Pure openness and total boundedness are not for such as us.

And so it is balances – ones that refuse rigid distinctions between the modern and the atavistic, the progressive and the regressive, bounded forms of life and vulnerable ones – that I locate in past texts as they relate to the present. If being modern means insisting on these distinctions, then I would suggest not only that we have never been modern, but that we would not want to be. If Foucault is right, though, modernity is not a single thing. It is an 'abundant ramification' of things.[72] If I have implied in the last few pages that there is more than one Habermas – if I have, earlier, shown that republican thought has left us more than one legacy – so also is there more than one way of being modern, more than one history of the present that can – and should – be written.

Notes

1. Adams says this in a letter to Mercy Otis Warren written on 8 August 1807. Quoted in David Wootton's introduction to *Republicanism, Liberty, and Commercial Society, 1649–1776* (Stanford, CA: Stanford University Press, 1994), 1.
2. Jonathan Scott, *Commonwealth Principles: Republican Writing of the English Revolution* (Cambridge: Cambridge University Press, 2004), 2.
3. See Pocock's 'Historical Introduction' to *The Political Works of James Harrington* (Cambridge: Cambridge University Press, 1977), 15.
4. *Republicanism, Liberty, and Commercial Society*, 1.
5. Peltonen's argument can be found in *Classical Humanism and Republicanism in English Political Thought, 1570–1640* (Cambridge: Cambridge University Press, 1995).
6. While Patterson's work on republicanism attends mostly to materials dating from after 1640, her *Shakespeare and the Popular Voice* (Oxford: Basil Blackwell, 1989) argues for a pro-republican Shakespeare; her account of *Coriolanus* I attend to below. Hadfield's literary work will arise time and again over the course of this book, but perhaps the most relevant stretch of text that details the presence of republican vocabulary in pre-Civil War political theory can be found in *Shakespeare and Republicanism* (New York: Cambridge University Press, 2005), esp. 17–90. Cheney's work on the topic is *Marlowe's Republican Authorship: Lucan, Liberty, and the Sublime* (New York: Palgrave Macmillan, 2009).
7. Cheney, for instance, makes this assumption in *Marlowe's Republican Authorship*. For another argument that republicanism is, above all, anti-monarchical, see Nigel Smith, *Literature and Revolution in England, 1640–1660* (New Haven, CT: Yale University Press, 1994).
8. See Patrick Collinson, 'The Monarchical Republic of Queen Elizabeth I', in *Elizabethan Essays* (London: Hambledon, 1994), 31–58. For a sense of the influence Collinson has had, as well as of the problems raised by his work, see John F. McDiarmid (ed.), *The Monarchical Republic of Early Modern England: Essays in Response to Patrick Collinson* (Burlington, VT: Ashgate, 2007).
9. Alan Cromartie, *The Constitutionalist Revolution: An Essay on the History of England, 1450–1642* (New York: Cambridge University Press, 2006).
10. Victoria Kahn, *Machiavellian Rhetoric: From the Counter-Reformation to Milton* (Princeton, NJ: Princeton University Press, 1994), esp. 55–7.
11. J. G. A. Pocock, *The Political Works of James Harrington* (Cambridge: Cambridge University Press, 1977), 23.
12. *Commonwealth Principles*, 9.

13. See Quentin Skinner, *Liberty Before Liberalism* (Cambridge: Cambridge University Press, 1998), 119.
14. See especially Skinner's 'Classical Liberty and the Coming of the English Civil War', in Martin Van Gelderen and Skinner (eds), *Republicanism: A Shared European Heritage*, vol. II: *The Values of Republicanism in Early Modern Europe* (New York: Cambridge University Press, 2002), 9–28. Skinner demonstrates, among other things, that in the *Philippics* (directed against Marcus Antonius) and in *De Officiis*, Cicero does advocate freedom as non-domination (10–11).
15. Skinner, *Hobbes and Republican Liberty* (New York: Cambridge University Press, 2008), 213.
16. See Skinner's Introduction to *Republicanism: A Shared European Heritage*, vol. II, 2–3.
17. *Republicanism: A Shared European Heritage*, vol. II, 1–6.
18. Both *Liberty Before Liberalism* and *Hobbes and Republican Liberty*, for instance, end by posing (but not answering) the question of the adequacy of liberty conceived of as the lack of interference.
19. Philip Pettit, *Republicanism: A Theory of Freedom and Government* (New York: Oxford University Press, 1997), 5.
20. John W. Maynor, *Republicanism in the Modern World* (Cambridge: Polity, 2003), 45.
21. Quoted in Isaiah Berlin, 'Two Concepts of Liberty', 118–72, in *Four Essays on Liberty* (New York: Oxford University Press, 1970), 127.
22. Charles Taylor, 'Cross Purposes: The Liberal-Communitarian Debate', 181–203 in *Philosophical Arguments* (Cambridge, MA: Harvard University Press, 1995), esp. 192.
23. *Commonwealth Principles*, 8.
24. *Republicanism, Liberty, and Commercial Society*, 7.
25. Blair Worden, 'Marchamont Nedham and the Beginnings of English Republicanism, 1649–1656', in *Republicanism, Liberty, and Commercial Society*, 46. See also *Literature and Politics in Cromwellian England: John Milton, Andrew Marvell, Marchamont Nedham* (New York: Oxford University Press, 2007).
26. Michael J. Sandel, 'America's Search for a Public Philosophy', 9–34, in *Public Philosophy: Essays on Morality in Politics* (Cambridge, MA: Harvard University Press, 2005), esp. 27. See also 'The Procedural Republic and the Unencumbered Self' and 'The Limits of Communitarianism', 156–73 and 252–62 of *Public Philosophy*, as well as *Democracy's Discontent: America in Search of a Public Philosophy* (Cambridge, MA: Harvard University Press, 1996) and *Liberalism and the Limits of Justice* (Cambridge: Cambridge University Press, 1998).
27. 'Cross Purposes', 192.
28. 'Cross Purposes', 192.
29. 'America's Search for a Public Philosophy', 11.
30. Developing what he calls 'republican liberalism', Richard Dagger makes a similar argument, connecting autonomy and civic virtue, self-concern and communal concern. In doing so, Dagger might be said to reconcile neo-Roman and communitarian thought. See *Civic Virtues: Rights, Citizenship, and Republican Liberalism* (New York: Oxford University Press, 1997).

31. Thomas Smith, *De Republica Anglorum: A Discourse on the Commonwealth of England* (Cambridge: Cambridge University Press, 1906), 20.
32. Philip A. Knachel (ed.), *The Case of the Commonwealth of England, Stated* (Charlottesville, VA: University Press of Virginia, 1969), 31.
33. Thomas G. West (ed.), *Discourses Concerning Government* (Indianapolis, IN: Liberty Fund, 1996), 22 and 512.
34. *The Case of the Commonwealth of England, Stated*, 67.
35. *Discourses Concerning Government*, 6.
36. *The Case of the Commonwealth of England, Stated*, 64.
37. George Buchanan, *De jure regni apud Scotos*, 1680, 22.
38. *Discourses Concerning Government*, 140.
39. See J. G. A. Pocock (ed.), *A System of Politics*, in *The Commonwealth of Oceana and A System of Politics* (Cambridge: Cambridge University Press, 2001), 273.
40. See *The Commonwealth of Oceana*, in *The Commonwealth of Oceana and A System of Politics*, 64.
41. To begin to get a sense of this influence, see Neal Wood's *Cicero's Social and Political Thought* (Berkeley, CA: University of California Press, 1988), particularly the introduction to that book, which details the process by which Cicero became known to an early modern English audience. For more on this, see also Wood's 'Cicero and the Political Thought of the Early English Renaissance', *Modern Language Quarterly* 51:2 (1990), 185–207. Many of the republicans discussed here invoke Cicero explicitly, almost always in approbation, and, as the following discussion will show, could be called neo-Ciceronian in several respects. Wood, for his part, places most emphasis on Cicero's defence of private property; but this defence, like other aspects of Ciceronian thought invoked by liberals and communitarians, is compatible with the vulnerabilities that Cicero valorises.
42. For an account that focuses on Cicero's influence on rhetoric – so great that his treatises provoked an anti-Ciceronian backlash in the Renaissance – see John Leeds, 'Against the Vernacular: Ciceronian Formalism and the Problem of the Individual', *Texas Studies in Literature and Language* 46:1 (2004), 107–48. For some other accounts of Cicero's influence in the domain of rhetoric, see Ronald Witt, 'Civic Humanism and the Rebirth of the Ciceronian Oration', *Modern Language Quarterly* 51:2 (1990), 167–84, and John Ward, 'Renaissance Commentators on Ciceronian Rhetoric', in James J. Murphy (ed.), *Renaissance Eloquence: Studies in the Theory and Practice of Renaissance Rhetoric* (Berkeley, CA: University of California Press, 1993), 126–73. For an account of Ciceronian friendship that resembles Leeds's study of rhetoric in that it traces a developing reaction against Cicero's influence, see Robert Stretter's 'Cicero on Stage: Damon and Pithias and the Fate of Classical Friendship in English Renaissance Drama', *Texas Studies in Literature and Language* 47:4 (2004), 345–65.
43. James E. G. Zetzel (ed.), *On the Commonwealth and On the Laws* (New York: Cambridge University Press, 1999), 30.
44. *De Republica Anglorum*, 12–13.
45. *The Case of the Commonwealth of England, Stated*, 7.
46. *On the Commonwealth*, 19.
47. *De jure regni apud Scotos*, 12.

48. Julia Annas (ed.), *On Moral Ends*, trans. Raphael Woolf (New York: Cambridge University Press, 2001), 41–2.
49. *The Commonwealth of Oceana*, 22.
50. *On the Commonwealth*, 2.
51. *The Case of the Commonwealth of England, Stated*, 31.
52. Mary Dewar (ed.), *A Discourse of the Commonweal of This Realm of England* (Charlottesville, VA: University Press of Virginia, 1969), 16–17.
53. *Discourses Concerning Government*, 511, 25.
54. The relevant quotation is in *Discourses Concerning Government*, 510.
55. See M. T. Griffin and E. M. Atkins (eds), *On Duties* (Cambridge: Cambridge University Press, 1991), 3.
56. Charles Taylor, *Sources of the Self: the Making of the Modern Identity* (Cambridge, MA: Harvard University Press, 1989).
57. Taylor draws this distinction on p. 3 of *Sources of the Self*.
58. Jerrold Seigel, *The Idea of the Self: Thought and Experience in Western Europe since the Seventeenth Century* (Cambridge: Cambridge University Press, 2005).
59. *The Idea of the Self*, 603–31.
60. *The Idea of the Self*, 31, 17.
61. Timothy Reiss, *Mirages of the Selfe: Patterns of Personhood in Ancient and Early Modern Europe* (Stanford, CA: Stanford University Press, 2003).
62. *Mirages of the Selfe*, 3, and passim.
63. Reiss himself turns to work on Ghanaian culture by figures such as Kwasi Wiredu and Kwame Gyekye (10–11).
64. See, for instance, David Aers, 'A Whisper in the Ear of Early Modernists; or, Reflections on Literary Critics Writing the "History of the Subject"', in Aers (ed.), *Culture and History: Essays on English Communities, Identities, and Writing* (New York: Harvester Wheatsheaf, 1992), 177–202, and Lee Patterson, *Chaucer and the Subject of History* (Madison, WI: University of Wisconsin Press, 1991).
65. See Greenblatt's *Renaissance Self-Fashioning: From More to Shakespeare* (Chicago: University of Chicago Press, 1980), 175.
66. Michel Foucault, 'Critical Theory/Intellectual History', in Lawrence D. Kritzman (ed.), *Politics, Philosophy, Culture: Interviews and Other Writings, 1977–1984*, trans. Alan Sheridan (New York: Routledge, 1988), 35–6.
67. 'Critical Theory/Intellectual History', 35–6.
68. 'Critical Theory/Intellectual History', 28–9.
69. 'On the Ways of Writing History', in James Faubion (ed.), *Essential Works of Foucault, 1954–1984*, vol. 2: *Aesthetics, Method and Epistemology*, trans. Robert Hurley (New York: New Press, 1998), 293, and 'The Art of Telling the Truth', in *Politics, Philosophy, Culture*, 95.
70. Jürgen Habermas, *Reason and the Rationalization of Society*, vol. 1 of *The Theory of Communicative Action*, trans. Thomas McCarthy (Boston, MA: Beacon, 1984), 65–6.
71. We should bear in mind as well that when Habermas does want to disentangle myth and enlightenment, non-modern and modern, he does so in hopes of elaborating a concept of reason that is not subject-centred, that does not only focus on how speaking can further secure bounded selfhood.

See *The Philosophical Discourse of Modernity*, trans. Frederick Lawrence (Cambridge, MA: MIT Press, 1987), especially 'The Entwinement of Myth and Enlightenment: Max Horkheimer and Theodor Adorno', 105–30, and 'An Alternative Way out of the Philosophy of the Subject: Communicative versus Subject-Centered Reason', 294–326.

72. 'Critical Theory/Intellectual History', 28–9.

Chapter 2

'Without Respect of Utility': Precarious Life and the Politics of Edmund Spenser's *Legend of Friendship*

Introduction

In this chapter I lay out a general theory of the open subject by looking into what friendship does to us. I think about friendship in both its personal and civic incarnations, about whether it renders us more vulnerable than we otherwise imagine ourselves; and I think about whether it should.

To see the issue through, I read book IV of *The Faerie Queene* alongside classical, early modern and contemporary friendship theory. I show how friendship shapes selfhood in theory and in Spenser's epic – how friends respect and reinforce each other's boundaries but also disregard and dissolve them. The *Legend of Friendship* explores how best to calibrate subjectivity and intersubjectivity, self-interest and self-sacrifice, bounded, unencumbered selfhood and its exposed, unbounded opposite. This will become, in part, a question of the place of Spenser's friendship theory in his political present – and, specifically, of whether his theory can be called republican. I will argue that it can, and that Spenser's republicanism has bearing on his place in our political present, on whether he speaks more to liberal friendship theory or to its radical counterpart. I argue that Spenser speaks to both but that he speaks more, and more instructively, to the radicals.

Much has been written about Spenser's attitudes toward bounded selfhood. The influential work of Stephen Greenblatt and Andrew Hadfield, for example, focuses on Spenserian selves who aspire toward a way of being in the world defined by clear personal boundaries, self-control and the use of force against those understood to threaten that control. My sympathies rest with another tradition of understanding Spenser, wherein Spenserian selfhood is defined by boundaries that do not hold, by a vulnerability to others that undercuts self-control and that is intractable. But I attend to how book IV entertains both sorts of self-hood, treating them as a dialectic.

In book IV, bounded selfhood comes to be by following a basic structure evident in numerous models of friendship in the Renaissance and in contemporary thinking, including that of Jürgen Habermas and Hannah Arendt; for friendship thus conceived, initial acts of self-sacrifice, and initial disavowals of friendship's utility, lead to self-fortification and fulfilled self-interest.[1] In book IV, the stories of Cambel and Triamond and of Placidas and Amyas follow just this structure. At times, Spenser does valorise such friendships – in which selves give things up only to get them, and much more, in return – but he is also, I argue, wary of what these friendships so often require to attain a happy ending: an instrumental approach to others, one that involves the manipulation and sometimes even the elimination of those who do not share a deep commitment to individual interests, and the personal boundaries that permit those interests to come into being. Spenser dramatises such a sequence when a nameless woman disregards her own safety entirely, allowing for the preservation of another set of friends, Amoret and Aemylia, only to be hated by Belphoebe and then shunted out of existence.

If this means that Spenser can be critical of the bounded selfhood represented in ostensible moral centres such as Belphoebe and Cambel, Spenser also displays interest in others ways of being in the world, and in other work that friendship can perform. He shows definite investment, I argue, in friendships that fully assume the sacrifice that in Cambel's case is only avowed, friendships driven by intense forms of self-abandonment – as they are, for example, in Britomart's bed scene with Amoret in canto i and in her exposure to an already exposed Artegall when they battle in canto vi. In the first scene, interior existence is emptied out in an ecstatic affective outpouring of being 'twixt'; in the second, Spenser portrays the English commonwealth itself as dependent, at its very foundation, not on aggrandised subjects but on selves subject to extreme openness, to lost will and shared plight. In these scenes, Spenser suggests a politics of friendship founded not on disciplined English self-fashioning, as Greenblatt and a host of other critics contend, but on intersubjective self-unfashioning – on a 'between' that can be overwhelming but that is nevertheless good. For Spenser, in other words, vulnerability ought to be at the core of community at least as much as it ought to be the thing that community casts out.

In portraying the precarious, yet liveable (and even luxuriant) experience of lost will and shared, circulated weakness, Spenser's thinking helps illuminate a tradition of friendship theory with similar emphases, one that culminates in the work of Georges Bataille and Judith Butler, and that, in several crucial respects, reaches back at least as far as the classical republican Cicero. So while Hadfield, following Greenblatt, locates Spenser's republicanism in his advocacy of a violently bounded form of life, I argue that in so far as Spenser develops Cicero in the ways that I claim he does, his republicanism has links, however unlikely, with current radical thought. This being so, I hope to begin in earnest the thinking together – of the republican and the radical – urged in my first chapter.

Recent Criticism and Spenserian Friendship

For three decades 'self-fashioning' has occupied a prominent place in early modern studies. Since its publication in 1980 no book, arguably, has had more influence on the field than has Greenblatt's *Renaissance Self-Fashioning*, and no piece of Spenser criticism has made greater impact than Chapter 4 of that book, 'To Fashion a Gentleman: Spenser and the Destruction of the Bower of Bliss'.[2] There, Greenblatt claims that Spenser, in love with the use of force, promotes self-control that can be cultivated through two practices: 'renunciation and the constant exercise of power' (173–4). Focusing primarily on Guyon's destruction of Acrasia's bower in book II, Greenblatt reads her bower as the offer and real allure of non-purposive passivity, relinquished will and self-loss; and in Spenser's eyes the offer must be resisted as 'the not-self', as 'all that lies outside, or resists, or threatens identity' (177). To construct and maintain a clear, bounded sense of himself, accordingly, Guyon must discipline or destroy his undisciplined, unbounded others – coded female, Irish and of the New World.

Since its initial articulation, this basic structure of self-fashioning – within which Spenserian subjects strive for an empowered, clearly delineated existence, often through the exercise of violence – has been pursued by numerous critics. Within the current domain of Spenser studies, Hadfield is probably the most prominent critic who sees a version of self-fashioning as quintessentially Spenserian. In *Spenser's Irish Experience*, for example, Hadfield argues that Spenser's work 'revolves around the question of identity, individual and national, painfully aware that borders exist which can all too easily be transgressed and always need to be policed'.[3] Like Greenblatt's account and a host of others, Hadfield sees Spenserian selves labouring toward disciplined, bounded embodiment and coherent, clearly demarcated social identity.[4]

Thus understood, Spenser's conception of selfhood has entailed a specific structure for Spenserian friendship. If bounded selfhood is that which, for good or ill, Spenser advocates, then true friends maintain distinct identities; in fact, friendship ought to draw the distinction in sharp relief. Hadfield, for example, argues that the friendship between Triamond and Cambel in book IV is about achieving 'stable units' to be contrasted with Lust's grotesque disregard for personal boundaries.[5] In his own, more generous picture of Spenserian selfhood, Richard Chamberlain has claimed that Spenser often imagines friendship as 'a democratic recognition of the other's alterity, powers and capacity', that for Spenser 'friendship's value lies in its semi-detached or contiguous juxtaposition of both parties.' Chamberlain, following Harry Berger, Jr, argues that book IV's narratives of friendship imagine relationships in which the self neither dominates nor subsumes the other.[6]

The tone of Chamberlain and others suggests that, just as Spenserian self-fashioning implies a certain form of friendship, so can friendship serve as a model for political belonging. When bounded selfhood is the foundation and end of such belonging, though, the politics of Spenserian friendship is usually understood much more darkly than Chamberlain does. For Greenblatt, Spenser offers only a violently xenophobic politics of friendship; political community is possible only with those who are similarly committed to selfhood – specifically, to disciplined, civilised, boundary-respecting forms of English selfhood.[7] Various others have an appeal that must be rejected, that must be understood as the enemy's false allure.

Against this background, Hadfield has traced the consequences of Spenser's attitude to others, especially the Irish, for his possible republican commitments. Like the scholars of early modern republicanism that I treated in Chapter 1, Hadfield describes how Renaissance texts advance forms of bounded selfhood from which contemporary political theory can learn; with respect to Spenser, he admires the very fact that Spenser critiques a monarch's authority over subjects.[8] Hadfield outlines Spenser's investment in 'notions of citizenship, liberty, and the need for active virtue', and though he is careful not to equate the republicanism of any early modern figure, Spenser included, with democracy, he and others have suggested how nascent notions of individual rights that create the legal fiction of boundedness – rights to political participation, self-propriety and personal property – can be found in the latter half of the sixteenth century.[9]

But Hadfield also sees a serious downside to Spenser's republicanism and his commitment to the boundaries of English subjects and English identity. 'After all,' he writes, 'the most aggressive policies and systematic slaughter in Ireland were carried out by English republicans, showing that republicanism was not always a good or a nice thing.'[10]

Unlike other figures of focus for 'republican' critics – who I treat in subsequent chapters – Spenser is typically seen as exhibiting the dark side
of bounded selfhood: as exhibiting the dangers, better handled by these
other figures, of a politics of friendship committed to such selfhood.
Thus, when most critics describe appealing aspects of republicanism,
Spenser is not often mentioned.[11]

Critics of other stripes, however, argue that Spenser is not so obviously invested in bounded selfhood and in doing so have opened routes
for alternative models of Spenserian friendship. In one of the few mon-
ograph-length studies of book IV, published one year after *Renaissance
Self-Fashioning*, Jonathan Goldberg argues that Spenser details the self's
constitutive incompletion. In Goldberg's account, friendship produces
'a society of loss'. Self-assertion in *The Faerie Queene* can only be a
cover for not having a self; the object that would grant a sense of self-
completion functions, finally, only as 'an otherness that overwhelms
and subverts the self'.[12] For Goldberg, the epic is Spenser's story of the
impossibility of bounded selfhood – of how self-identity, self-control
and self-sufficiency elude us and of how the societies we form must lack
all three.

Goldberg has several fellow travellers within Spenser studies, particularly among critics concerned with gender and sexuality. In this
group are Lauren Silberman, Dorothy Stephens and Kathryn Schwarz.[13]
Goldberg, Silberman, Stephens and Schwarz all devote critical energy
not just to how Spenser attempts to further secure personal boundaries,
but also to how he is well aware of the exposure of self that friendship
can occasion.

I will put my critical energy to similar use. According to Greenblatt
and most republican critics, Spenser's political instructiveness consists largely in the extent to which his writings are symptomatic of
the tendency of bounded, modern identity to be accompanied by
self-hardening, self-defensive violence. Such critics have shown how
this is often true; I will suggest, however, that by remaining silent (as
Greenblatt is) on book IV and by claiming (as Hadfield does) that the
book mostly endorses the violence that secures selfhood, these critics
have underestimated the extent to which Spenser is aware and even critical of the dangers that bounded selfhood can present. I will also suggest
that in his implicit equation of republican selfhood with bounded selfhood, Hadfield misses out on some of Spenser's affinities with Cicero, a
republican who makes vulnerability central to civic friendship.

This chapter, like studies such as Goldberg's, will focus on the vulnerability of Spenserian subjects. But I will want to re-assess what this
focus brings into view. What follows, in stark contrast to Goldberg, will

focus neither on the textuality of undone selfhood nor on its negative aspects.[14] Unlike Goldberg and his fellow travellers, I will hone in on how vulnerability can serve as the basis for an attractive, wide-reaching politics of friendship in which Spenser shows definite investment.[15] To explain these points – to give precision to the forms of relation relevant to book IV, to identify the possibilities, limits and dangers of those forms, and to lay out some terms by which we might regard friendship defined by undoing as of political appeal – I preface each reading of book IV with a consideration of what happens to selves within traditions of thinking about friendship.

'More then for my owne sake': Self-Aggrandising Rhetorics of Self-Sacrifice

Renaissance theories of friendship often emphasise bounded selfhood, even though, just as often, the opposite seems so. To be sure, Renaissance figures regularly describe friendship as what would seem to undermine various features of boundedness, such as of discrete belief, will and desire. For Thomas Elyot, friendship only occurs between those of identical opinion and inclination, since 'where is any repugnance, may be none amitie, sens frendshippe is an entire consent of willes and desires' that makes the friend 'the other I'.[16] Francis Bacon, similarly, writes that '[a] friend is another himself.'[17] And Montaigne, for his part, recommends that friends 'hate and banish from their thoughts these words that imply separation and difference: benefit, obligation, gratitude, request, thanks, and the like'.[18] The Renaissance paradigm of openness, which developed not only from Christian but also from Aristotelian and Ciceronian modes of thought, can pervade psychological and social spheres, and even pass into corporeal ones, blurring the boundaries that secure social identity and bodily integrity alike.[19] Such blurring nullifies many ways that bounded selfhood comes to be, whether by possessing distinct physical and psychological demarcations and capacities, by being recognised as a discrete entity in the field of social visibility, or by being invested with the legal fictions that help individuals consider themselves possessive individuals.

In obvious ways, Elyot, Bacon and Montaigne's ideas seem opposed to the Greenblattian conception of self-fashioning, and to any account in which friendship fosters bounded selves capable of either self-control or self-interest. If friends agree on all scores they would seem, literally, unable to think for themselves, to form discrete personalities and act according to clearly delineated will; and if pure other-concern defines friendship, there is no room within friendly space for the pursuit of individual aims. Such an open-hearted love, in Bacon's phrase, is thus 'without respect of utility' (41). Along the same lines, Montaigne writes that his connection with Etienne de la Boétie

> possessed itself of my will, and led it to plunge and lose itself in his; which possessed itself of his whole will, and led it, with a similar hunger and a like impulse, to plunge and lose itself in mine. I may truly say lose, for it left us with nothing that was our own, nothing was either his or mine. (97–8)

If admitted into sociality more broadly, Montaignean friendship would serve as the basis for a society of loss, one devoid of the personal boundaries and capacities that make self-possession thinkable and individual property possible.

And yet in much Renaissance friendship theory, including Elyot's own, momentary abandonment of individual boundaries and discrete self-interest works to further both, a point that Lorna Hutson has demonstrated in another context.[20] Consider one story well known in early modernity (and, we will see, directly relevant to book IV), told by Boccaccio and then by Elyot: that of Titus and Gisippus.[21] In their bizarre story, Titus, a Roman, and Gisippus, an Athenian, grow up together in Athens, developing a sameness of outlook that leads both to fall in love with the same woman, Sophronia. She has already been promised to Gisippus, and so Titus pines to the point of being bedridden (169). When Gisippus discovers the cause of his friend's malady, though, he arranges a bed-trick, showing disregard for property and propriety alike, and displaying extreme self-unconcern which, he knows, Athenian society can only shun. Given Sophronia, and restored to himself, Titus returns to Rome. But Gisippus, having sacrificed his place in Athens, resolves 'as a wilde beste to wander abrode' (180), spending a night in a Roman barn, a night which proves quite fateful indeed. For it so happens that that night a murderer plants his murder weapon, a knife, on Gisippus. Brought to trial, Gisippus confesses, hoping to seize the chance to be put to death. Titus, however, happens to be close by, and in his own act of self-sacrifice, he also confesses, a gesture which inspires the murderer – who also happens to be nearby – to furnish his own confession. Most impressed by such gestures, the Roman Senate declines to attach the crime to a single agent and instead absolves all three. To end the story, Titus takes Gisippus back to Athens, and threatens to sack the city unless his friend's 'landes and substaunce' are 'stablysshed him in perpetuall quietenes' (183). They are; Gisippus gets his 'substaunce' back, and so Titus returns to Rome.

Most remarkable to me about Elyot's retelling of this tale is that, despite its quite flagrant violations of individual difference and stable identity – despite the identical desire, the bed-trick, the triple confession, and the pardon which makes law appear like anything but that which individuates – the story still ends with re-empowered, proper-tied, consolidated selves. Titus and Gisippus end up more discrete than ever, living in separate cities, each standing for himself. The difference between them is effaced only so as to further secure it; they sacrifice themselves only to end up aggrandised.

In this structure, the effacement of self-possession and even of discrete identity serves to bolster a bounded, possessive individuality under-stood as ultimate. In more mild and realistic forms, this line of thinking is evident not just in the Renaissance, but also in several theories of friendship circulating today. Here I have in mind theories voiced from a variety of perspectives, including those of Hannah Arendt, John Rawls, Jürgen Habermas and Francis Fukuyama.[22] All reconcile rigid forms of boundedness – for instance, the classically liberal version of possessive individualism that C. B. Macpherson describes – with more open or communitarian selfhoods.[23]

In her comparison of love and friendship, for instance, Arendt regards social connection not as that which undoes but as that which relates. Arendt thus offers a rather decorous theory of civic 'friendliness'. Whereas '[l]ove, by reason of its passion, destroys the in-between which relates us to and separates us from others,' Arendt writes, respect 'is a kind of "friendship" without intimacy and without closeness; it is a regard for the person from the distance which the space of the world puts between us'.[24] Civic 'friends' ought to see themselves in others, as Titus and Gisippus do, but only in so far as they recognise those others as being similarly bounded, discrete and delineated; Arendt condenses the narrative of Titus and Gisippus, their movement from indistinction to distinction, into a single instant – the moment of civic recognition – and so does without the element of risk that marks their tale prior to its happy ending.

Rawls, like Arendt, advances a practical ideal of fraternity based in a similar recognition, one driven by 'the idea of not wanting to have greater advantages unless this is to the benefit of others who are less well off'.[25] Those who accept this ideal could form a 'reasonable society', which 'is neither a society of saints nor a society of the self-centered'.[26] Individuals are free to be bounded, possessive individuals so long as they do not impinge on others' abilities to be the same; as in Arendt's formulation, we ought to see others as deserving of the same protections and entitlements as us.

For a final example, one that more closely approximates the

temporality of Elyot's tale, we might look to Habermas and his basic claim, following Mead (following others), that individuation is not 'the self-realization of an independently acting subject carried out in isolation and freedom'; instead '[i]ndividuality forms itself in relations of intersubjective acknowledgment and of intersubjectively mediated self-understanding.'[27] For Habermas, as for Elyot, the solidification of self in distinction from others requires a prior opening up to those others.[28] For all of these thinkers, civic virtue enables the recognition and reinforcement of individual boundaries. For them, sociation allows for individuation; intersubjectivity deepens subjectivity; momentary sacrifice serves the purpose of future reward. Fraternity furthers self-concern even as it curbs or ostensibly forgets it.

Two stories of friendship in book IV, those of Cambel and Triamond and of Amyas and Placidas, follow precisely this pattern. The story of the first pair, Cambel and Triamond, begins by presenting the dangers of total enclosure. The two are stalemated in their fight over Cambel's sister, Canacee – not because they are too vulnerable but because neither one is vulnerable enough. By rather different routes, these two have stockpiled so much power as to have become almost invincible. Triamond achieves better boundaries, paradoxically, through an indistinction his mother, Agape, has bargained for; when his brothers, Priamond and Diamond, die, their souls enter him. When their one and two become Triamond's three, he is made fantastically formidable. For his part, Cambel – who wants to keep all three of the brothers -mond from being with his sister – wears a ring that stanches wounds.[29] The ring so numbs him to the world outside that having his head split open cannot keep him down for long (4.3.34).[30] Cambel and Triamond's preternaturally resilient personal boundaries, though, give them access to only the most awful experience:

> Long while they then continued in that wize,
> As if but then the battell had begonne:
> Strokes, wounds, wards, weapons, all they did despise,
> Ne either cared to ward, or peril shonne,
> Desirous both to have the battell donne;
> Ne either cared life to saue or spill,
> Ne which of them did winne, ne which were wonne.
> So wearie both of fighting had their fill,
> That life it selfe seemed loathsome, and long safetie ill.
> (4.3.36)

What keeps them from losing makes them indifferent toward winning. Their standoff – their battle that seems always just starting – cannot stop until Cambina administers the nepenthe that reconciles them and opens them up to others again. Until then they are, irreparably and invulnerably, what they are; and it is then that they begin to resemble the heroes of Elyot's tale closely. Cambel and Triamond resemble Titus and Gisippus – first, in their temporary dependence on a third party, Cambina, who not only supplies them with the nepenthe that turns them into friends, but also, later, gets together with Cambel.[31] Whereas in Elyot's tale Sophronia allows the two to strengthen their connection, Cambel and Triamond depend on Cambina in order to forge their relationship to begin with; in the one tale, a love object inevitably shapes friendship, while in the other, that object is necessary for friendship's genesis. But in both tales (and this is the crucial point) the others that shape subjects and their desires for *philia* – that briefly undermine their capacity for self-possession – none the less end up serving those subjects. When they do, Titus and Cambel regain self-control. When Titus has Sophronia and Cambel Cambina, self-possession, however illusory, also comes into play; the correct object ends up in the hands of the correct, newly fortified subject.

After Cambina administers the nepenthe, Cambel and Triamond enter a cycle like that experienced by Titus and Gisippus, within which the more self-control and individual integrity they momentarily lose, the more of both they receive in return. We see this in Satyrane's tournament, when the two imperil themselves by standing in for each other against great odds. Triamond finds himself too wounded to participate in the second day of combat, and Cambel, 'though he could not salue, / Ne done vndoe' Triamond's wounds, decides to don his friend's armour and enter the fray, 'to salue his name, / And purchase honour in his friends behalue' (4.4.27.1–4). Cambel upends Satyrane but finds himself 'enclosed round' by a hundred knights who hope to take him prisoner. Triamond gets wind of it, ignores his injury and, having donned Cambel's own armour, breaks into the enclosure, presumably to show that he and his friend cannot be isolated individually. They are not simply in this together, but are in this together as each other. What transpires next is quite curious:

> As when two greedy Wolves doe breake by force
> Into an heard, farre from the husband farme,
> They spoile and rauine without all remorse,
> So did these two through all the field their foes enforce.
> . . .
> Fiercely they followd on their bolde emprise,
> Till trumpets sound did warne them all to rest;
> Then all with one consent to yeeld the prize
> To *Triamond* and *Cambell* as the best.
> But *Triamond* to *Cambell* it relest.

And *Cambell* to *Triamond* transferd;
Each labouring t'aduance the others gest,
And make his praise before his own preferd:
So that the doome was to another day differd.
                    (4.4.35.6–9, 4.4.36)

There have been self-sacrificial gestures: in donning the other's armour, and assuming the other's identity; in Cambel's willingness to subject himself to the harsh blows of a hundred knights (just as Titus offers to take Gisippus' place on the scaffold); and in the refusal, after their triumph that day, of a form of recognition. And yet we are told that what we have here is not two lambs, but two greedy wolves[32] – not two beings emptying themselves out but two beings feeding, filling themselves up.

Donning the other's armour falls short of self-loss. And so Cambel and Triamond find themselves in an awkward position at the day's end, for then they are assumed to be essentially inseparable; the day's prize is given to them both. The assumption here is that in wearing the outward signs of someone else, and in risking oneself for the sake of that someone, each is willing to admit personal indistinction. But the assumption is one that Cambel and Triamond reject; they have stood for each other, yet they refuse to share their reward. Instead, both want to give the prize to the other, want to insist that they are not the same. Now that quite a bit of honour has accrued to them, they do not want their names, which they themselves have interchanged, to remain interchangeable. After all, there would be little point in saving the other's name if that name – and, it so happens, one's own – were considered indistinct, unimportant, unsaved at the end of the day.

In this, their story shares much with the contemporary friendship theory discussed above. To the extent that Cambel and Triamond realise that to accept the prize as the superlative knight would not redound to the other, would only benefit the self, we might say that they follow John Rawls's prescriptions. They are not straightforwardly self-centred. But they are also hardly saints. To recall Hannah Arendt, they do insist on the 'in-between' that sharing the girdle would destroy no less than love would. They respect the distance that the world places between selves – that relates them to yet separates them from others. This means that for them sociation serves the purpose that it does for Habermas in the essay on Mead; it individuates. Cambel and Triamond come to be recognised through a literal enactment of intersubjectivity's emblem, by occupying the other's position, then returning to and insisting upon the positions that can be properly called their own.

Calidore, the hero of book VI, does something similar to what Cambel and Triamond do. Though Calidore surpasses his rival for Pastorella's love, Coridon, in almost everything, he cedes his reward time and again. (For instance, he allows Coridon to lead a dance he was to lead, putting the 'flowry garlond', which Pastorella gave him, on his rival's head; when he outwrestles Coridon, he also gives the oaken crown to him (6.9.41–6).) But this apparent largesse – this pretence of shifting from the position of winner to loser – is practised in the hope that Calidore will receive the recognition he really wants: that he will, in appearing selfless, 'winne the loue of the faire *Pastorell*' (6.9.46.2). The difference with Cambel and Triamond is that they both get what they want. Their moment of seeming self-refusal and ostensible generosity is equally a moment in which they cling to individual difference. Paradoxical as it sounds, the two will not allow their existence for – even their identification with – each other to end in recognition which is other than individual or other than individuating. As in Elyot's tale, the momentary self-sacrifice of both eventuates in the aggrandisement of each. Cambel and Triamond's story shows how others can stand in for us so that we can stand for ourselves, that indistinction does not have to always undermine distinction, but can instead sustain it, can create a ricochet effect by which, with each blow struck, the reputation of each receives extra marks.

Triamond stands in for Cambel and Titus for Gisippus to keep the friend from being undone. In canto viii of book IV Placidas takes the place of Amyas to do the same. Like Titus, Placidas replaces his friend not in an armoured, martial sphere but in an erotic one. Amyas, we discover, has been taken prisoner by Poeana – who has been trying, thus far unsuccessfully, to seduce him. Since Placidas looks exactly like Amyas, he is able to foil Poeana's plan altogether, managing to take his friend's place in captivity so that Amyas might reunite with his true love, Aemylia. In this story, like that told by Elyot, friends do not let friends stay incarcerated, do not allow them to be enclosed in a way that could entail their elimination – by a hundred knights, by a would-be lover, by self-consuming obsession. Friends recognise friends as those who deserve better boundaries, who ought to be seen, and see themselves, as free agents capable of owning their desired objects. And friends place themselves at risk to help the project along.

When Placidas attempts to make his own escape, Poeana's father, Corflambo, nearly kills him. He is saved only because Arthur happens to be nearby and is happy to kill the enraged patriarch. Surely Placidas puts himself at risk. He also gives himself over to Poeana's erotics, bending his sexual mores to hers; and this latter 'sacrifice' clarifies a limit of

the idea in many of the friendship discourses covered so far. Placidas'
account of his initial encounter with Poeana includes self-sacrificial
rhetoric, but with a slip:

> My former hardnesse first I faire excusd;
> And after promist large amends to make.
> With such smooth termes her error I abusd,
> To my friends good, more then for my owne sake,
> For whose sole libertie I love and life did stake.
> (4.8.60.5–9)

Placidas seems to claim that his interest here is not in an erotic relationship from which he might benefit. He seems to claim quite the contrary
– that his love of his friend's 'sole libertie' moves him to altruism. This
is the only solace he takes in tricking this dominatrix. Later, of course,
Placidas receives reward; Arthur convinces him to marry his former
captor and assume control of a reformed Poeana's lands. The walls of
her prison are replaced with a better set of boundaries; Arthur manages
to 'shut vp all in friendly loue' (4.9.15.1). For the second time in book
IV, the offer of self-sacrifice, of being imprisoned and conceivably killed,
ends in self-possession and additional possessions.

   However altruistic Placidas seems, his reward is hardly incidental,
and if we put pressure on his words the gap between sacrifice and profit
closes completely. He submitted, he says, 'To my friends good, more
then for my owne sake'; in using 'more then' rather than 'not' he equivo-
cates, admits that he does what he does, in part, simply because he
enjoys his flirtation with Poeana. Even more: Spenser's choice of 'then'
allows the word to be read not just in a comparative register (as 'than')
but in a temporal one as well, in which case Placidas may reveal that he
does what he does at that moment more on his own behalf – for his own
liberty, love and life – than on Amyas's. It is as though he knows that
the business of friendly self-sacrifice may not be as serious as friendship
discourses often claim – or as he himself seems to claim. It is as though
he has been tipped off as to what is in store for him, what the point of
his story shall be. It is as if Spenser is writing, and Placidas is speaking,
under the weight of so many stories of friendship, that some inexorable
logic lets both know how these stories ought to end.

'foule and lothsome' friendship: Spenser's self-critique

I have suggested that in the story of Amyas and Placidas, Spenser seems
self-conscious about book IV's placement within the canon of friendship

discourse. Nevertheless, the two stories just discussed seem to suggest that book IV accedes to the logic that works to friends' advantage. Spenser seems to assume that friendship's project is to practise the magic by which self-sacrifice becomes self-aggrandisement, to make interaction foster autonomous action. Otherwise, the story of Titus and Gisippus would not be so thematically and structurally central.

But their story is only one. Much friendship theory, including some of Spenser's own, takes Bacon and Montaigne's statements about self-effacement very seriously. Such theory has a long history and extends into a range of more recent work as well – such as that of Georges Bataille, Maurice Blanchot, Jacques Derrida, Judith Butler and many others. All have turned away from bounded selfhood. In part, we will see, they do so because they believe vulnerability to be of inherent value. They also, as I detail in Chapter 3,[33] eschew boundedness because of the wrongs that self-fortifying friendships sometimes require. For initial loss to end in gain, they point out, some third party often bears the cost; for temporary vulnerability to lead to strengthened personal boundaries, that vulnerability is often displaced on to objects which are then sacrificed or threatened with sacrifice. These theorists see this process at play in the contemporary political context, but we can also see the process at work in the story of Titus and Gisippus, where objects that bear displaced vulnerability include Sophronia (whose desires are disregarded), and the Athenians whom Titus would like to obliterate.

Spenser, I want to argue, displays an awareness comparable to that of the theorists mentioned above. In his portrayal of Cambel and Triamond and of Placidas and Amyas, Spenser seems to endorse the logic of which radicals are wary, and even to assume that female figures such as Aemylia and Poeana exist only to be owned, only to help male friends make good on the possessive individuality that they offer each other. In another tale, though, Spenser seems more aware – and, I would hazard, even critical – of the fact that some third (again, female) figure often has to be possessed, manipulated or exposed in order to secure self-fortification. In canto vii, we find Amoret trapped in Lust's cave. She discovers a fellow captive lying beside her, sighing and sobbing, and when she expresses interest in this voice – when she voices what sounds like other-concern – the answer she gets is that she ought to abandon such concern: 'Ah wretched wight / That seekes to know anothers griefe in vaine, / Unweeting of thine owne like haplesse plight: / Selfe to forget to mind another is oversight' (4.7.10.6–9).

The voice here is Aemylia's; the advice, in a place where each moment presents the threat of being devoured, may well strike us as sound. It is the sort of advice that Redcrosse forgets when, in book I, he is deceived by Duessa's weeping; he is 'swallowed vp vnwares/ Forgetfull of his owne, that mindes anothers cares' (1.5.18.7–9). Here, however, no advice is necessary, for Amoret is not at all in a self-forgetting frame of mind. She gives no sign that she asks questions about Aemylia's sufferings out of concern for her fellow captive. Amoret asks questions aimed at illuminating her own situation; specifically, she wants to know how Aemylia has managed to remain 'from [Lust] vnknowne / Thine honor sau'd, though into thraldome throwne' (4.7.19.4–5). Lust exacts only the most awful undoing – his practice is to rape, then eat those he captures – and so Amoret, desiring to preserve her chastity, speaks out of (entirely justified) self-concern. The figure for self-abandonment, Aemylia reveals to Amoret, is a nameless woman who, in offering herself up to Lust, saves their honour: 'Through helpe . . . of this old woman here / I have so done . . . / For ever when he burnt in lustfull fire, / She in my stead supplied his bestiall desire' (4.7.19.6–9).

Aemylia and Amoret never forget themselves or abandon self-concern, as does this old woman. And because this woman does what she does, Spenser's characters abandon her utterly. After Belphoebe defeats Lust and all three captives are freed, the nameless woman is described but briefly, in terms which – given her sacrifice – cannot fail to strike us as unkind: 'A foule and lothsome creature did appeare; / A leman fit for such a lover deare. / That mou'd Belphebe her no lesse to hate, / Then for to rue the others heauy cheare' (4.7.34.4–7). Belphoebe hates this woman – the lone figure here who makes a sacrifice that serves no useful purpose for her, the one figure who gives without expectation of return. Once we know what Belphoebe thinks, this woman vanishes from the poem.

If subjects fail to counterbalance self-sacrifice with self-control and self-concern, the narrative seems to say, they cannot enter the community of friends. One way to interpret this scene – one guided by classic Greenblattian conceptions of self-fashioning[34] – would be to see Spenser rejecting Lust and the nameless woman alike, he for recklessly disregarding others' borders and she for disregarding her own. Such disregard renders the two irredeemable. Belphoebe, Aemylia and Amoret, more temperate, know the importance of healthy self-containment; missing this, figures such as Lust and our 'lothsome creature' put themselves outside the human domain.

Spenser portrays Lust as utterly repugnant, but I am not sure that he does the same with the nameless woman. The obvious irony here – that the figure who in this epic seems the friendliest of all is not befriended by any, that the most other-concerned ends up abjected as wholly other – is lost on Spenser's characters. But clues exist which suggest that the irony is not lost on Spenser himself. Despite announcing that Lust and the nameless woman are fit for each other, the canto invites us to see more resemblances between Amoret, Belphoebe and Lust – a self who uses others as he sees fit – than between him and the old woman whom he ravishes. Amoret, for instance, flees from Lust 'like a ghastly Gelt' (4.7.21.3); and when Belphoebe pursues Lust, he flees 'with ghastly dreriment' (4.7.29.8). Spenser does not invite a simple equation of Amoret's desire to protect her borders with Lust's desire to expand his by engorging himself; but he does suggest that the two, in the desperation with which they cling to themselves, are more alike than the figure who has no name and willingly lets go of everything. In this Spenser does suggest that Amoret is more like Lust than this nameless woman, this loathsome creature who has acceded to vulnerability completely.

After Belphoebe kills Lust, she too reacts in a way that aligns her with him: 'ouer him she there long gazing stood, / And oft admir'd his monstrous shape, and oft / His mighty limbs, whilest all with filthy bloud / The place there ouerflowne, seemed like a sodaine flood' (32.6–9). Arguably, Lust is what tempts Belphoebe and what she temperately refuses – what, however fascinating, must be other to her way of being in the world. But to read this way we have to overlook the fact that Lust occasions not Belphoebe's amazement, or not only that, but also her admiration. She gazes at him for so long in this attitude, admiring his monstrously swollen body, unconcerned that his self-swelling has led only to a sudden bloody overflowing. A figure who questions others but never herself, Belphoebe's interest in the repellent figure of Lust betrays her momentary identification with him, and her virtue with his. In Spenser's portrayal, Lust's way of being in the world is never other than abhorrent, and in this instant – just before she scorns the nameless woman – Belphoebe identifies with his abhorrence.

In allowing the reader to question Belphoebe, Spenser constructs canto vii to foreclose readerly ability to adopt any likely figure as a model for self-fashioning or for fashioning friendship. The canto's least loathsome figure may well be the loathsome creature who herself attaches no value to her self and so quickly disappears. Canto vii follows a ghastly logic that Spenser portrays as bankrupt; either you engage in grotesque self-swelling (Lust), or you protect yourself (as Amoret does) – an enterprise that only succeeds when someone else is utterly exposed. Either you commit to personal boundaries and might go on living (as Amoret does) so long as someone else does not, or you are so uncommitted to those boundaries that you cease to exist.

Considered together, the tales of friendship discussed thus far put book IV's theory of friendship in a strange place. Cambel and Triamond follow the path of sacrifice that reaps rewards; so do Amyas and Placidas. In portraying them, Spenser exhibits some scepticism about the rhetoric of self-sacrifice – about whether the declared and actual content of friendship coincide. In the episode of Lust's cave, Spenser allows us to see how self-protective structures of friendship can have more to do with other-sacrifice. As a group, the friendships of book IV discussed so far call into question the story of Titus and Gisippus by foregrounding the dubious support on which the friendships depend. And if they suggest limits and dangers of friendship that furthers bounded selfhood, they also suggest the need for other models of relation.

Many critics have overlooked this point. In his reading of Lust's death, for example, Hadfield focuses not on the nameless woman but on Lust himself, on his 'lack of restraint and bestial sexual appetite', and on how, for Spenser, Lust's way of being in the world must be met with and superseded by more civilised forms of violence.[35] Hadfield exposes the self-defensive violence used to secure English identity, but in neglecting the nameless woman, he underestimates the extent to which Spenser is not just conscious, but also is critical, of the practices by which selves construct boundaries of identity. This is why Greenblatt overstates in saying that Spenser simply 'loves power';[36] and why Spenser is not, as Hadfield puts it, always only 'painfully aware that boundaries exist which can all too easily be transgressed and always need to be policed'.[37] Greenblatt and Hadfield overlook what Spenser, in his self-criticism, at times seems to say in book IV: that, too often, friends do not take friendly intersubjectivity as seriously as they say they do – that, too often, the figures of his poem fail to allow for the opening and undoing that ought to occur when they are together.

So far I have suggested this only by negation – by pointing to what I take to be Spenser's dissatisfaction with the very commonplaces of the Renaissance friendship discourse that he at times employs. But I do not believe that Spenser's project was primarily a critical or a simply equivocal one – that in his book of friendship he meant to tepidly endorse a dominant model of Renaissance friendship, undermine that model and stop there. Quite the contrary; much of book IV prompts and even constitutes a radical rethinking of what friendship can be. In hating the nameless woman, Belphoebe would have us believe that when we enter into relation, we must keep the maintenance of disciplined, bounded selfhood in view, that if we fail to do so, we will end up ravished and swiftly eliminated, as the old woman is. Inhabiting worlds of dangerous excess, subjects thus must fashion themselves and be fashioned as disciplined English subjects. This, not unlike the world of book II as Greenblatt presents it, is the danger that Lust presents. Often, however,

Spenser sees this line of thinking as blinkered in its view of friendship's possible functions. Often, I will now show, he invites us to realise worlds in which the consequences of openness – of vulnerability and a non-instrumental, self-squandering form of life – are not so dire.

Without Respect of Utility

A concern discussed above – about the wrongs that often secure bounded, possessive existence – has helped motivate many theorists to privilege friendship's potential to undo boundaries, and to show how the 'useless' experience of undoing may be a good one. Derrida, for instance, has explored the notion of 'a friendship without hearth, of a *philia* without *oikeiotes*'; whereas 'so-called political friendship is grounded in association or community in view of the useful,' Derrida explores the possibility of aneconomic friendships. He imagines a 'minimal community' founded on *philia* that is older than subjectivity and its borders, friendship prior to that which we would normally recognise, without regard for contract, mutuality or agreement. Derrida thus calls for a friendship without fraternity – a groundless, useless politics of friendship, but one that is none the less fundamental and ineffaceable.[38]

If Derrida calls for community that loses sight of the useful, Butler locates such loss at the core of human relation. She writes that our connections to others, whether or not we imagine them as such, often simply arrive, beyond control and consent;[39] and so, as long as friendship is supposed to foster self-possession and possessive individualism, friendship runs the risk of being useless. Butler even extends the point, observing that we cannot be useful to each other in this way because our being in the world, our bodies and our identities alike, are constituted through social orders that precede and exceed us. Vulnerability and incapacity – not autonomy and acquisition – are thus interaction's inevitable but also potentially valuable outcome. We are, necessarily, beings 'attached to others, at risk of losing those attachments, exposed to others, at risk of violence by virtue of that exposure'; '[w]e're undone by each other,' Butler writes; '[a]nd if we're not', she adds, 'we're missing something.'[40] What we miss when we fail to see how we undo each other – and how a politics of friendship must take undoing into account – is the opportunity to reflect on how to inhabit our vulnerability without resorting to the reactive, self-defensive violence by which we so often try to compensate for the fact that we are vulnerable. Butler advocates a meditation upon how precarious all lives must be, and how precariousness can – and must – be lived.

Underlying Butler's advocacy is the assumption, evident in earlier theorisations such as those of Blanchot and Bataille, that our existence as vulnerable, incomplete beings might actually be desirable. In his reading of Bataille, Blanchot writes that being recognised as discrete and delineated is just the opposite of the self-dissolution that we all, in our own way, are after. 'A being', Blanchot writes, 'does not want to be recognized, it wants to be contested,' called into question, broken apart. More than a sense of ourselves as distinct individuals, we want to experience life 'as an existence shattered through and through, composing itself only as it decomposes itself constantly'.[41] Communication is thus 'an opening to the outside and an opening to others' without regard for consent or reciprocal recognition, without regard for bounded selfhood. For Blanchot, friendship itself is a movement to dissolution (22).

In his own work, Bataille similarly claims that friendship occurs as a form of ecstasy, and that entering into friendship equals self-loss. Of the difference between this and love, Bataille writes that while the latter involves two subjects who possess each other as objects, ecstasy involves pure passage, a communication that moves not from one subject to another but that folds whatever existence we have as bounded subjects into our existence in a pure between. This folding renders impossible a detached, possessive, instrumental relationship to the world and renders inconceivable the division of that world into sets of subjects and objects.[42] Accordingly, Bataille conceives of friendly sacrifice not as that which serves utility's sake, but as that which, in Bacon's words, must be 'without respect of utility'. Bataille takes the self-sacrificial aspect of friendship completely seriously – friendship occurs only when we give without receiving, when we become more like solar energy than stable subjects, when we exist as pure expenditure, utterly incapable of conserving ourselves.[43]

Friendship thus imagined might seem naïve, utopian, or simply unliveable. But the theorists just discussed do not dispense with personal boundaries entirely; those boundaries simply lose the privileged status that they have in stories such as that of Titus and Gisippus, in some theories of Spenserian self-fashioning, and in some liberal theory. In Butler's view, for example, individual demarcations are and should be fabricated partly through the elaboration of rights – not only or primarily to protect bounded individuality but also to enable salutary experiences of vulnerability.[44] Bataille is far more radical, for he does not make the kinds of concessions that Butler does. But even he does not just abandon boundaries. He objects only to the notion of boundaries that exist so as to protect or bolster selves rather than to intensify aneconomic experience. Whereas the tale of Titus and Gisippus employs momentary sacrifice in service of self-fortification, for example, Bataille urges us to use such fortification not to guard against but to further sacrificial ecstasy; if, as he writes, '[l]ife is a result of disequilibrium and instability,' '[s]table forms are needed to make it possible':

> We have to stake out courses that are stable enough. To shrink from fundamental stability isn't less cowardly than to hesitate about shattering it. Perpetual instability is more boring than adhering strictly to a rule, and only what's in existence can be made to come into disequilibrium, that is, to be *sacrificed*. The more equilibrium the object has, the more *complete* it is, and the greater the disequilibrium or *sacrifice* that can result.[45]

Bataille's investment in constructing stable forms for the purpose of exploding them is founded on the belief that we can handle it; we are structured such that the erosion of personal boundaries does not mean death.

In a sense, at issue in all of the foregoing – in friendship theory now and in the Renaissance, in Spenser and critical treatments of him – is how we can be in the world, and what the world is for us. From one perspective the world is one of scarcity and so of necessity, one in which resources should be stockpiled, and in which drawing the distinction between self-willing subjects and manipulable objects becomes critically important; in such a world, the compromise of the self and its possessions contains fatal potential.[46] In one politics of friendship, then, Titus needs his scarce love object and Gisippus needs his lands returned to him in order for both to go on living; bounded individuals need final control over themselves and what they regard as theirs. When such a politics is operative in Spenser, as I have noted, the maintenance of boundaries often necessitates violence. As Greenblatt claims, Guyon must destroy the bower of bliss in order to establish and maintain self-control; as Hadfield argues, to maintain control over Ireland and over bounded English identity, the English must control the unruly Irish.

In the opposing perspective, Bataille's own, the world is essentially one of surplus, of excess resources, of energies that surpass our needs and that thus, one way or another, not only can but must be wasted. From this vantage, the self always has reserves of energy that exceed what is required to maintain life; an instrumentalised orientation to the world – the division of that world into clearly delineated subjects and objects – becomes unnecessary. The self's reserves allow for the unworking and reworking of its boundaries, only so as to unwork, rework and unwork them again. These are reserves, in other words, that allow vulnerability, not boundedness, to be given privilege.

The world made in *The Faerie Queene* – as I will demonstrate and as every reader who sees superfluous energies in Faerie Land must know – resembles this world at least as much as the one defined by scarcity. One legitimate Spenserian question, then, is whether we might want to be given over to sacrifice, inhabiting our vulnerability, giving up the idea that we are centres of freely willed, acquisitive action in a world of clearly bounded subjects and objects. The question is whether we might want to let go of control and allow ourselves to be undone by others, might want to know how it feels to 'squander' energy – to put aneconomic activity at the heart of our politics of friendship. The question is whether the recognition we give and are given should, first and foremost, confirm and strengthen us or should be of the vulnerability that we share; whether personal boundaries exist above all to bolster our sense of ourselves as discrete and delineated, or should set off the experience of *jouissance* when those boundaries are undone; whether self-possession, when we develop it, should further possessive individualism or should instead enable greater self-sacrifice.

The question is by no means new with Spenser or with the Renaissance. In fact, it is not unfamiliar to the republican tradition that, when viewed a certain way, would seem at odds with friendship theory that privileges sacrifice of self. But when we bear in mind, as I do in Chapter 1, that republican traditions are multiple, we can find strong resemblances between ideas just discussed and those of, say, the Roman republican Cicero. In some respects, to be sure, Cicero is an odd fit with contemporary radical thinking. His writing has a Stoic strain, one that privileges self-control; and Cicero would find alien or repulsive a few of the notions described above and explored below – for instance, that friendship should be without fraternity, that it should involve squandering anything, and that friends desire *jouissance* above all. Cicero believes, too, that advantage often grows out of friendship, even as his letters waver, wildly, between the languages of calculating self-interest and of boundless self-sacrifice.[47]

But as the letters suggest and as *De Amicitia* bears out, Cicero is far from systematic in his thinking; and his sense of the work of friendship shares much with radical theory. For Cicero (following Aristotle),[48] friendship simply is not true friendship – nor citizenship true citizenship – when self-interest assumes primary or ultimate status; friendship, he writes, 'cannot under any circumstances be derived from any calculation of potential profit'.[49] Even a more balanced approach, one that conforms 'friendship to an equal exchange of services and feelings', none the less 'reduces it to a too mean and narrow calculation of payments and receipts meticulously balanced'. Friendship 'is not going to keep a close watch on whether it pays out more than it receives' (205–6).

Quite the contrary. The friend is going to try to pay out more than he receives. We should, according to Cicero, 'take as our model the fertile fields, which bring forth much more than they have received',[50] and to do so the Ciceronian friend must resemble the friend in Bataille, at least in so far as he moves within an abundant world, has more than he needs, and so has deep reserves to expend. Describing Scipio Africanus, Laelius (*De Amicitia*'s speaker) remarks that Scipio was a great friend not despite but because of his self-sufficiency, his utter lack of dependence on others; because he had 'the very least need of anyone else', Scipio could perform acts of friendship without asking for any in return (194, 204). In this, Cicero offers a solution to the problem, posed by Plato in *Lysis*, as to why self-sufficient men bother making friends to begin with.[51] For Cicero the good man renders the world one of surplus – it is not simply given, as in Bataille, but can be achieved by the good man – and so for Cicero, friendship is as Derrida would like it to be: openly aneconomic. The friend believes and acts as though – and enjoys acting as though – friendship involves loss more than gain, and in this way is without utility.

This means embracing the hazards that friendship, not to mention community membership, entail.[52] In his praise of the story of Orestes and Pylades – it, like the story of Titus and Gisippus, involves one friend being willing, before a judge, to sacrifice his life for the other – Cicero admires not that these friends escape unscathed, that the risk undertaken in friendship is rewarded, but rather that they are willing to undergo total risk for each other (189). To demonstrate great republican spirit, Cicero counsels, 'you should vigorously undertake difficult and laborious tasks which endanger both life itself and much that concerns life';[53] in *De re publica*, as noted above, Cicero claims that he 'did not hesitate to subject myself to the greatest tempests, even thunderbolts, of fate' for Rome's sake (18). For Blanchot, friendship is a movement toward dissolution; so for Cicero to be a friend or fellow citizen is to be willing to undergo dissolution. And while Blanchot regards such alacrity as a matter of desire, Cicero sees it as one of duty.

The embrace of peril in Cicero begins as do the best connections in Butler: with a recognition of shared vulnerability. The self, however invulnerable he might be on his own, not only recognises his own vulnerability in the friend; whenever the friend suffers, the self suffers with him. Friendship relieves the self of suffering alone. 'Should things go wrong,' Cicero writes, 'your misfortunes will indeed be hard to bear without someone who suffers as badly as yourself, or even worse.'[54] Friendship thus 'will inevitably involve distress, and quite often at that' (203).

Besides which, if one wished to avoid friendship for the shared worry and pain that it brings, being in the world ensures – as Butler would argue so much later – that such a wish remain unfulfilled. 'Somehow or other', Cicero writes, 'friendship inserts itself into all our existences. However we choose to live, there is no escaping it' (219). Butler believes that our connections with others arrive whether we will them or no, and Cicero's belief is no different. We cannot help but form connections. Nor can we tell whether or not we ought to have done so until the connection already exists: 'the friendship comes first and the material for estimating its desirability only becomes accessible later on; it is impossible to try out one's friends in advance' (208).[55] We undertake friendship in that risk and prove it most when self-loss enters the field of possibility.

And yet self-loss, for Cicero as for Butler, does not imply a destructive politics of friendship. If the risk of friendship is the risk of non-existence, the existence of the social structure depends on our embracing that risk: 'Take away the bond of kindly feeling from the world', Cicero writes, 'and no house or city can stand' (189). It seems counter-intuitive to say that the strongest social structures are held together by weakness, but in one sense this is precisely Cicero's point; those structures stand on the basis that those who make them might and must be willing to fall. 'We must', he remarks in *De Officiis*, 'be more willing to risk our own than the common welfare.'[56]

I have discussed how many of those interested in English republicanism describe republican selfhood as bounded selfhood. But Cicero says that the strongest friends are those for whom self-sufficiency gives way to susceptibility; all forms of life depend on friendship, and republican friendship at its best, like friendship as presented by Butler, Bataille and Blanchot, means being vulnerable – means privileging and embracing vulnerability, allowing it to be the content of community even as its more odious forms are what community rules out. For the balance of this chapter I will show how Spenser occupies, explores and expands upon the dimensions of this position, pursuing its complexities along radical and republican lines.

Headless Knights: Book IV's Battles

Earlier, I noted that as Triamond gains strength, battle unexpectedly becomes more difficult. A life more tolerable – more fleeting but also more open – is the one he leads with his similarly named brothers, those whose deaths make him a repository of incredible, invulnerable but intolerable power. Much more pleasurable is the indistinction of this prior life, in which Triamond and his brothers 'loue each other deare, what euer them befell' (4.2.53.9). These three, who 'with so firme affection were allyde' (4.2.43.2), do not care who ends up with Canacee, do not care which subject has her: 'never discord did amongst them fall . . . / And now t'increase affection naturall, / In love of Canacee they ioyned all' (4.2.54.2–5). They view their relation as one not founded on the calculation and calibration of individual interests, and so rather than introduce antagonism, love of Canacee only increases their affection for each other. Individual benefit has no meaning for them because they cannot conceive of benefit as other than mutual. Whereas Triamond later becomes, with Cambel, united in a commitment to individual difference, the brothers -mond are now like Montaignean friends; they lack the vocabulary of separation and difference. They cannot see their association as other than antithetical to individuation.

When it comes to that other, more total sort of indistinction – the mingling of their souls – Spenser celebrates not strength but shared weakness. When Diamond dies, for example, most remarkable is not the infusion of strength into Triamond. Rather, what fascinates Spenser is the moment of Diamond's dying. When Priamond dies, his soul enters Diamond's, and because of this, when Diamond's time comes, boundaries are shown to be eroded – not just between subjects, but between life and death; it is a moment of complete incapacity in which a figure still stands, not for himself as a bounded self but for being without a self. Diamond is decapitated by Cambel:

> from his shoulders quite his head he reft:
> The headless tronke, as heedlesse of that stower,
> Stood still a while, and his fast footing kept,
> Till feeling life to fayle, it fell, and deadly slept.
> . . .
> They which that piteous spectacle beheld,
> Were much amaz'd the headlesse tronke to see
> Stand up so long, and weapon vaine to weld . . .
>   (4.3.20.6–4.3.21.3)

What most amazes those watching occurs prior to the moment in which Priamond and Diamond's souls fortify their brother; what amazes them most, and what arouses their pity, is this moment for Diamond – headless, faceless, self-less but not dead, not yet. What amazes most is not the invulnerability that Triamond takes on, but the utter exposure of a head taken off. The shared existence of Priamond and Diamond provides support that astonishes those who are its witness. Through the brothers -mond, Spenser raises the question of how it might be possible to inhabit 'headlessness': to be incapable of calculation, willed action or even thought (let alone thinking for oneself). In so far as they have not been calculating the brothers -mond have always led a headless life, and that headlessness is brought to an extreme, amazing end when Diamond keeps his footing.

This is not to say that Spenser longs for a world in which we slice off each other's heads so that onlookers can experience the momentary sublimity of decapitated bodies that can still stand. But it is to say that Spenser, like Cicero and contemporary theorists of friendship who share with him, is less impressed by the strengthening of the self's boundaries than by genuine sacrifice, by the erosion of those boundaries in vulnerability. There almost seems an elegiac tone, a note of regret in his dilation of the moment of Diamond's death, a desire to linger evident in the halting syntax that describes his fall: he 'Stood still a while, and his fast footing kept, / Till feeling life to fayle, it fell, and deadly slept.' If only, the text suggests, Cambel had not been so strong, did not cling to himself and his sister so grimly; if only moments of sinking below self-consciousness, and soaring beyond self-concern, did not mean death.

How else might the brothers -mond have lived out their indistinction and lack of self-concern, their ability to love the same thing in the way that Ciceronian friends love virtue: a way so uncompetitive and unacquisitive as to multiply their affection for each other? Cicero writes that 'when friendship is measured by the affection it generates from within, there is nothing to surpass it.'[57] If this is our measure, nothing can surpass the friendship between these brothers. They fulfil other Ciceronian criteria too. 'Man's peculiar virtue', Cicero avers, 'is fortitude, of which there are two main functions, namely scorn of death and scorn of pain'; the friendship between the brothers -mond lets them scorn both.[58] And if they are to be understood as offering a model of belonging, they not only, like Cicero's ideal republican citizens, have no concern for individual gain – not only do not keep a close watch on whether they give more than they receive – but even undertake a task that, they know, endangers their lives.

In other respects, of course, their example does not fit the Ciceronian model. First of all, for Cicero the ideal friend – and the ideal citizen – is self-sufficient in that he is so outside the sphere of need that he no longer needs to consider himself a discrete, bounded subject in a world of scarce objects. For all that the brothers -mond do not exist as discrete subjects, they nevertheless perceive, and desperately pursue, a scarce object. What is more, they do so objectionably. There are two objects in their world, one of love – Canacee – and one of hate – Cambel – and both are viewed as Cicero contends friends and fellow citizens never should be viewed, as 'cattle', possessions to be either hoarded or destroyed.[59] They lack rationality as Cicero defines it in *On Moral Ends* (and as I discuss above);[60] while they do seem drained of self-concern, reason does not lead them to extend bonds of affection ever outwards, to embrace all. Their world instead is one where friends are contrasted with enemies. Presenting their interests as irreconcilable, the encounter between Cambel and the brothers -mond dramatises the gap between, and the difficulty of bridging, one Ciceronian ideal – the transcendence of individual interest in friendship (between the brothers themselves) – and another – achieving that transcendence in broader, more inclusive terms.

Priamond and Diamond perish in the space of this gap: the battlefield. Spenser returns to the space time and again, in ways that both follow and depart from Ciceronian lines of thought: for example, in Satyrane's tournament. In a sense, the tournament re-enacts the struggle between Cambel and the brothers -mond. It presents groups of 'friends' united against groups of enemies in a world of irreconcilable interests, and just as Cambel and the brothers -mond are battling over Canacee, the apparent end of the tournament is a prize, Florimell's 'gorgeous girdle' (4.15.6).

Here, however, the object of desire is not just, or even primarily, the girdle but is also the regard that winning the girdle would give. In fact, Spenser presents a struggle between opposing impulses wherein the girdle is hardly primary: the impulse to be recognised as heroic and whole, and the impulse to be contested and broken apart. In the tournament, these impulses are always intertwined and clarify what, for Spenser, can be achieved from battling. When Cambel and Triamond take part in the tournament, I have suggested, a process of self-aggrandisement begins as willing self-sacrifice. For others, though, attempted aggrandisement leads only to self-loss. Silberman sees these dynamics in a negative light, in circuits of mutual comparison and pointless recognition – in a stupendously unproductive pissing contest – and to an extent she is doubtless right.[61] Still, I wonder if figures other than Cambel and Triamond gain more from contestation and undoing than from recognition, and further, if desire for the latter intensifies the experience of the former. For example, the more that combatants such as Satyrane insist on winning (and being seen as winners), the more they are undone, and the more impressive the squandering of energy seems to be. Spenser describes Satyrane's first encounter in the tournament, with 'Bruncheual the bold', as such:

> So furiously they both together met,
> That neither could the others force sustaine;
> As when two fierce Buls, that strive the rule to get
> Of all the heard, meete with so hideous maine,

That both rebutted, tumble on the plaine:
So these two champions on the ground were feld,
Where in a maze they both did long remaine,
And in their hands their idle truncheons held,
Which neither able were to wag, or once to weld.
                                        (4.4.18)

The stanza's first five lines accord with the idea that the tournament is a competition for only the most primal recognition and control over spoils. If the tournament thus seems driven by an instrumental economy, however, once the 'champions' are on the ground they enter an economy. They remain in mazes; singularly incapable of erect being, they cannot even attempt to find their way out. Pursuit of recognition produces *jouissance* that unmans them, plunges them into states of extravagant incapacity within which they cannot wield (or even wag) the instruments by which they would triumph. If Bruncheval and Satyrane are after the girdle, they enact the folly of acquisitive individuals as Cicero describes them and fall far short of the ideal man, who does not nominate things as goods 'because the enjoyment of them seems to him slight, the use minimal, and the ownership uncertain'.[62] If they are after recognition, similarly, they not only are not going to get quite what they want, but exist in the state of dependency that, according to Cicero, the desire for glory always occasions.[63]

For all its folly, though, this encounter between Bruncheval and Satyrane is not a straightforward illustration of how they fail to conform to Ciceronian ideals. Their immobilising encounter, for instance, sounds rather like the undoing of Scudamour and Amoret when they embrace at the climax of the 1590 *Faerie Queene*: '[n]o word they spake, nor earthly thing they felt, / But like two senceles stocks in long embracement dwelt' (3.12.45a.8–9). For Amoret and Scudamour this senseless state is an ultimate outcome, so much so that in 1596, with book III no longer at the epic's end, Spenser would strike their climax from the text. For Bruncheval and Satyrane, such a state is simply life as lived within the tournament; it eclipses the importance of the final outcome. This agon assumes precedence over the self-'salving' acts of friendship that Cambel and Triamond offer to one another. If one looks beyond what combatants ostensibly want to what they are asking for – and are exposed to over and over – the greatest enemies here turn out to be the best of friends.

At its outset, Satyrane's tournament shows how the assertion of self leads to intense undoing, undoing all the more intense in its contrast to the stability that immediately precedes it. Earlier, I mentioned how theorists like Bataille do not pose the question of the erection and erosion of strong personal boundaries, of the construction and destruction of stable forms, as absolute. Though Bataille believes exposure, ecstasy and instability to be superior to closure, self-possession and stability, he also believes that the initial imposition of more stable forms can make the ensuing instability more liveable and luxuriant.[64] A similar logic is at work in Satyrane's tournament. Spenser does not pose the problem of selfhood as requiring an irrevocable choice between fortifying and undoing ourselves. Rather, he considers whether the latter should be put in service of the former – as Cambel and Triamond do, activating a possessive, instrumental economy and way of being in the world – and whether the process ought instead to be reversed, whether self-enclosure and assertion ought to foster exposure and life that is aneconomic.

For Satyrane and Bruncheval, what looks like a desire to prove the self's strength and stability serves only extravagant idleness – serves only felled identity, radical disequilibrium, life lived below the level of self-concern. And unlike Priamond or Diamond, this does not bring the end of life; the battles of the tournament are more innocuous than this. Though we do not hear more from Bruncheval, Satyrane survives and fights again. Battles such as this suggest that one reason for fashioning ourselves – for assuming a world of subjects and objects that we might then possess – lies in the unfashioning that follows.

Being encased in armour strengthens the contrast when others split that armour open, and as Spenser develops this insight, we can observe the collision of the thought of a republican like Cicero and that of a radical like Bataille. If the two share in rejecting possessiveness, they collide here over proper forms of undoing. For even as the tournament shares with Cicero in presenting the dangers of being possessive – of wasting energy and of losing what you would possess – Spenser dotes upon those dangers as Bataille does: as appealingly extravagant. Spenser's portrayal of the tournament undermines one aspect of republican thinking even as it reinforces another, challenging Cicero's belief that the self's undoing ought always to be in performance of some duty, personal or civic – whether to the friend, to the republic or to virtue itself. During the tournament, worthwhile undoing extends to those who lack worth – and extends no further than the experience of being on their backs. So for all that I explore overlap between radical thought and its republican counterpart, the tournament allows us to see how the former displays a limit of the latter.

'Twixt themselves alone': Britomart and Amoret

Spenser dotes on figures lost to an instrumentalised world of subjects and objects and to the closure that such a world might provide.[65] But so far the appearance and reappearance of objects – Canacee, Florimell's girdle, the title of champion – limit (even as they enable) possibilities for the undoing of these subjects. Aneconomic moments of incapacity and self-loss have led either to death or to an all too quick resumption of self-interested action.

In stanzas 21–24 of the book's first canto, when the speaker describes Ate's home, he muses about the 'sad effects of discord' that take place in a world understood as one populated by scarce objects. Hung on Ate's walls are signs of 'sad Ilion, / For memorie of which on high there hong / The golden Apple, cause of all their wrong, / For which the three faire Goddesses did strive' (4.1.22.3–6). The speaker longs here to be rid of discord's sadness, to eliminate the notion of golden apples, to see instead an abundant world in which the self can sacrifice its resources – and expend itself – without real harm. Within such a world, to adopt an instrumental, self-concerned approach would be misplaced, would be to misconstrue so much of the world's offer. Selves could instead enter Satyrane and Bruncheval's wandering mazes to experience vulnerability not alone but together, as something shared and good.

Twice in book IV, Spenser constructs scenarios of this sort, ones that bring together meanings of friendship in radical and republican thought. The first, which culminates in a bed scene between Britomart and Amoret, is set in motion during the book's first battle, between Britomart and a nameless 'iolly knight'. Both seek entrance to a couples-only castle, and so the battle is over Amoret. The knight swears

> That fairest Amoret was his by rights,
> And offred that to iusitife alowd.
> The warlike virgine seeing his so prowd
> And boastfull chalenge, wexed inlie wroth,
> But for the present did her anger shrowd;
> And sayd, her loue to lose she was full loth,
> But either he should neither of them have, or both.
> . . .
> So foorth they went, and both together giusted;
> But that same younker soone was ouerthrowne,
> And made repent, that he had rashly lusted
> For thing unlawfull, that was not his owne;
> Yet since he seemed valiant, though unknowne,
> She that no lesse was courteous then stout,
> Cast how to salue, that both the custome showne
> Were kept, and yet that Knight not locked out,

That seem'd full hard t'accord two things so far in dout.
. . .
The Seneschall was cal'd to deeme the right,
Whom she requir'd, that first fayre Amoret
Might be to her allow'd, as to a Knight,
That did her win and free from chalenge set:
Which straight to her was yeelded without let.
Then since that strange Knights love from him was quitted,
She claim'd that to her selfe, as Ladies det,
He as a Knight might iustly be admitted;
So none should be outshut, sith all of loues were fitted.
                                                    (stanzas 10–12)

In some respects, this battle seems unremarkably structured; two masculine, warlike figures fight over lawful right to a feminine object. The structure seems zero-sum; whoever wins the joust wins the prize, Amoret. Britomart guards Amoret quite jealously; her world, at this moment, is a world of subjects and objects. She claims that the jolly knight has been unlawful in trying to seize an object belonging by rights not to him, as he claims, but to her.

Still, Britomart is not always only possessive of herself and what she identifies as her own. The situation with the jolly knight – for her, anyhow – is not zero-sum; if in losing to Britomart the jolly knight loses Amoret, he gains Britomart when she takes his arm, when she makes sure that the castle they enter is one from which 'none should be outshut'. And so when she removes her helmet, all within the castle walls are 'with amazement smit' (14.2). In occupying two subject positions – in being a female knight, assuming the 'inclusive identity' which Schwarz has so carefully described[66] – Britomart shows how she can both possess and be possessed in passing yet revocable ways. She makes this openness valuable and even virtuous for herself and those around her.

The jolly knight, 'doubly overcommen', thus adores her. Overcome once on the battlefield and again when he beholds Britomart's face, he gives her '[t]en thousand thanks', having delighted in his double loss (4.1.15.3–5). If Butler is right to say that we are missing something when we fail to see how we are undone by each other, the jolly knight – inhabiting defeat, ravished by the sight of Britomart – misses nothing. The scene allows Amoret to open up as well. No longer worried that her knight-protector will want to ravish her in Lust-like, self-swelling fashion, Amoret can give Britomart '[m]ore franke affection' (15.4–7). She can follow Britomart to bed. There, losing control makes sense, and so we see what Stephens, rightly, calls the poem's 'one happy bed scene', a scene in which Britomart, having occupied all subject positions, now occupies none:[67] 'Where all that night they of their loues did treat, / And hard aduentures twixt themselves alone, / That each the other gan with passion great, / And griefull pittie priuately bemone' (4.1.16.1–4).

Until this moment subjects and objects, in however limited and flexible a fashion, have remained in play. Notions of possession (if not rigid forms of self-possession and possessive individualism) have remained in operation. But not so now. After fixed, clear positions have become difficult to establish, personal frontiers are the next to go. Ambiguity abounds in these lines: about who or what excites passion; about what it could mean to be 'twixt themselves alone'; about which hard adventures are in question; about whether they take place now or have already taken place.[68] Self-disclosures do not give selves the closure of clear delineation; their friendly confessions do not stabilise or even locate them as individuals. The 'right safe assurance' (1.15.9) achieved during the bed scene does not solidify or strengthen them in any recognisable way. It instead yields the vexed state of shared suffering that Cicero regards as a necessary – not to mention a beautiful – part of genuine friendship, and that Guyon promises to Amavia in book II's opening canto, when he offers to 'die with you in sorrow, and partake your griefe' if he cannot help her (2.1.48.9). As Guyon promises to be, Britomart and Amoret are exposed, 'twixt themselves alone', in a state of disorientation that generates an excruciating emotional outpouring. These two cannot give each other self-assurance but are instead assured, for this night, of being both between and alone, outside themselves but also outside any easy, restorative unity, undone and unjoined at once. Being so occasions the 'passion great' that Spenser recuperates, that defines the one happy bed scene in *The Faerie Queene*. Previously, one might have thought that for these two, in pursuit of lost love objects, the world was one characterised by scarcity; yet discussing these lost objects has led to an affective abundance which, overflowing, carries them beyond that world.

Through discourse, what had been a world of clearly delineated subjects and objects becomes something else for Britomart and Amoret; talking together inside the castle, insides and outsides, being 'twixt' and being 'alone', cannot be told apart. Being unbounded ('twixt') is not the means to the end of being bounded ('alone'); instead, the two coincide as internally related, simultaneous processes. In bed, Britomart and Amoret's friendly intersubjectivity cannot work toward the bolstering of personal boundaries. Talking about their lost objects, Artegall and Scudamour, unworks their sense of themselves as subjects. The hard adventures about which they worry shade into those that they have with one another. They nullify, if only for this night, their interest in the future altogether.

Britomart and Amoret's shared dwelling undoes their possessive impulses similarly. They escape the dangers of possessiveness of which Cicero warns in favour of the sharing that he praises as integral to the ideal friend and citizen. All of Britomart's self-fashioning – her cultivation of preternatural control – serves the purpose that self-sufficiency does for Cicero: that of giving, of friendship's outpour. We see, as well, not love's mutual self-possession but lost love eclipsed by ecstasy as Bataille defines it, pure passage, a communication that does not move from one subject to another but that folds existence 'alone' into existence 'twixt'. These two escape the poverty of possessive, future-directed outlooks and prompt us to imagine the form that their community might take were it to extend beyond their bedroom's walls.

We should not forget that the scene is but brief. Within a few lines morning arrives and the two start searching again for Artegall and Scudamour; they resume the attempt to possess. Still, in her refusal to draw distinctions – to fix the jolly knight in the loser's position, to subdue the enemy completely, or to insist on a difference between life that is between and life that is alone – Britomart opens a space in which she and Amoret can experience vulnerability, even luxuriate in it, without being quickly eliminated as the nameless woman is. And their friendship could become our politics were we to assume that our life with others affords exposure and outpour, the erosion of our boundaries: were we to assume that others exist not only to strengthen us but also to share in our weakness, and to allow us to share in theirs. Their bed scene, expanding on the brothers -mond in a way, offers a form of life that makes respect for utility – makes a possessive relationship to oneself or one's world – unthinkable. According to Cicero, 'the benefits that friendship offers almost defy description, they are so great';[69] when these friends move beyond calculation, similarly, friendship's value becomes incalculable.

'their beuers up did reare': Britomart and Artegall

There is one more episode, with which I would like to end, in which Spenser again sees importance in armour coming off: the episode in which Britomart and Artegall behold, in turn, the other's face.

In their bed scene, Britomart and Amoret recognise each other's suffering not in order to be healed but to move beyond, or between, the concerns of persons. For these two, recognising weakness means sharing it. Recognition so conceived is also at the core of Butler's treatment of Levinas in *Precarious Life*. There, she examines how exposure to the face of the other exposes us by placing demands, 'ones that we do not ask for, ones that we are not free to refuse'; in Butler's formulation '[t]o respond to the face, to understand its meaning, means to be awake to what is precarious in another life or, rather, the precariousness of life itself' (131, 134). For Butler and Levinas alike, to enter into relation with the face of the other is to become incapable of killing (138); for Butler, any politics of friendship depends upon keeping vulnerability in mind and acknowledging that that vulnerability is shared, that it is ever-present, that all life is precarious. An encounter between Britomart and Artegall in book IV, I will now show, suggests such a politics. And whereas the scene between Britomart and Amoret occurs entirely privately, here Spenser puts the recognition of shared vulnerability – one that stays swords and induces complete incapacity – at the inception of England itself.

Britomart topples Artegall near the end of Satyrane's tournament, but a more crucial moment occurs afterward, in canto vi, when they fight again. Artegall splits open Britomart's helmet but finds that he cannot strike the final blow. Actually, he cannot control himself at all. The face before him disarms him utterly:

> And as his hand he vp againe did reare,
> Thinking to worke on her his vtmost wracke,
> His powrelesse arme benumbed with secret feare
> From his reuengefull purpose shronke abacke,
> And cruell sword out of his fingers slacke
> Fell downe to ground, as if the steele had sence,
> And felt some ruth, or sence his hand did lacke,
> Or both of them did thinke, obedience
> To doe to so diuine a beauties excellence.
> . . .
> . . . trembling horrour did his sense assayle,
> And made ech member quake, and manly hart to quayle.
> (4.6.21, 4.6.22.8–9)

Artegall's somatic response to Britomart drains him of his will to avenge himself. Benumbed, powerless, he drops his sword. It is as though the fierce agency that Artegall has had has left him altogether and has entered the sword that promptly deposits itself on the ground, or as though his ability to think and decide has been displaced on to his hand and sword. Faced with Britomart's utter openness, he is undone extremely and to his extremities; appendages now are actors, independent of his wishes. Her loss fails to become his gain; her exposure affords him no closure. Her vulnerability is his.

Horror takes hold of him. It seems that Britomart has again gained the upper hand – that the 'golden border' of her hair has saved her. He and Scudamour, on their knees, 'their beuers up did reare' (4.6.25.8–9).

And now that Artegall is exposed at his most vulnerable, she becomes vulnerable once again. His exposure reactivates hers, for his is a face that Britomart has seen in a crystal ball. Recognising him, she loses power too:

> Therewith her wrathfull courage gan appall,
> And haughtie spirits meekely to adaw,
> That her enhaunced hand she downe can soft withdraw.
> . . .
> Yet she it forst to have againe vpheld,
> As fayning choler, which was turn'd to cold:
> But euer when his visage she beheld,
> Her hand fell downe, and would no longer hold
> The wrathfull weapon gainst his countenance bold:
> But when in vaine to fight she oft assayd,
> She arm'd her tongue, and thought at him to scold;
> Nathlesse her tongue not to her will obayd,
> But brought forth speeches myld, when she would have missayd.
> (4.6.26.7–9, 4.6.27)

Her hand, like his, refuses what she wills. Even her voice acts on its own, without regard for what she would wish. In this case, as in Artegall's, the other's face – the exposure of the other, the openness to having life ended, the complete accession to weakness – fails to consolidate the self supposedly in control. The desire for triumphal recognition quickly becomes the intimate recognition of another's precariousness. Beyond will, beyond words, beyond any modicum of control, vulnerability is shared; action, reprieve, occurs in the absence of actors.

The incident is not alone. Characters in *The Faerie Queene* often are disarmed by the fragility evident in another's face, and even when the face is for Spenser the face of evil, he does not disapprove of the disarming. After his encounter with Britomart, for example, Artegall himself battles with and is ready to decapitate Radigund, an enslaver of men, until he unlaces her helmet and 'as he discouered had her face, / He saw his senses straunge astonishment' – as though in looking at her and seeing her face bathed in blood, he sees himself, sees in her his own astonishment at what he has done and at what might be done to him (5.5.12.1–2). So he throws away his sword; he yields to her. The epic approaches its very end with a yielding of this ilk; in the Mutabilitie cantos, Jove has the chance to destroy Mutabilitie herself – to end change, perhaps to eliminate precariousness altogether – but 'when he looked on her louely face' '[h]e staide his hand' (6.31.1–5).

In these moments, the weakness of others weakens selves, makes them unable to kill; unlike the case of Britomart and Artegall, though, losing one's will arguably produces or would produce problems – for instance, when Artegall gives Radigund the upper hand and is promptly enslaved. But if this sequence in book V demonstrates the danger of imagining that being together means passing power around from one self to another, the scene between Artegall and Britomart in book IV locates value in political belonging where vulnerability is shared and power relinquished as a thing that selves possess.

In this, the scene offers a compelling picture of what can occur when will is not one's own. When we consider the notion in unproblematic terms we sometimes find, as in Elyot, 'an entire consent of willes and desires'[70] or, as in Cicero's more utopian moments, 'a complete identity of feeling'.[71] In this framework, wills may be indistinct but always accord; therefore, they never need to be curbed. But the encounter between Britomart and Artegall takes up the question, noted above, of what happens and what ought to happen when – as invariably occurs if friendship gets translated to broader forms of belonging – wills become plural and even irreconcilable.[72] How can we move forward from the fact of such difference, from the fact that Britomart and Artegall initially want to vanquish each other?

One way to deal with the issue, implicit in Arendt and Rawls, is to recognise, respect and accommodate the plurality of individual interests when possible and to curb individual will only when necessary. This is what it means to respect the space that the world puts between us, to be a society neither of saints nor of the self-centred. But the scene between Britomart and Artegall presents another way to deal with the problem of plurality, implying as it does that Arendtian and Rawlsian frameworks underestimate the degree to which wills can come into conflict so bitter as to make mutual respect impossible. The desire for self-preservation, Spenser shows, can lead to the wish to exterminate. Having one's will often means depriving another's. With such weight put on the pitfalls of the world in which wills are plural – on how, at times, we cannot move forward from the fact of such difference so long as individual will exists – we are forced to consider what might occur were will lost.

For Britomart and Artegall what occurs, I have suggested, is this: vulnerability is recognised as – and is – shared in a way that saves them both. The decision to drop swords arrives from outside; the only decisions in this scene, if we want to call them that, are Britomart's decision in Artegall, and Artegall's decision in Britomart. Unlike the ideal citizen in Cicero, who willingly gives himself over to danger, these two, unable to harm and so open to harm, are forced into friendship and its risks. But Spenser dramatises here what Cicero knows, that this is how friendship often happens; before we know it, it is upon us, and what counts for the self is suddenly the outside of self – not what these two can do as autonomous individuals but what passes between them, what undoes autonomy. So long as the outside of self is what counts for both Britomart and Artegall, harm cannot occur.

As far as Spenser is concerned, what counts for them is also what counts for English community. I have pointed out how for Cicero Rome would crumble without friendship, and how friendship depends on susceptibility, on eschewing self-concern and relinquishing well-bounded selfhood. In the mythos of *The Faerie Queene*, Britomart and Artegall are Elizabeth I's ancestors, and so for Spenser, similarly, it is precisely the failure of self-sovereignty that makes the English nation possible. In so far as he shares with and elaborates on Cicero's position here, we can call Spenser's position a republican one.

Since what qualifies as 'republican' is so open a question, I want to close with a word more about what it means for me to categorise Spenser as such. I described in Chapter 1 how a central – perhaps the central – concern of republican thought is how to keep citizens from being exposed to arbitrary, tyrannical will, how to protect against the Lusts and the Radigunds of the world. One republican response, detailed in Chapter 1 and evident in Cicero's *Philippics*, is to limit the reach of the tyrant's will by protecting the subject's will, by providing the positive liberties and negative freedoms that secure a space of individual freedom. I have not focused on the point, but Spenser seems well aware that those in Lust's cave are in desperate need of such provisions; without them, the nameless woman gets sacrificed. So this response to the threat of tyranny at times may well be Spenser's own – even as we also see, in that same episode, Spenser's awareness of some dark sides to characters' stringent insistence on self-protective, bounded selfhood.

Another republican response to the threat of tyranny, one that bulks large in book IV as well as in the radical theory discussed here, is to view will itself – especially when it is ascribed supreme value – as a possible source of tyranny. Cicero is wary of anyone who does not take others into account and regards will as unfettered; indeed, he declares such an outlook unnatural. Thus Cicero writes that,

> for one man to take something from another and to increase his own advantage at the cost of another's disadvantage is more contrary to nature than death, than poverty, than pain and than anything else that may happen to his body or external possessions

and nothing, according to Cicero, runs more contrary to nature than doing violence to someone else for one's own advantage.[73] When we understand will itself as a potential threat, one might put into place stronger rights against that threat, as does Rawls, while still upholding (fettered) individual will as a supreme good. But one might also do as Spenser does and question whether discrete self-will is of great worth.

Spenser does so when Britomart and Artegall attempt to assert themselves and fail. Spenser creates a scenario, as he does so regularly in episodes that I have discussed, where to assert one's will, to pursue one's own interests without regard for others, would mean being a tyrant, ending not just in the neglect but in the ruin of someone else. The scenario also offers a way out, not on the level of legislation but on the level of lived experience. It brings into view how reconciliation occurs when individual will is not of much account, when decision is as it is above: not that of self-willing actors, but the other's decision in the self. Spenser offers a powerful image of how decisions can be – and sometimes should be – so made. And he prompts us to make the meeting between Britomart and Artegall into a distinctly Ciceronian practice of the self, a republican duty of radical abandon: a choice to let the other make a choice in us, doing as Cicero and theorists of friendship who follow him recommend, deciding always with the other – literally – in mind.

Britomart and Artegall present an image of this ideal, one that sharpens the distinction – if not the incompatibility – between traditions of republican thought explored in this book. What Spenser portrays here is not how tyranny might be defeated, and how selves might be reconciled, through the legal structures of the republican polity. Instead, he portrays how both can occur in a visceral, lived encounter that takes place below or beyond those legal structures. Spenser, in other words, presents here not the need for provisions that limit vulnerability, but rather a vision of those given over to it, in an encounter at once Ciceronian and radical – a weakness circulated and shared, a displacement of self-will by the other inside us, the seeming enemy who turns out to be the friend. Cicero and Butler are right to point out that we cannot avoid such situations, cannot know in advance the friend who will undo us. But Spenser, for his part, leads us to think about seeking those situations out. Because Britomart and Artegall make each other weak, they cannot, at least not in this moment, engage in the sort of self-defensive violence that Guyon practises and that Andrew Hadfield describes; whenever Britomart beholds Artegall, she cannot hold her wrathful weapon. The republicanism they represent is unlike that described by Hadfield, when perceived or possible openness leads to the most awful kinds of violence, a reassertion of boundaries gone wrong. The republicanism of book IV is instead one for which we can be glad.

For much of the Renaissance friendship theory discussed here, the work of friendship and the work of possession – of oneself, of one's words and one's will, of the things we understand as ours – go hand in hand. But this is not, finally, the world that Spenser most wants in book IV. There, he asks us to approach friendship as that which gives us over to self-abandonment, and to consider whether the most intense – and perhaps the most important – experiences have little to do with proving one's power, with securing personal boundaries and possessions, with the self's triumph. Spenser, like Cicero and others after him, thus urges us not to ask that political community only hide or minimise our vulnerability, but also to embrace that vulnerability as virtue, as vital to community's very being.

Notes

1. While the concept of self-interest is often attached to developments that post-date Spenser (for instance, in C. B. Macpherson's famous *The Political Theory of Possessive Individualism* (Oxford: Oxford University Press, 1962)), recent scholarship by figures such as Jill Phillips Ingram has argued that investment in self-interest (specifically, in notions of 'credit' and personal property) can be identified much earlier. See *Idioms of Self-Interest: Credit, Identity, and Property in English Renaissance Literature* (New York: Routledge, 2006).
2. Stephen Greenblatt, *Renaissance Self-Fashioning: From More to Shakespeare* (Chicago: University of Chicago Press, 1980), 157–92.
3. Andrew Hadfield, *Spenser's Irish Experience: Wilde Fruit and Salvage Soyl* (Oxford: Clarendon, 1997), 7. For an earlier account of self-fashioning in response to Greenblatt that also takes up Spenser in particular, see Louis Montrose's 'The Elizabethan Subject and the Spenserian Text', 303–40, in Patricia Parker and David Quint (eds), *Literary Theory/Renaissance Texts* (Baltimore: Johns Hopkins University Press, 1986).
4. For an excellent overview of Spenser's attitudes to various 'others', an overview which includes perspectives both compatible and incompatible with self-fashioning as Greenblatt understands it, see Patrick Cheney and Lauren Silberman (eds), *Worldmaking Spenser: Explorations in the Modern Age* (Lexington, KY: University Press of Kentucky, 2000), esp. sections II-IV, 'Spenser and the Continental Other', 'Spenser and the English Other' and 'Policing Self and Other: Spenser, the Colonial, and the Criminal'. For some other recent statements of Spenser's relationship to Ireland, see Willy Maley, *Salvaging Spenser: Colonialism, Culture and Identity* (London: Macmillan, 1997); and Richard McCabe, 'Ireland: policy, poetics and parody', in *The Cambridge Companion to Spenser* (Cambridge: Cambridge University Press, 2001), 60–78.
5. See Hadfield, '*The Faerie Queene*, Books IV–VII', in *The Cambridge Companion to Spenser*, 126–8, and *Spenser's Irish Experience*, 137–45.
   For another reading that sees Spenserian friendship as, at its best, occur-

ring between selves who possess self-control and clearly delineated personal boundaries – as occurring in a world where chastity can be clearly recognised, aggression plays no part, and friendship can be perfected by justice – see Mark Heberle's 'The Limitations of Friendship', in *Spenser Studies* VIII (New York: AMS, 1990), 101–18.

6. Richard Chamberlain, *Radical Spenser: Pastoral, Politics and the New Aestheticism* (Edinburgh: Edinburgh University Press, 2005), 86, 89; and Harry Berger, Jr, 'The Spenserian Dynamics', in *Revisionary Play: Studies in the Spenserian Dynamics* (Berkeley, CA: University of California Press, 1988). Berger argues that Spenser advances a notion of *discordia concors*, according to which 'the opposition of contrary sexes is mingled with a crucial similarity, namely, that both lovers are separate, equal, and unique selves' (34).

   For a reading that sees these stories of concord – for instance, between Cambel and Triamond, and Amyas and Placidas – as not radical in any redeemable way, see 'Social Concord in Miniature', Chapter 5 of James W. Broaddus's *Spenser's Allegory of Love: Social Vision in Books III, IV, and V of* The Faerie Queene (Madison, NJ: Fairleigh Dickinson University Press, 1995), esp. 110.

7. Specifically, Greenblatt writes that, for Spenser, the enemy 'is as much a tenacious and surprisingly seductive way of life as it is a military force, and thus alongside a ruthless policy of mass starvation and massacre, he advocates the destruction of native Irish identity' (187). Hadfield, similarly, claims that within the Spenserian imaginary, cultural others offer an unsustainable loss of control, a bloody undoing of self and other. Hadfield has described how the maintenance of bounded English identity often requires dominating or simply eliminating those understood to threaten that identity. See especially 'Reading the Allegory of *The Faerie Queene*', 113–45, in *Spenser's Irish Experience*.

8. Hadfield, 'Was Spenser Really a Republican After All?: A Response to David Scott Wilson-Okamura', *Spenser Studies* 17 (New York: AMS, 2003), 275–90, esp. 280. The recent controversy over Spenser's republicanism was occasioned by Hadfield's earlier 'Was Spenser a Republican?' in *English* 47 (1998), 169–76.

9. 'Was Spenser Really a Republican After All?', 280.

10. 'Was Spenser Really a Republican After All?', 279. Elsewhere, Hadfield acknowledges the possibly internal relation between active virtue and martial activity: for instance, in his discussion of 'Mutabilitie' in *Shakespeare, Spenser, and the Matter of Britain* (New York: Palgrave Macmillan, 2004), 141–2. For this reason, Hadfield has no interest in equating republicanism and democracy.

11. David Norbrook, for example, writes most substantially about Spenser in his first book, *Poetry and Politics in the English Renaissance* (London: Routledge & Kegan Paul, 1984). In that book, according to Norbrook, Spenser becomes less radical (which is to say, less admirably republican) over the course of his career (144). Patterson, similarly, believes that, whereas works such as *The Shepheardes Calender* espouse a civilising 'pedagogy of outreach', Spenser's radicalism on this score was abandoned by the time he wrote *The Faerie Queene*. 'Couples, Canons and the Uncouth:

Spenser-and-Milton in Educational Theory', *Critical Inquiry* 16:4 (1990), 773–93, esp. 787, 793.

12. Jonathan Goldberg, *Endlesse Worke: Spenser and the Structures of Discourse* (Baltimore: Johns Hopkins University Press, 1981), 86, 103.

13. Silberman argues, for instance, that the masculine attempt to assure order in *The Faerie Queene* is, in Spenser's view, ill-conceived, and indeed that the book's characters 'flourish or fail according to their openness to risk' – according, in a way, to their willingness to be open subjects. See *Transforming Desire: Erotic Knowledge in Books III and IV of* The Faerie Queene (Berkeley, CA: University of California Press, 1995), 10, 125, 142.

Stephens argues that the poem registers 'the possibility of discovering its own debt to an essentially monstrous, essentially feminine imagination' but displays 'an investment in the erotic exchanges between this feminine disorder, and the masculine borders that would wish to contain it'. *The Limits of Eroticism in Post-Petrarchan Narrative: Conditional Pleasure from Spenser to Marvell* (Cambridge: Cambridge University Press, 1998), 61.

Schwarz, for her part, claims that characters such as Britomart, who figures importantly later in this chapter, 'reveal the precarious foundations on which conventions of identity rest, displaying oppositions and hierarchies in their natural if only potential state of collapse'. See 'Dressed to Kill: Looking for Love in *The Faerie Queene*', Chapter 4 of *Tough Love: Amazon Encounters in the English Renaissance* (Durham, NC: Duke University Press, 2000), 161.

For an argument that takes up the theme of 'the instability of female identity' in the Spenserian imagination but that focuses on ways that Spenser would like to eliminate such instability, see Tracey Sedinger, 'Women's Friendship and the Refusal of Lesbian Desire in *The Faerie Queene*', *Criticism* 42:1 (2000), 91–113.

14. For some examples that illustrate the difference between Goldberg's approach and my own, see his treatments of Lust's cave, which appear on 58, 87 and 109 of *Endlesse Worke*.

15. Usually, Goldberg suggests that Spenser does cast vulnerability in such a light through the vocabulary of desire he employs; for Goldberg, the Spenserian self's lost integrity is typically felt as a 'wound' (79), as 'lack' (85). Relatedness is experienced 'devastatingly' (85) and can be understood along the lines of 'disease' (87). I, by contrast, will focus on the salutary aspects of lost integrity.

I supplement Silberman, Stephens and Schwarz by showing how the undoing of personal boundaries in book IV need not be discussed primarily in terms of sexuality and gender, and can instead be profitably discussed as an exploration of the politics of human interaction more generally, as those politics appear from antiquity up until the present moment. Indeed, I will suggest that focusing on gender or sexuality too narrowly leads critics such as Silberman (and, to a lesser degree, Stephens) to dismiss some interactions (such as those that take place during Satyrane's Tournament) that may in fact be valuable.

16. *The Boke Named The Governour* (New York: E. P. Dutton, 1907), 163–4.

17. 'Of Friendship', in Sidney Warhaft (ed.), *Francis Bacon: A Selection of His Works* (Indianapolis, IN: MacMillan, 1965), 118.

18. 'Of Friendship', in *Essays*, trans. J. M. Cohen (New York: Penguin, 1958), 99.

19. Cicero writes, for instance, that 'friendship is nothing else than an accord in all things, human and divine, conjoined with mutual goodwill and affection.' See *De Amicitia* in *De Senectute, De Amicitia, De Divinatione*, trans. William Falconer (Cambridge: Harvard University Press, 1938), 131. Aristotle, similarly, writes that the good man 'extends to his friend the same relation that he has towards himself (for a friend is another self)'. See *The Ethics of Aristotle: The Nicomachean Ethics*, trans. J. A. K. Thomson (New York: Penguin, 1976), 294.

20. See *The Usurer's Daughter: Male Friendship and Fictions of Women in Sixteenth-Century England* (New York: Routledge, 1994).

21. Elyot's rendition, which I summarise here, can be found in 166–186 of *The Boke Named the Gouvernour*. For Boccaccio's version, see the eighth story of the tenth day in *The Decameron*, trans. Mark Musa and Peter Bondanella (New York: W. W. Norton, 1982), 640–55.

22. See Fukuyama, *Trust: The Social Virtues and the Creation of Prosperity* (New York: Free Press, 1995), esp. Chapter 23, 'Eagles Don't Flock – or Do They?', 269–82.

    For some recent studies that argue for the compatibility of civic virtue and self-interest, see Richard Dagger, *Civic Virtues: Rights, Citizenship, and Republican Liberalism*, and Thomas Spragens, Jr, *Civic Liberalism: Reflections on Our Democratic Ideals* (New York: Rowman & Littlefield, 1999), esp. Chapter 7, 'Civic Friendship in Liberal Society', 175–211.

23. See *The Political Theory of Possessive Individualism*. On 263–4 of that book, Macpherson lays out seven propositions that for him define possessive individualism and that emphasise boundedness. For an argument that insists that possessive individualism and communitarianism are false alternatives, see Jack Crittenden, *Beyond Individualism: Reconstituting Liberalism* (New York: Oxford University Press, 1992).

24. See Arendt, *The Human Condition* (Chicago: University of Chicago Press, 1958), 242–3.

25. Rawls, *A Theory of Justice* (Cambridge, MA: Harvard University Press, 1971), 105–6.

26. Rawls, *Political Liberalism* (New York: Columbia University Press, 1996), 54. See also li.

27. Habermas, 152–3 of 'Individuation through Socialization: On George Herbert Mead's Theory of Subjectivity', 149–204, in *Postmetaphysical Thinking: Philosophical Essays*, trans. William Mark Hohengarten (Cambridge, MA: MIT Press, 1993). See also 'Citizenship and National Identity: Some Reflections on the Future of Europe', *Praxis International* 12:1 (1992), 1–19.

28. Laurie Shannon's recent recuperation of sameness in Renaissance friendship, *Sovereign Amity: Figures of Friendship in Shakespearean Contexts* (Chicago: University of Chicago Press, 2002), follows a similar structure in so far as exposure to the other, paradoxically, reinforces individual borders. Shannon emphasises how only sovereign selves are capable of

opening their borders and letting the other in so as to reconsolidate those borders, so that friends can remain sovereign, and critical, in relation to the monarch (17–53). What Shannon designates as primary – nourishing sameness – secures what she designates as secondary: critical autonomy. Accordingly, we might say that while Shannon wants her readers to refrain from 'judging early modern likeness from a postliberal perspective' (21), this is ultimately so that likeness can be reconciled with liberalism and with concepts of rational consent and dissent.

29. It may be worth pointing out that the ring in one of Spenser's sources, Chaucer's *The Squire's Tale*, presents an effacement of the human and animal worlds – allowing humans and animals to experience loss as something shared; Cambel's ring, by contrast, renders him completely distinct.

30. All citations are from Thomas Roche (ed.), *The Faerie Queene* (New York: Penguin, 1978).

31. For more on their dependence on Cambina, see Silberman, *Transforming Desire*, 87–97.

32. Though I would not press the point too much, Cambel and Triamond may here resemble a more successful version of Sans loy, who in book I is described in similar terms when the fawns and satyrs come upon him and he is forced to give up Una:

> As when a greedie Wolfe through hunger fell
> A seely Lambe farre from the flocke does take,
> Of whom he meanes his bloudie feast to make,
> A Lyon spyes fast running towards him,
> The innocent pray in hast he does forsake . . .
> (1.6.10.3–7)

33. I lay out this theoretical position in the section entitled 'Recent Theory and the Forms of Self-Undoing'.

34. As will become clear below, this is essentially the reading of Spenser offered by Hadfield, although he does not attend to the nameless woman.

35. *Spenser's Irish Experience*, 141. His reading of the scene extends from 137–45.

36. *Renaissance Self-Fashioning*, 174.

37. See *Spenser's Irish Experience*, 7 (quoted above) and *Shakespeare, Spenser, and the Matter of Britain*, 141–2.

38. Derrida, *Politics of Friendship*, trans. George Collins (London: Verso, 1997), 200, 155, 236. For a discussion of how Derridean *aimance* could avoid the repellent forms of border-drawing I have described, and could instead be 'a relationality prior to any activation or instantiation in the act of befriending', see A. J. P. Thomson, *Deconstruction and Democracy: Derrida's* Politics of Friendship (New York: Continuum, 2005), 15. For an excellent account of the aneconomic opening to the other that friendship is, see Jody Greene, 'The Work of Friendship', *GLQ* 10:3 (2004), 319–37, esp. 324. For an interesting account that, rightly or wrongly, reconciles Arendt and Derrida, see 'The Problem of Love', the introduction to James R. Martel's *Love is a Sweet Chain: Desire, Autonomy, and Friendship in Liberal Political Theory* (New York: Routledge, 2001).

39. Another interesting discussion of the decisions that others make in us – of

decisions that occur outside traditional voluntaristic notions – can be found in Simon Critchley's 'The Other's Decision in Me (What Are the Politics of Friendship?)', in *Ethics – Politics – Subjectivity: Essays on Derrida, Levinas, and Contemporary French Thought* (New York: Verso, 1999), 254–286.

40. Butler, *Precarious Life: The Powers of Mourning and Violence* (New York: Verso, 2004), 20, 23.
41. Blanchot, *The Unavowable Community*, trans. Pierre Joris (Barrytown, NY: Station Hill, 1988), 6.
42. Bataille, *Inner Experience*, trans. Leslie Anne Boldt (Albany, NY: SUNY, 1988), esp. 58–60.
43. Bataille, *Theory of Religion* (New York: Zone, 1989), 49–50, and *The Accursed Share*, vol. 1 (New York: Zone, 1991), 28–9 and 55–9. For another discussion of Bataille's that touches on friendship, see 'Friends', 11–48, in *Guilty*, trans. Bruce Boone (San Francisco, CA: Lapis, 1988).
44. See *Precarious Life*, 24–26, for one of Butler's concessive statements to the value of rights. For Butler's statements of how too much legislation to protect personal boundaries is a problem, see both the sections of *Precarious Life* referred to above, as well as *Excitable Speech: A Politics of the Performative* (New York: Routledge, 1997), which I treat more directly in Chapter 4.
45. *Guilty*, 28–9.
46. For one of Bataille's explorations of these issues, see the 'Theoretical Introduction' to *The Accursed Share*, 19–41.
47. To get a sense of such wavering, see, for instance, *Letters to Atticus, Books I-VI* (Cambridge: Harvard University Press, 1980), trans. E. O. Winstedt, and *Letters to Friends*, vol. 1, trans. D. R. Shackleton Bailey (Cambridge, MA: Harvard University Press, 2001). Anthony Everitt's recent biography, *Cicero: The Life and Times of Rome's Greatest Politician* (New York: Random House, 2001), uses these letters to dramatise Cicero's internal struggle over self-promotion and self-sacrifice.
48. See *The Ethics of Aristotle: The Nichomachean Ethics*, trans. J. A. K. Thomson (New York: Penguin, 1976), 258–72.
49. See *On the Good Life*, trans. Michael Grant (New York: Penguin, 1971), 226, 191. Here I use Grant's translation as I find it more compelling than that offered by Falconer in the Loeb translation.
50. See M. T. Griffin and E. M. Atkins (eds), *On Duties* (Cambridge: Cambridge University Press, 1991), 20.
51. *Lysis* is 146–68 of Edith Hamilton and Huntington Cairns (eds), *The Collected Dialogues of Plato* (New York: Pantheon, 1963). There, Socrates argues that if only virtuous individuals are capable of friendship, and if virtuous individuals are self-sufficient, the virtuous would not seek friendship. And yet nearly all of us, Socrates points out, have known friendship, implying that we must have an imperfect understanding of its features.
52. To be sure, Cicero believes that commonwealths only remain commonwealths to the degree that they remain communities of interest, but his greatest praise is for self-sacrificial figures such as Cato, who recognise that the outside of self – in this case Roman community – 'has a claim on the largest and best part of our minds, talents, and judgment for her own

use', and even fantasises about sacrificing himself. See James E. G. Zetzel (ed.), *On the Commonwealth and On the Laws* (New York: Cambridge University Press, 1999), 5.

53. *On Duties*, 27.
54. *On the Good Life*, 188.
55. Certainly, Cicero wishes the case were otherwise. He believes, for instance, that 'decisions about friendships should be taken after we have reached full physical and intellectual maturity' (*De Amicitia*, 213). But he also acknowledges the impossibility of putting the decision off.
56. *On Duties*, 33.
57. Julia Annas (ed.), *On Moral Ends*, trans. Raphael Woolf (New York: Cambridge University Press, 2001), 54.
58. *Tusculan Disputations*, trans. J. E. King (Cambridge, MA: Harvard University Press, 1945), 195.
59. See, for example, p. 13 of *On the Commonwealth*, where Cicero praises the man who never values possessions as 'goods' and – more directly to the point – p. 189 of *De Amicitia*, where Cicero denounces those who 'regard their friends as they do their cattle'.
60. *On Moral Ends*, 41–2.
61. A number of critics have seen the tournament, and its relation to recognition, in a negative light. Thomas Roche, Jr, for example, sees it as illustrative of Satyrane's deficiency: 'Like Proteus he cannot grasp the true significance of Beauty; he can see only its exterior, and for this reason he is deceived by the false beauty of the False Florimell at the contest for the girdle.' See *The Kindly Flame* (Princeton, NJ: Princeton University Press, 1966), 166.

    Silberman herself, as I have suggested, sees the battles as 'pointlessly unproductive', in part because of false recognitions as can be found in the mutual comparison between knights; in doing so, the knights try and fail to 'assert fixity and control over the intractable to-and-froness of desire' (99, 102).
62. *On the Commonwealth*, 13.
63. *On Duties*, 28.
64. *Guilty*, 28–9.
65. Spenserian narration more generally is, of course, notorious for its deferral of conclusive ending, deferral evident from the start, when Redcrosse's defeat of Error in *The Faerie Queene*'s first canto seems only to produce a series of further errors. For a classic account of how such open-endedness may be endemic to romance in general (and to *The Faerie Queene* in particular), see Patricia A. Parker's *Inescapable Romance: Studies in the Poetics of a Mode* (Princeton, NJ: Princeton University Press, 1979), esp. 3–15 and 54–113.
66. See *Tough Love*, esp. 168.
67. Stephens, *The Limits of Eroticism in Post-Petrarchan Narrative*, 38.
68. For two recent discussions of these themes, see Stephens (esp. 36–40) and Schwarz (esp. 168–9). Stephens, cannily, points out that the 'self-sufficiency' in this scene has to do with Britomart and Amoret's interaction, not their status as selves.
69. *On the Good Life*, 188.

70. *The Boke Called the Gouvernour*, 163–4.
71. *The Good Life*, 187.
72. For a recent explication of this difficulty, one in basic accord with Rawls and Arendt, see Chapter 7 of Spragens's *Civic Liberalism*.
73. *On Duties*, 108–9.

Chapter 3

Unbuilding the City: *Coriolanus, Titus Andronicus* and the Forms of Openness

Introduction

In the previous chapter, I argued that Spenser follows Cicero in making shared vulnerability a definite good. For the bulk of this chapter, I focus on how Shakespeare portrays the founding of the Roman republic in *Coriolanus*; there, however, the emergence of the republic coincides not with the adoption of vulnerability as virtue but with a resolute (if empty) emphasis on the protection of Roman citizens. While Spenser suggests that the members of a polity must be open to self-risk, Shakespeare portrays a polity that offers to do the opposite: minimise vulnerability as much as possible.

In *Coriolanus*, Shakespeare views this offer as empty (that is, as both insincere and undesirable). And so he, like Coriolanus himself, searches for an alternative – one in which secure personal boundaries are, as in Spenser, not of primary importance. In the Rome of *Coriolanus*, this world would be socially unrecognisable, partly because Shakespeare presents such a dark picture of the construct of boundedness as to yearn to abolish the construct altogether. I hope to show, however, that if this makes *Coriolanus* the most utopian of my texts of focus, it also makes the play the most forceful statement both of the pitfalls of bounded selfhood and of the possible value of vulnerable life.

Typically, *Coriolanus* is read in a quite different fashion. At a couple of points I have said that for a large body of recent criticism, the political utility of early modern texts hinges on the degree to which they can be read as republican in a way that prefigures modern liberalisms and liberal subjectivities. Such a judgement lies behind Annabel Patterson's recuperation of *Coriolanus*, which reads the play as one that eschews absolutism, demonstrates the value of giving voice to all citizens, and – most importantly for my purposes – advocates an English republic that would foster subjects who are recognised as bounded, discrete and delineated.[1]

I will call readings such as Patterson's into question on the grounds of both their textual accuracy and their appraisal of bounded selfhood. A wide range of recent theoretical work has identified dangers inherent in the notion of personal boundaries central to republican arguments, and in *Coriolanus* many of these dangers – including those described in Giorgio Agamben's accounts of the state of exception – indeed plague republican Rome.[2] Shakespeare, I argue, represents the birth of Roman republicanism as the birth of a state that, in the name of securing personal borders, uses law to place individuals outside the law, thus making life within the city into what Agamben calls 'bare life' – life that can be killed without recourse to more recognisably legal channels.[3] Advancing a pro-republican reading of *Coriolanus* is thus quite difficult to do.

But if we cannot read the play as a pro-republican or proto-liberal document, it may still be a politically appealing one, particularly if we look to Coriolanus himself. As an exploration of the emerging appeal of bounded selfhood, *Coriolanus* has proven exceptionally provocative to early modernists; and while the play's eponymous hero is usually read as the character most attracted to the wish for such selfhood, he is, I argue, just the opposite: a figure who represents practices of self-undoing that could clear a path out of the state of exception, however tortuous that path might prove. He gestures toward life after and outside its production in Rome as bare life, toward ways of speaking and acting that do not depend on the construct of personal boundedness through which the republic can locate and manipulate its subjects. Shakespeare shows Coriolanus standing at one gateway leading outside the state of exception, directing us toward a specifically sexual 'world elsewhere' (III, iii, 136).[4] Coriolanus – who bears a historical likeness to Jonathan Goldberg's sodomite[5] and a theoretical likeness to Leo Bersani's gay outlaw[6] – points the way to a life that is openly vulnerable but also liveable, to a Sodom whose residents would renounce the constructs of discrete social identity and bodily integrity alike, a place in which subjects would perish but life would not.

Unlike most of my texts of focus, then, *Coriolanus* engages with republican thought only to reject it in favour of what is more radical, and unexchangeably so. Shakespeare never imagines a republic that could accommodate a figure such as Coriolanus. As I show in the chapter's last section, however, Shakespeare is hardly consistent in his attitude toward republican thought and, particularly, in his sense of what republicanism can be. Indeed, in his first Roman play, *Titus Andronicus*, Shakespeare embraces aspects of the alternative, 'open' version of republican selfhood that is this book's focus. In *Titus*, Shakespeare advances an intersubjective openness, one that is more limited than the openness articulated in *Coriolanus* and that can be found in Cicero and Livy in the classical period and in Habermas today. If the last chapter attended mostly to overlap between radical and republican thought, Shakespeare's first and last Roman plays suggest a disjunction between the two. But even as these texts suggest disjunction, they are most instructive in that they also suggest interplay, helping us to think through the complementarity of theorists such as Habermas and Bersani. We tend to think of the two as at loggerheads; when considered together, *Titus* and *Coriolanus* help us to jettison the idea, on the grounds that, unless and until we do, our efforts to inhabit our openness are bound to collapse.

Coriolanus and Early Modern Concepts of the Bounded Self

I have noted that in early modernity – as numerous critical and historical accounts, reaching back to that of Jacob Burckhardt, have variously shown – questions about selfhood were increasingly turning into questions about bounded selfhood.[7] According to many of these accounts, with the arrival of early modernity the subject was presented with new possibilities for cultivating a deeper, more clearly discrete existence. Among such possibilities were opportunities for individual interpretation afforded by the explosion of print; increased acquisition of personal property and the attendant rise of possessive individualism; expanding codes of civility; heightened Protestant emphasis on inwardness; and, most crucially for my purposes, the rise of a certain kind of English republicanism, one centred around ideals of participatory government and personal liberty.[8] In these accounts, the influence of humoral theory – for which the self was understood as being fundamentally open, psychologically and corporeally porous, permeable, unstable and volatile – was beginning to wane as the determining factor in the early modern subject's self-understanding.[9] The lines dividing inside from outside were instead hardening, amid heightened desires and needs to assert the difference between self and not-self, to enrich and demarcate one's mind and to cordon off one's body.

Whether or not they agree with the historical specificity of these accounts, many critics have read *Coriolanus* as a venture into the pitfalls and possibilities of bounded selfhood. When these critics focus on Shakespeare's portrayal of Coriolanus, the play's position appears markedly sceptical; for he, almost uniformly, is seen as aspiring toward an unreasonable, even absolute, degree of autonomy. Psychoanalytic critics – for instance, Janet Adelman and Cynthia Marshall – see in him a frantic, and failed, attempt to break from his phallic mother and secure a coherent masculine identity;[10] readings inflected by Marxism, such as Arthur Riss's and Michael D. Bristol's, see him mistakenly seeking to construct a territorialised, proprietary and private life for himself;[11] liberal critics of the play, including Leonard Tennenhouse and Stanley Cavell, argue that Coriolanus wishes for privacy even in the linguistic sphere, that he tries to live 'in a world of private signification' and to 'speak without conversing'.[12] These critics discuss his attempt at autonomy in different terms, but all see it as evident and quite excessive. For them, Coriolanus wants total boundedness, complete severance from community; in this case, the 'world elsewhere' he seeks is one in which he would be absolutely sovereign, a world either without others[13] or else, as Patterson and James Holstun argue, with his unanswering and unanswerable power over them, a world in which Coriolanus could live as the lonely dragon to which he compares himself (III, iii, 136; IV, i, 30).[14] When we focus on its title character, this criticism suggests, *Coriolanus* enacts a nightmare of radicalised subjectivity, giving voice to early modern anxiety about the subject's expanding interiority and solipsistic aspirations toward autonomy.

While many critics see Coriolanus's excessive, outlandish pursuit of autonomy as the play's abandonment of bounded selfhood,[15] not all do. Patterson and Holstun, for instance, see the play sorting good and bad methods for staking out a separable subject position. In their views, Shakespeare advances strategies, ones less uncompromising and more socially functional than Coriolanus's own, for establishing autonomy. Holstun argues that the play's citizens, quite reasonably, reject Menenius's inept fable of the belly and its coercive, disempowering model of incorporation.[16] For Patterson, the citizens seek a world elsewhere not by becoming social misfits, as Coriolanus does, but by cultivating distance, attaining the vantage that allows for critique; they openly articulate their complaint against the state which, they hope, will recognise them in turn. In particular, Patterson argues that while the citizens' complaint about a food shortage has to do with their bodies, Shakespeare 'does not leave them … clapping their hands spasmodically upon their stomachs' but instead shows them proceeding 'to discuss the political economy … not without considerable social perspective'; Shakespeare, that is, 'clearly shows us plebeians capable of reasoning from one thing to another', rising above the supposedly irrational corporeality that might justify their subjection.[17] In doing so, they hold the authorities accountable, refusing the false community of

Menenius's monarchical fable, wresting themselves from that fiction of the body politic in hopes of a life in which their own bodies would be truly, properly protected.[18]

For Patterson, Rome's citizens use their newfound sense of autonomy to be recognised and to secure their rights as Roman subjects. For her, *Coriolanus* advocates drawing borders around the self and in doing so calls for a new community, one that would jettison the notion of a body politic guided by an absolute sovereign in favour of a republic which actively fosters empowered, discrete subjects, the potential bearers of rights.[19] She believes we ought to celebrate this, since the forms of personal autonomy and republican community advocated by *Coriolanus* prefigure the liberal forms of subjectivity and polity that her work holds dear.[20]

Patterson's argument about *Coriolanus* is part of a much broader critical practice, detailed at various points in this book, of recuperating early modern texts not just as republican documents but as proto-liberal ones. In these accounts, we have seen, political community ought to maintain its members' borders; to borrow a phrase from Thomas Smith, good citizens speak and act so as to ensure 'the conservation of themselves aswell in peace and in warre'.[21] If the state fails to protect or unjustly infringes on subjects' edges, a critical populace – one capable of rejecting empty propaganda and of making distinctions between inside and outside, self and other, those who protect us and those who are indifferent or mean us harm – becomes all the more crucial. Put slightly differently, this critical movement shares a basic accord with the liberal reading of Jürgen Habermas, one that is rather different from the reading I offer at this chapter's end but that I take up in detail in Chapter 5. In this reading, the emergence of the public sphere has value largely because it marks the emergence of spaces in which individuals can come together, identify common interests and compel those in power to elaborate the rights needed to meet these interests. From this vantage and that of many scholars of republican thought, community ought to serve as ballast for such self-sovereignty.[22]

I believe that *Coriolanus* is not a republican or proto-liberal document. Its political utility, I will be arguing, lies elsewhere than in the discovery of a proper form of bounded selfhood to be contrasted with Coriolanus's supposed self-aggrandising. I will, in fact, make the opposite claims: that Coriolanus desires undoing, not autonomy, and that the political import of the character rests in our seeing just that. To make the most thorough case for this, I want to preface my analysis of the play with some recent theoretical arguments that identify dangers attached to the construct of discrete being, and that point toward new – less socially operative but also less dangerous – foundations upon which community might be built.

Recent Theory and the Forms of Self-Undoing

That communities ought to further the maintenance of subjects with deep, protected interiors may appear commonsensical because it is a view shared by both liberals and conservatives. However, a host of recent theoretical works by a number of authors, including Jean-Luc Nancy, Giorgio Agamben, Leo Bersani and Judith Butler, have issued challenges to taking the point for granted.[23] Each of these authors, as I suggested in the last chapter, indicates limits and dangers involved in making distinctions as to what is interior and exterior to the self; while they differ in their emphases, all are acutely aware of the coercive potential inherent in the shape of the bounded self. Butler, for instance, points out that in order to ascribe rights to individuals, societies must first subscribe to the autonomy mentioned above, according to which subjects have depth and delimitation, and so are capable and deserving of self-ownership.[24] If this provision at first sounds innocuous – as well as valuable in warding off some undesirable kinds of violence – it comes at a serious price. Both Butler and Bersani insist that once one adopts a rights-based perspective, viewing all relations in terms of property relations becomes quite likely, since once boundaries around subjects and objects are in place, possession of all kinds becomes possible; far too often, individuals exploit those whose rights either do not exist or can be easily ignored.[25] In the previous chapter, I discussed how such exploitation can take place in order to make what looks like self-sacrifice end up being self-aggrandising. But the grimness with which we can cling to bounded selfhood can also often mean rejecting the notion of self-sacrifice altogether. Butler, for instance, describes how the insistence on discrete being can become a refusal of our potential to be undone by others, how what she terms self-hardening can and often does lead to the harshest forms of censorship and violence.[26]

Agamben has contributed to this discussion by arguing that the state endangers its subjects in the very act of granting them rights. Paradoxical as such an argument may sound, he has gone so far as to say that Nazism itself can only be understood in the context of the self's – in addition to the nation's – supposed sovereignty; the biopolitics of the concentration camp, Agamben maintains, became thinkable once the declaration of rights brought what he terms 'bare life' to the centre of the political domain where, in antiquity, it had been only marginal.[27]

That is, once the state posited a life around which it should trace rights-bearing borders, it also reserved the right to erase those borders at any time; once the state gave the subject the right to life, it could also – under the pretence of self-righteous legality – begin to take it away.[28] Thus, for Agamben, 'once their fundamental referent becomes bare life, traditional political distinctions (such as those between Right and Left, liberalism and totalitarianism) lose their clarity and intelligibility and enter into a zone of indistinction.'[29] Liberal subjects can always be reduced to bare life because states of law are always already implicated in states of exception – in governments that abolish the distinction between legislative, executive and judicial powers; that blur the distinction between fact and law; and that thus open a space where even the most unconscionable acts can be sanctioned.[30] Worse, states of exception are, increasingly, becoming the rule; more and more, individuals are exposed to a limitless capacity to be killed, placed – under the guise of the juridically valid – into fundamentally extrajuridical spaces disturbingly similar to those of concentration camps.[31]

For Butler, an insistence on self-sovereignty leads to self-defensive violence. For Agamben, the declaration of rights leaves us defenceless against the violence of a larger sovereign, the state. For both, rights-based liberalism, from its inception, shares something with, and threatens to become, its coercive, totalitarian other; and while these two critique liberal thinking from different vantages (Butler, for instance, makes concessions to the protective potential of rights, whereas Agamben tends not to),[32] both argue that we doom ourselves to relationships of ownership and domination as long as we assume that political action at its best means to elaborate a right or that community membership, at its best, means to be one subject among many, the boundaries of all clearly drawn. They agree that democracy's shortcomings point toward the need for a broadening of our understanding of what counts as political, and of what constitutes viable community. They, along with theorists such as Nancy, have accordingly begun thinking of community outside the state of law, and so outside the rights-bearing subject.[33]

In their exasperation with the failings of bounded, supposedly socially operative selfhood, these theorists advocate openly non-functional, unproductive and even unrecognisable forms of speaking and acting. Nancy, for instance, argues that the 'singularities' that compose community should be understood as having neither borders nor depth. Whereas many liberal theorists advocate a framework wherein bordered subjects join communities so as to give voice to common social goals and thereby further secure members' borders, Nancy works from the premise that 'individual' and 'community' are conceptually and necessarily antithetical – that once community or 'being-with' exists, individuals do not.[34] For Nancy, accordingly, the bounded subject in which many republican critics are so invested becomes thinkable only after the exclusion of being-with.[35] In Nancy's view, that is, being-with cannot do what liberal theorists would like it to do; community cannot mean the coming together of subjects with borders and so cannot mean working to recognise, protect and strengthen those borders.[36] Community is not socially operative in this way, Nancy contends, and is valuable for precisely that reason, precisely because it unworks the subject through the simple experience of being-in-common. This experience, of the spacing and interweaving of singularities which are not subjects, presents to us the basic fact of our existence with each other; it affords the experience not of the awareness of a threshold surrounding the other – beyond which one must not pass – but of being exposed, 'the experience of the outside, of the outside-of-self'.[37] Thus, far from strengthening the social fabric and the individuals that make it up, community tears at both; it shows that the borders of self do not exist when we are with others, that all is external, surfacial. For Nancy, ecstasy – the ex-stasis of standing outside oneself – is all there is and all there ought to be.[38]

If Nancy's fascinating essays remain largely at the level of the abstract, a theorist such as Bersani has given form to the experience of undone subjectivity, claiming that the sexual, in particular, offers a gateway out of social functionality. Translated into Agamben and Nancy's terms, the sexual helps us out of the state of exception and into alternative, inoperative communities. Arguing in *Homos* that sexual relations are anticommunal, antinourishing and antiprotective – are, in other words, self-shattering and antisocial – Bersani describes a community of 'gay outlaws' who 'renounce self-ownership and agree to that loss of boundaries' that allows them, like Nancy's singularities, to become 'shifting points of rest in a universal and mobile communication of being'.[39] Doing so creates sameness and eliminates depth, and it brings about a state in which one '*is*, briefly, the contact between himself and the world', the self reduced to a bodily ego that has eroded its own borders.[40] This lack of differentiation produces a kind of lawlessness, for members of this new, utterly exposed community dispense with notions of interiority and so do not recognise the other's boundaries, let alone have regard for or act so as to ensure them. As in Nancy's community, Bersani's gay outlaws unwork the social.[41] Shattered, criss-crossed selves – possessing 'a potentially revolutionary inaptitude . . . for sociality as it is known' – could force a '*massive redefining of relationality*'; in this world of inoperative *jouissance*, friends and enemies, self-respect and dignity, meaning and abiding order, all are unimaginable.[42]

Despite their differing emphases, the theorists just discussed have much in common. Because they believe that a rights-based, socially 'operative' outlook consistently fails to make good on its promise to protect subjects, all ask that we confront and embrace the fact that our lives are vulnerable ones. All believe that by doing so we might avoid the violence that results from insisting otherwise. Accordingly, these theorists advocate an opening up of the subject and a turning out of the depths to which rights can be ascribed (and indeed, for some, this amounts to a recognition of that subject as depthless and as always already opened up). All promote a form of life that eschews disciplined, self-regarding interiority in favour of irresponsible superficiality.

In such a life, the situation of speech and action would undergo drastic change, taking unsanctioned forms that might none the less have value. Speech would not shape subjectivity by communicating meanings from one subject to another, would not work under the pretence of making a world in which all subjects' outlines are clear and well fortified; instead, it would unsettle and destabilise subjects. In place of the self's structural hardening would be its accession to susceptibility, and in place of the language that constitutes subject positions – that does the work, for good or ill, of interpellation – would be language that disorients and decontextualises us, speech that is our undoing. We would, similarly, no longer seek to protect or cordon off our bodies from others. We would instead deliberately expose ourselves before the state ever could, yielding our corporeality to its total openness, seeking new ways to be penetrable and permeable, new ways to undo ourselves. No longer socially workable, action would show only itself, unrelated to sanctioned ends. It would neither make nor preserve any boundary, since life would take place in a pure exteriority outside and without any law.[43] Rather than coming into relation with others, we would become that relation, given over to existence on the surface, to communicating nothing but the fact of our being-in-common.

The Rome of *Coriolanus*, or the State of Exception

I have chosen to relate this theoretical story at some length because I believe that it is, in several respects, the story of *Coriolanus*. To begin to demonstrate how this is so, we might look to Shakespeare's portrayal of Rome's regard for its citizens. The action of the play takes place after the expulsion of the Tarquins – the supposed end of absolute rule – and the subsequent creation of the tribunate. That creation, Patterson points out, 'issued in four and a half centuries of republican government', and a cardinal accomplishment of *Coriolanus*, for her, is that 'Shakespeare's audience is invited to contemplate an alternative political system.'[44] As we have seen, that alternative is republicanism, read as a signpost toward an equitable state of law, as a limited yet germinal version of participatory government and rights-based democracy. How *Coriolanus* could be said to make such an offer, though, is hard to grasp, since the tribunes make Rome resemble not a state of law but a state of exception, using appeals to one in order to produce the other. Consider, for instance, the terms by which Sicinius accuses Coriolanus of desiring the throne and posing a threat to the people. He says that Coriolanus

> hath resisted law,
> And therefore law shall scorn him further trial
> Than the severity of the public power,
> Which he so sets at nought.
>   (III, i, 268–71)

What Coriolanus has done is to decline to show his wounds to the citizens who are to ratify his consulship; to ask for their voices instead in a peculiar, uncivil manner; and to make a few statements that could be construed as sympathetic to monarchy. Yet this list suffices for the tribunes, with the people's support, to declare Coriolanus 'worthy / Of present death' (ll. 212–13). By insisting that law itself will prevent 'further trial', Sicinius claims that they act with lawful power in placing Coriolanus outside the law. Capturing him within the juridical order through this inclusive exclusion, Rome, as in the state of exception described by Agamben, exposes him as bare life, as life that can be killed without reference to usual legal channels. Given his prestige and preternatural record of service, Coriolanus seems an unlikely candidate for such exposure; that Brutus and Sicinius succeed so easily shows that in the emerging republic, even citizens once of great value to that republic may not be very far from being made into bare life.

This suspension of law can appear lawful because Brutus and Sicinius portray Coriolanus as a direct threat to the people. Their protection, the tribunes claim, means that violence can, indeed must, be used. When Menenius pleads with them to proceed by process, they respond that 'those cold ways, / That seem like prudent helps, are very poisonous / Where the disease is violent,' and that Coriolanus 'must be cut away' (ll. 221–3, 295). By fabricating an imminent threat to Roman lives, the tribunes bring the care for these lives within the state's purview. This renders lawful all measures undertaken in the name of defending Rome against its internal and external enemies, however unlawful those measures might appear. Thus, Sicinius says that law itself denies Coriolanus trial; this is how his fundamentally extrajuridical decision can come to seem legal; this is why guarding the borders of some citizens can seem to require killing Coriolanus. In Shakespeare's representation, at the moment of republicanism's birth – a birth celebrated by so much liberal criticism – is the *iustitium*, the supposed state of emergency that allows any and all actions in service of saving the city's true citizens.[45] If the play dramatises the transfer of sovereignty from a tyrant to the people as the tribunes represent them, it depicts this moment as one which preserves the exception – the placement of life outside the law – as a legitimate, lawful political act.

A critic like Patterson would, no doubt, demur by calling such an argument ungenerous to the unstable start of republican Rome. Patterson finds Brutus's and Sicinius's behaviour as unsalvageable as I do. For her, it is the citizens who point the way to the full flourishing of the republic; they are the figures in whom Shakespeare displays his hopes for a republican England, since they show how Rome could become a just state of law.[46] But this reading also falls short, in large part because the citizens themselves favour declaring a *iustitium*. They clamour for Coriolanus's death just as insistently as Brutus and Sicinius do ('Down with him! down with him!' (l. 230)).[47] If Patterson is right to say that the citizens create rational arguments to justify the 'undeniably physical content' which drives them, they none the less are as bloodthirsty as anyone.[48]

The Roman people do not understand the danger of their call for death. By declaring the *iustitium*, Brutus and Sicinius set off the chain of events that opens all Romans to extrajuridical killing and that leads to their own exposure as bare life in another state of exception: Antium. Banishing Coriolanus, using law to put him outside law, allows him to join with Aufidius and unleash a violence on Rome strong enough '[t]o unbuild the city' itself (l. 199). Cominius tells Brutus and Sicinius that they have helped 'to ravish your own daughters and / To melt the city leads upon your pates, / To see your wives dishonored to your noses' (IV, vi, 83–5); Rome, we are told, has given its enemy its shield (V, ii, 40). In their production of bare life, Brutus and Sicinius endanger the very borders – of Rome and its residents – that they claim to safeguard. One would not know, from reading *Coriolanus*, that the republic ever became stable.

For another example of how the play generalises Coriolanus's position, we might look to passages that begin as a family story but can be read much more broadly. I have in mind Valeria's description of young Martius: 'I saw him run after a gilded butterfly, and when he caught it, he let it go again, and after it again, and over and over he comes, and up again, catched it again. Or whether his fall enraged him, or how 'twas, he did so set his teeth and tear it! Oh, I warrant, how he mammocked it!' (I, iii, 60–5). From one vantage, the butterfly might stand for the Roman people, as it does when Cominius describes Coriolanus's assault on the Roman army. His soldiers

> follow him
> Against us brats with no less confidence
> Than boys pursuing summer butterflies
> Or butchers killing flies.
>
> (IV, vi, 94–7)

A republican reading would interpret this as a tendency toward tyrannical violence – one that runs in this problematic family and that sets them apart from citizens of more worth. But if Coriolanus seems to reduce others to the state of annoying and fragile forms of life when he ought to respect their humanity, we ought to bear in mind that it is the Romans' respect for their own humanity (and consequent disregard for his) that enables the situation. Cominius's comparison shows a being destroying the 'brats' who, in banishing him, also become less than human; to Cominius, the problem is less with Coriolanus and his kin than with those who singled him out and who now face his wrath. The problem, in other words, is with those who have insisted on a distinction – between who qualifies as human and should be protected, and who does not and can be torn apart. And as Menenius observes, having wings can mean more than one thing, can mean being more, not less, than human: 'There is a differency', he explains to Sicinius, 'between a grub and a butterfly; yet your butterfly was a grub. This Martius is grown from man to dragon. He has wings; he's more than a creeping thing' (V, iv, 11–14). The play figures both Coriolanus and the Roman people as wingless and as winged, and it confuses the meaning that Romans would like to attach to those categories. Indeed, this seems to be the point – that there is no point in trying to tell boy from butterfly, aside from the undesirable violence that always seems to follow. Everyone (and no one), the play suggests, is the boy; everyone (and no one) has wings. At times, that boy will seem defenceless, as Coriolanus does at the play's end; at times, he will be destruction's agent. Winged creatures will likewise both tear and be torn by humanity. Since they act equally heinously, it matters little which is which.

There is no telling between friend and foe, human and inhuman, in a state of exception, 'th' city of kites and crows' (IV, v, 45) to which the play's characters are exiled. There, such distinctions are so tenuous and reversible as to be virtually empty of content. They signify only as political tools, ways to mobilise a people's bloodthirstiness, to identify the 'viper / That would depopulate the city' (III, i, 264–5) and that must itself be killed. *Coriolanus* suggests that states doom themselves in constructing the human as they do, through arbitrary decisions about which beings merit protection and which do not. Roman citizens are both birds of prey and insects torn to bits; the state of nature is not what the city excludes but what is always already within its walls.

If I am right to argue that Rome is a state of exception in *Coriolanus*, we might direct our reading of the play with a new set of questions about its possible politics. Patterson's *Coriolanus* responds to the question of what form the state of law ought to take, offering a republican way out of absolutist and other monarchical political structures dominant in early modern England.[49] But if the play displays no investment in the state of law, the appropriate question can no longer be about which of these states *Coriolanus* portrays as best. The appropriate questions instead become something like the following: Does the play suggest ways to live in a world in which life is produced as bare life without also subscribing to the controlling fiction of sovereign selfhood? Does it suggest ways to escape, and to begin to dissolve, states of exception? What form of life might emerge in the aftermath? Awakening from the dreams of bounded life and just law, as I believe *Coriolanus* asks us to do, how can we speak and act without exposing others to the unlimited capacity to be killed? To see how the play addresses these questions, it is to Coriolanus himself that we have to look.

Coriolanian Being – A 'Thing of Blood'

As noted above, critics often read Coriolanus as aching for an extreme version of the bounded selfhood being articulated in early modernity. If he does, then he – a caricature of the play's other characters – clings to a central fiction by which states of exception operate. But I do not think that Coriolanus clings to this fiction, even when he seems to in his interactions with Roman citizens. He repeatedly maligns the populace – perhaps most flagrantly in Act III, when he complains about nourishing the 'cockle of rebellion' (III, i, 70) by giving the people voice. Such moments could be seen as attempts to demarcate the Roman nobility, including himself, as discrete persons in contrast to a many-headed multitude. Yet in his first invective against the citizens, Coriolanus admonishes them for wishing to be discrete, a wish that he, implicitly, does not share:

What would you have, you curs,
That like nor peace nor war? The one affrights you,
The other makes you proud. He that trusts to you,
Where he should find you lions, finds you hares;
Where foxes, geese.

(I, i, 166–70)

Coriolanus despises the citizens because they are inconsistent and unsure on most scores, yet are absolutely sure about avoiding risky positions, shrinking from a touch like recalcitrant, self-protective rabbits. Their chief concern is to guard personal borders, even as '[w]ith every minute' they 'do change a mind' (l. 180) as to how to do so. Coriolanus cannot stand this; during the battle which gives him his name, he remarks that 'He that retires, I'll take him for a Volsce, / And he shall feel mine edge' (I, iv, 28–9). In order to qualify as a 'Volsce' or enemy to Coriolanus, strangely enough, alliance to a particular state is not necessary; to Coriolanus, the commitment that matters is the one to a retired life, to avoiding the battlefield and its risks. If this implies a belief that the Roman people do not know their place, that place is simply the one where he too imperils himself. He objects here not to the erosion of class stratification and the attendant threat to identity; quite differently, he objects to withholding oneself, to retreating into the depths of the city where one mistakenly feels safe.

Coriolanus hates the citizens' voices because whenever they speak, they do so to aggrandise and protect themselves. A citizen makes this clear when outlining the process by which Coriolanus can become consul: 'He's to make his requests by particulars; wherein every one of us has a single honor, in giving him our own voices with our own tongues' (II, iii, 42–4); this same citizen goes on to remark, to Coriolanus's great dismay, that 'if we give you anything, we hope to gain by you' (ll. 70–1). He asserts self-ownership; he wants recognition as a discrete Roman subject, one given specific powers, entitlements and protections. Rome, he assumes, ought to foster self-sovereignty.

Coriolanus assumes just the opposite. He wants to keep to battlefields, for there he can exist beyond protective imperatives. There, he can erode the borders of his social and bodily self. Consider, for instance, what he says of his Volscian archrival, Aufidius:

Were half to half the world by th' ears and he
Upon my party, I'd revolt, to make
Only my wars with him. He is a lion
That I am proud to hunt.

(I, i, 231–4)

To fight Aufidius is what Coriolanus wants, and his commitment to warring with him supersedes all others: to Rome, to family, to the mother who taught him how to withhold the heart in the bid for its invincibility. For Coriolanus, war does not consolidate ideas of individual and group identity; instead, it suspends them. He accepts his agnomen and recognition from Rome almost against his will; he serves as Rome's shield but does so only incidentally. And so when he calls for soldiers to join him in battle, he appeals first not to the thought that 'his country's dearer than himself' but instead to being the sort of soldiers who love blood, who 'love this painting / Wherein you see me smeared' (I, vi, 73, 69–70). Coriolanus believes war to be beautiful not because it protects or strengthens Rome and its residents but because it smears him into bloody existence on an otherwise blank canvas. Battle turns the corporeal self inside out; it does what the public square does not, makes of him surfaces without depths, a being no longer clearly or only Martius (as he is then called) but undifferentiated. He becomes exposed to the outside-of-self, mixed with the blood of others. Being on the battlefield makes him not a soldier in wrenching relations but an entity that somehow is those relations and that returns as no more than their residue.

Smearing himself, Coriolanus renders his loyalty to Rome and his status as Roman unrecognisable; this, in the moment when the state might reasonably expect both to become most apparent. Ostensibly he fights for Rome, yet he largely fails to attach his behaviour to shoring up individual and national identity. The play never even makes clear whose blood is on him, whether it came from Romans or Volscians, or that Coriolanus cares which is the case. Equivocating about the source, if not the effect, of this blood, he says that it 'is rather physical / Than dangerous to me' (I, v, 18–19); but later, when he meets Aufidius, he claims that ''Tis not my blood / Wherein thou seest me masked' (I, viii, 9–10). This stated certainty, though, may just be meant to antagonise Aufidius so as to mix his blood further with others, for still later in the play Coriolanus says that 'I have shed my blood, / Not fearing outward force' (III, i, 76–7). His friend Cominius warns him that he should: you return from battle too late 'if you come not in the blood of others, / But mantled in your own' (I, vi, 28–9). Menenius remarks that the blood that Coriolanus 'hath lost . . . / . . . is more than that he hath' (III, i, 299–300), that there is somehow more of Coriolanus's most vital fluid outside, than inside, his body. But Coriolanus himself seems pleased to have accessed such a radical form of bodily openness and unworried about whether blood has flowed out of rather than on to him. This, unlike the public commemoration that would imbue his wounds with social closure, is 'physical' to him. Wanting contact, he negotiates his relationship to other bodies in absolute irresponsibility, as indifferent to others' boundaries as he is to his own. He loves war not because it permits him to prove his loyalty to Romans in risking himself against Volscians, but because taking that risk makes Romans and Volscians indistinguishable and, to that extent, alike. Coriolanus is selfless not in the sense typically attributed to soldiers, but only in the sense that, in the words of Cominius, he becomes non-human, unrecognisable as a self: 'From face to foot / He was a thing of blood,' a thing that 'struck / Corioles like a planet' (II, ii, 107–8, 112–13).

Time and again, Coriolanus seeks such self-undoing. When Corioles is empty of Romans, he enters; when the time comes to show himself worthy of the consulship, he speaks in terms that seem absolutist, helping the tribunes toward their goal of having him thrown off the Tarpeian rock; and later, when he is supposed to solidify his alliance to Antium, he instead sides with his Roman mother. Rather than act to preserve an aggrandised existence, he says and does whatever will accelerate his unravelling. This, above all, is why he acts. This is what he uses words to do, and why his acts and words get misconstrued. Indeed, openness to the blood of others and indifference – to the borders of both state and self – are what make Coriolanus's form of life so very different; letting go of the notion of discrete being turns him into a misfit. Just as Romans misrecognise his uses of his body as patriotic, so they misrecognise his use of language as akin to their own. When he delivers his speech about being a blood painting (I, vi, 68–70), for instance, he gets the wrong reaction: '*They all shout and wave their swords, take him up in their arms, and cast up their caps*' (l. 76 sd). 'O, me alone!' Coriolanus complains. 'Make you a sword of me?' (l. 77). The soldiers give Coriolanus recognition for his speech when that is the last thing he seeks and seemingly the least pleasurable thing he can imagine. The proper response, in his view, would be to withhold this form of acknowledgement and accord him the regard reserved for forged metal.

About being commemorated in language, he says the following: 'I have some wounds upon me, and they smart / To hear themselves remembered' (I, ix, 28–9); 'oft, / When blows have made me stay, I fled from words' (II, ii, 71–2); 'I had rather have one scratch my head i' th' sun / When the alarum were struck than idly sit / To hear my nothings monstered' with praise (ll. 74–6). When Menenius counsels him to 'desire them / To think upon you,' Coriolanus responds that he 'would they would forget me' (II, iii, 54–6). The citizens want to use language to designate themselves as individuals; language gives them the 'honor' (l. 43) of speaking so that Coriolanus and Rome more generally will see them as possessing discrete political power, each of them with a voice that counts. Coriolanus, on the other hand, wants his 'nothings' (II, ii, 76) to remain what they are, not things that can be used to solidify or advance his position, not things that can aggrandise him. If he can help it, his nothings will not be made into monstrous creatures, fantastic myths surrounding him and serving as his legacy – his preservation, in language, as heroic and whole.

Accordingly, Coriolanus also conceals his wounds. While smearing himself in blood is meant to show others the appeal of being undone, displaying his wounds would mean acceding to a process of social exchange that leads to the public fabrication and recognition of separable identities. He cannot let the citizens speak for his wounds, cannot permit a socially recognisable rendering of them. Desiring to be corporeally undifferentiated means that Coriolanus does not want to be made meaningful. He speaks in order to be undone; he wants words to make him into a sword, not a respected Roman citizen; he hopes that opening his mouth will relieve him of the supposedly safe borders and acknowledged agency of which the people seem so covetous.

Hoping to speak himself into objecthood, Coriolanus does not object to giving himself over to being handled, even when doing so means being, sometimes, not the edge of a sword but also a body exposed to one, as he is when he offers his throat to Aufidius. Coriolanus, in other words, realises that his life is bare life. To find an existence after and outside the state's controlling fictions, the play suggests, we may first have to become things of blood. For a time, we may have to inhabit our lives as bare lives – as unprotected lives that can, at any moment, be killed. Embracing this danger offers escapes: an escape from citizenship, its boundedness and its imperative to speak and act in a socially identifiable, workable way; an escape, too, from the cultivation of fashioned selfhood which Brutus and Sicinius need in order to do well as tribunes, to appropriate the 'stinking breaths' (II, i, 231) of the citizens for their own purposes. Coriolanus inhabits his life as bare life instead of pretending it is something else, and in so doing he loses his identity. In one respect, he finds the way out of Rome; he becomes unlocatable as a subject, a being that has already, and on its own terms, undone itself – turned inside out, edges eroded, a bloody object lost in the 'vast world' (IV, i, 42).

The question is whether his way out allows him to reach a world elsewhere. We might question how lost he actually gets. Being open to his own vulnerability and willing to renounce control, Coriolanus spends most of the play killing at the behest of one state or another, Rome or Antium; at the end of the play, he is himself killed. He refuses the constructs of corporeal and social boundedness; content to be a sword instead of a citizen, he becomes unrecognisable as a discrete body or a defined social individual. But if he cannot be found as a subject of the state, that state still captures him in crucial ways. He is still Rome's tool; Rome still employs him in its logic of killing. Whatever becoming a thing of blood accomplishes, he fails to pry himself completely from politically operative community. In this sense, inhabiting his life as bare life makes him all the more manipulable. Does *Coriolanus* suggest that there is, ultimately, no outside to states of exception? Or does the play indicate a way for Coriolanus to be made into something aside from a sword, something that the Brutuses and Aufidiuses of the world cannot wield?

Fisting Each Other's Throat: A Sodomitical Outside

The play does offer an outside, does indicate a path to life after bare life.[50] Opened by Coriolanus, this path requires connections potent enough to undo not just given individuals, as battle can, but the very social orders in which they exist. I want to argue that in Shakespeare's play these connections are specifically sexual and that, in his refusal of boundedness, Coriolanus is the figure who produces them.[51] Consider, for instance, Brutus's characterisation of him after the triumph at Corioles, just before he is to be made consul: 'All tongues speak of him, and the blearèd sights / Are spectacled to see him' at the Capitol (II, i, 200–1). When Coriolanus brings others together, they abandon the tasks that make Rome what it is for someone such as Brutus. A 'prat-tling nurse / Into a rapture lets her baby cry, / While she chats him' (ll. 201–3); she abandons her infant charge – that most sensitive material for social reproduction – to its own screams, preferring to speak of Coriolanus rather than worry about Rome. Filthy women come out of kitchens to see him, literally climbing the walls in which their lives are confined: 'the kitchen malkin pins / Her richest lockram 'bout her reechy neck, / Clamb'ring the walls to eye him' (ll. 203–5). To be near him, more comely,

> veiled dames
> Commit the war of white and damask in
> Their nicely guarded cheeks to th' wanton spoil
> Of Phoebus' burning kisses.
> (ll. 210–13)

Wanting to be seen, they lift their veils, forgetting self-preservation, giving up the appearance of flawlessness in favour of being exposed to the world that would ravish them. Priests, '[s]eld-shown flamens' (l. 208), emerge looking to shed their marks of distinction and lose themselves in crowds (l. 208); 'variable complexions' come together (l. 207). 'Stalls, bulks, windows / Are smothered up' with people longing to see him, distracted from all else (ll. 205–6). They stand on Rome's rooftops; containers – roofs, veils, walls – fail to contain anything; the partitions which separate Romans from one another start to crumble.

Brutus sees Coriolanus creating a sexualised community which disrupts social order. The scene just described takes place mainly between Coriolanus and the women who want to see him (although men, too, are present), but in a way that is hardly potentially procreative or socially reproductive. Shakespeare's scene wrenches Roman life so that social marks, those which would guarantee differential subject positions, have little meaning, get lost in 'the popular throngs' (l. 209). I have argued that Coriolanus escapes to the battlefield as a way out of bodily and social identity; here, for once, the city serves the same purpose for the Roman people. Figures drawn to Coriolanus – those within an unstable orbit whose centre is itself always a site for undoing – find their identities unsettled. Relieved of their normally appointed tasks, they forget their roles, forget who they ostensibly are as Roman men and women.

Like Bersani's gay outlaws, Coriolanus unworks the social; he exhibits a prodigious indifference to and disregard for personal borders of all kinds; through sexual relation, he allows others to exhibit an inaptitude 'for sociality as it is known'.[52] To account for the inclusiveness of the scene at hand, however, I must invoke a figure of early modernity, one who shares much with Bersani's outlaw – the sodomite. As Alan Bray has demonstrated, sodomites represented a force beyond order, the possibility 'that the chaos of the first day of Creation when "the earth was without form, and void" might come again'.[53] Those engaged in nonprocreative, nonmarital sexual activity were often presumed to be undermining social structures and identities more broadly; as Goldberg points out, they were frequently identified as heretics, spies and traitors.[54] Like gay outlaws, sodomites threaten the social not just by using sex to threaten alliance but by 'fully negat[ing] the world, law, nature', by refusing to protect or maintain subjects or engage in sanctioned sociality of any sort.[55] In this view, sodomites are beings from a world elsewhere, who threaten to bring that world to England, beings who wish to usher in disordered forms of life. They seek to dissolve the boundaries of England's subjects and, indeed, to do away with the human altogether, to collapse distinction into sameness of a most horrifying sort. As Bray notes, sodomites, werewolves and basilisks were literally spoken of 'in the same breath'.[56]

Brutus sees this inhuman, sodomitical world unfolding in front of him. He refers to people astride roof ledges as 'ridges horsed' (l. 206); what he claims to witness, to his horror, are people using Rome's buildings as they would animals. He claims to witness an exceptional moment, one in which the city seems not man-made; as I have argued, however, humanity itself (life deserving protection) can always become inhumanity (life that can be annihilated) in Rome, a city animalised (as one of kites and crows) from the start. And contrary to what Brutus believes, the city he sees here – unlike the one he seeks to make – may be the most liveable city that the play can imagine, the only one in which life would no longer become bare life. When veiled dames give themselves over to the sun's 'wanton spoil' (l. 212) – when they forget their place in Rome – they are worthless in Brutus's eyes; this scene suggests that malice such as his would vanish if all Romans forgot the distinction between Roman and non-Roman, human and inhuman. The scene offers a life outside law, one in which we stop working to uphold the borders of self that can at any moment be violently torn down, a life in which we instead embrace a more salubrious undoing. Were it to take hold, this sodomitical city would destroy not bare life but the possibility for its production. In the unbuilt city, all life would be openly unprotected and so no life would be singled out and ended as bare. Without effort, Coriolanus gives social order over to pleasure, martial conquest over to sex, and the quest to save the self over to its exposure; only then does he stop killing and fully suspend the state of exception. If only, the play seems to wish, there were no Brutuses, no citizens inside the city walls to make public life into something else. If only sociality were always as it is in this scene at the Capitol.

That Coriolanus might have been thought of – and that we might want to think of him – as a sodomite has received little critical attention.[57] Indeed, Goldberg's analyses of the play are among the few that argue in anything like these terms.[58] But to see how the play represents a community with political appeal, the best place to look may indeed be the relational structure or 'sodometry' that *Coriolanus* offers in scenes such as the one just described. The play says more about the way out of Roman life – about what it would take in order for Sodom to overtake Rome in a more than merely momentary way – in its portrayal of Coriolanus's relations with Aufidius. The latter remarks that, 'If we and Caius Martius chance to meet, / 'Tis sworn between us we shall ever strike / Till one can do no more' (I, ii, 34–6). In fact, they meet many times during the course of the play, and only at the end does Aufidius make good on the promise. In *Coriolanus*, upholding vows and honouring one's commitment to the state has unpalatable meanings. For

Brutus, it means women confining themselves to the kitchen, or wearing veils until told otherwise; as we have seen, it also means defending the city against its identified enemies. Keeping the Roman promise, staying loyal to oneself and one's country, often means killing. But relations founded on the broken promise, on being a sexual enemy to the social covenant, often means living. *Coriolanus* questions the promise to value distinctions essential to being a loyal subject: distinctions between Roman blood and Volscian blood, friends and enemies, life that must be protected and life that can be killed, citizens and sodomites, my body and yours.

What if, the play asks, we began by promising nothing except to become 'a kind of nothing, titleless' (V, i, 13), promising nothing except to break every other promise? Existence might enter the state Aufidius dreams of. He asks Coriolanus to

> Let me twine
> Mine arms about thy body, whereagainst
> My grainèd ash an hundred times hath broke,
> And scarred the moon with splinters. Here I clip
> The anvil of my sword, and do contest
> As hotly and as nobly with thy love
> As ever in ambitious strength I did
> Contend against thy valor.
> . . .
> Thou hast beat me out
> Twelve several times, and I have nightly since
> Dreamt of encounters 'twixt thyself and me.
> We have been down together in my sleep,
> Unbuckling helms, fisting each other's throat,
> And waked half dead with nothing.
> (IV, v, 110–17, 125–30)

They are about to pour 'war / Into the bowels of ungrateful Rome' (ll. 133–4). If characters in any Shakespeare play can be marked as sodomites, Coriolanus and Aufidius seem as likely candidates as any. Like sodomites, they seek to dissolve personal boundaries, want to become able to fist each other's throat; they want their interiors emptied out, to reduce themselves to surfaces. Like sodomites, they displace alliance by way of sexualised relation, and they do so in the context of a broader undoing of the social order. Their connection does not merely coincide with a tear of the social fabric but itself produces the tear; it makes Coriolanus traitor to Rome and Aufidius traitor to the families of those who have died at his rival's sword.

At first, it may seem that sodomy cannot keep either from being promised to states of exception. If Coriolanus is enemy to Rome, he is friend to Antium, and Aufidius only binds himself to Coriolanus in order to betray him; he only betrays Antium, that is, in the service of its strengthening. From this vantage, both only break promises in order to forge other, politically recognisable and functional ones. Aufidius, in particular, may fall short of the sodomitical ideal of undoing. He keeps a malicious secret, secures his triumph – and consolidates his Volscian identity – by being more than surface. With Coriolanus, the case is different. For his promise to Antium is not one that he ultimately upholds. He can only pour so much war into Rome before he finds himself delivering a kiss to it, the 'kiss / Long as my exile, sweet as my revenge' (V, iii, 44–5). This kiss, I want to emphasise, does not effect a simple reversal, a completion of the circuit from one city to the other. The beauty of Coriolanus heeding the call of family lies in its permitting a kiss that grants forgiveness and turns on Aufidius, yet does not ally him with Rome; Coriolanus intends to return to Antium. The kiss he would give to his wife remains a betrayal – this kiss would establish him as friend and enemy to all, and so, from Roman and Volscian perspectives, to none. With this kiss, he becomes traitor to Rome and Antium alike; in relenting towards his wife and family he has embraced and betrayed both places and so cannot be identified with, or tolerated by, either. He makes himself into an absolute traitor, a traitor to every promise and to every border of identity. Unidentifiable and unidentified, he cannot kill; in his least violent moment, Coriolanus becomes a model sodomite.

The tragedy of the play is that for Coriolanus, this kiss is the kiss of death. For us it can be exemplary, but for Rome and Antium it cannot. Never again can he make sense within either's walls, and since he cannot again be used as an instrument of killing, he cannot again enter either city without being killed. The effect of the kiss cannot last. Coriolanus's sodomy, his sexual undoing of all promises and identities, is the way out of the state of exception, and so – an outlaw captured by a supposed state of law – he must die. Agamben observes that 'a being radically devoid of any representable identity would be absolutely irrelevant to the State' and that irrelevant beings, those who do or will not belong, are 'the principal enem[ies] of the state'.[59] In the moment of delivering the kiss that promises himself to everyone and thus to no one, Coriolanus does not affirm an identity, but rather affirms his life as belonging to no one. That neither Rome nor Antium can render him recognisable makes his death inevitable, just as in Agamben's description the refusal of identity inevitably results in a scene like the one at Tiananmen Square, inevitably ends in borders being violently, paradoxically, redrawn.[60]

Coriolanus asks its audience to cast off this inevitability, to create the world elsewhere that its eponymous hero brings about, however fleetingly. It asks us to insist on connections which expose our radical vulnerability and erode our social identities, even if these connections must be continually renewed and cannot be made to last. Doing so would initiate the overhaul of relationality for which Bersani calls, one that certainly could not qualify as socially operative,[61] rendering unthinkable both falsely bounded subjects and the states that fabricate them. Replacing them in the space of the thinkable and possible would be the realisation of Aufidius's dream. Forgetting valour and contesting with one another's love, helms would be unbuckled. Waking 'half dead with nothing', we could not pretend that the question of our lives is one of protection; there could not be a question of when domination is necessary, when biopolitics makes sense, or who ought to be thrown off the Tarpeian rock. We would not expect states (and undertake our own endeavours) to solidify our borders.[62] The wager, for *Coriolanus* and the theorists I have discussed, would be this: by seeing that the state produces life as bare life while claiming to safeguard it – and by seeing that nothing can save us from the fact that we are, necessarily, vulnerable beings – a possibility would arise. A possibility to reflect on what it entails, exactly, to fist each other's throats and to be given over to sodomitical sameness. A possibility for thinking through how we ought to live out our exposure, how we can manage and inhabit open life.

Radical and Republican Thought in Shakespeare's Romes

In *Coriolanus*, Shakespeare rejects republicanism in so far as republics and those who speak for them claim to foster a citizenry of bounded selves. And though, as I have argued, republican selves need not be bounded ones, the sexual undoing that Coriolanus offers is none the less also anti-republican, a fact easily observed in Coriolanus's relationship to Cicero, a Roman republican featured prominently in *Open Subjects*. Though Cicero values vulnerability, he hates Coriolanus. The latter surfaces in *De Amicitia*; for Cicero, Coriolanus being in league with Antium makes him irredeemable. 'Such alliances of wicked men', Cicero writes, 'not only should not be protected by a plea of friendship, but rather they should be visited with summary punishment of the severest kind.' Such punishment is requisite 'so that no one may think it permissible to follow even a friend when waging war against his country'.[63]

This is a limit of friendship in some Ciceronian thought: knowing who one's friends are and observing the boundary that cordons them off from enemies. In his willingness to expose his vulnerability, perhaps, Coriolanus shares with Cicero's ideal citizen; but since Coriolanus also seeks to erode his social identity, that willingness cannot equate to virtue for Cicero. Roman community, according to him, 'has a claim on the largest and best part of our minds, talents and judgment for her own use';[64] since the community Coriolanus would found would do away with the distinction between Roman and non-Roman, his selflessness could never bolster a larger communal identity in the way that Cicero sometimes imagines. Besides which, most of what Coriolanus stands for – relations founded on the broken promise, undoing the distinction between man and animal, the replacement of Rome with Sodom – flies rather ridiculously in the face of the moral theory articulated in texts such as *De Finibus* and *De Officiis*. Cicero would not want gay outlaws within Roman walls; *Coriolanus* is not, on most scores, a republican text, and so one implication of this chapter is that Renaissance texts need not be recognisably 'republican' in order to be politically instructive.

But Shakespeare's attitude toward republicanism, as toward most things, is hardly uniform. In *Shakespeare and Republicanism*,[65] Andrew Hadfield demonstrates this. With good reason, Hadfield avoids extended discussion of *Coriolanus*. But he shows how a wide range of Shakespeare's works – including *The Rape of Lucrece*, the first tetralogy, *Julius Caesar* and *Hamlet* – takes up questions of governmental structure and the scope of citizenship. Hadfield shows how these works address issues of monarchical power, its limits, and the need for political representation of less powerful citizens; he shows as well how they, at least arguably, seem republican in many of the ways that Patterson believes *Coriolanus* is. Shakespeare, Hadfield helps us see, is far from systematic in his thinking about republicanism that offers bounded selfhood.

Nor, I want to argue, does Shakespeare always present more open forms of life as anti-republican. Shakespeare registers awareness, in *Coriolanus*, of the fragile nature of the solutions that his eponymous hero offers. That the play's world elsewhere is so fleeting suggests that Coriolanus's openness is bound to crumble in the lived world unless it receives a supplement. *Coriolanus* remains incomplete as an expression of the Shakespearean alternative to bounded selfhood as offered by Brutus and Sicinius. This being so, I want to end by considering another facet of open selfhood in Shakespeare, one that makes reference less to Shakespeare's last Roman tragedy than to his first, *Titus Andronicus*, and the form of vulnerability embraced there. The form shares more with Habermas than with Bersani; moreover, it shares with Cicero as well as with the republican Titus Livius. Considered together, Shakespeare's first and last Roman plays suggest the need for one strand of republican thought even as they focus on the pitfalls of another, and they spur us to think about theorists such as Habermas and Bersani in conjunction rather than in opposition. To explain what this means, allow me to preface my reading of *Titus* by specifying which Habermasian ideas are relevant here.

In my second chapter, I claim that Habermas privileges individuation over sociation, self-enclosure over openness. This is true of the essay on Mead and – as my final chapter argues – in his early work on the public sphere; but as Chapter 1 shows, Habermas sometimes places more value on being open to others. This is especially evident when he considers intersubjectivity as realised in dialogue. For Habermas, violence 'begins as a spiral of distorted communication', one leading from reciprocal mistrust to the breakdown of communication and to the abandonment of negotiation as such.[66] So for Habermas, our response to any violence must involve a re-commitment to communicative action – to intersubjective, open argument guided by the unforced force of superior reasons. Only then can we minimise the distortion – the failure of understanding, deceit and coercion – that produces scenarios in which 'communication' involves, say, the razing of skyscrapers, or the sacking of Rome, or the killing of Coriolanus. If we commit to models of mutual understanding by which we assume roles both of speaker and of hearer, if we inhabit both our position and another's, what Habermas calls a 'fusion of horizons' can occur. Considering the option of violence, we might respect the epistemic fact of difference but still attempt to arrive at a shared interpretation as to whether violence makes sense.

So doing, we commit to the possibility of compromise. And we become open subjects; having been both speaker and hearer, we can move beyond the rigid divisions between subjects that that binary implies (36–7). Able to exist at once as ourselves and as outside ourselves, bounded and unbounded, we are plunged into a state where, in Habermas's formulation, 'one subject can know itself to be one with another subject while still remaining itself.'[67] This form of openness is thus less total than those urged by radical theorists and has some subjective protection built in; individuals can, for instance, maintain a certain distance, can be themselves by adopting a critical attitude toward the other's utterances. At the same time, though, the self can be transparent to and feel at one with that other – on common interpretive ground, open to persuasion, vulnerable to the other and her words. Plunged into intersubjectivity, violence becomes implausible, maybe even unthinkable, since elements that often precede violence – for example, the inflexible boundaries between self and other that permit self-hardening and aggression – no longer are in place.

Titus Andronicus lends itself to Habermas because much of the tragedy of that play is driven by failed attempts at intersubjectivity. In the play's opening scene, for instance, Titus prepares to execute Tamora's son, Alarbus, and as she pleads she begs Titus to inhabit both his place and his enemy's. In occupying the position of a Roman as well as that of a Goth, he might discover a shared rationale that would make violence less sensical: 'if thy sons were ever dear to thee', she says 'O, think my son to be as dear to me!' Why, Tamora asks, 'must my sons be slaughtered in the streets / For valiant doings in their country's cause?' (I, i, 110–11, 115–16).[68]

If Titus comes to adopt Tamora's perspective, even for the briefest of moments, he would see that what she values in her sons (valour) is what he values in his. Set with her against a shared background, he might regard the antagonism between Romans and Goths as to some extent artificial or imposed. He has lost twenty-one sons; soon he will have only one still living. But even after he turns from Rome, Titus will remain locked into the position for which all others are either friends to be protected or enemies fit for elimination. For Titus, equality is only ever equitability, had by the balancing of death with death; Alarbus thus cannot live. If the experience of intersubjectivity makes counting more difficult – makes one of two yet preserves two as two – for Titus tallying the dead is all that counts.

Violence in *Titus* almost always depends on quickly foreclosed inter-subjective potential. Sometimes, one character silences another: for example, during the forest scene in which Titus's daughter, Lavinia, is undone. She begs Tamora and her sons, Demetrius and Chiron, for mercy. They refuse each plea, but in anxious fashion. Lavinia gestures toward something shared ('O Tamora, thou bearest a woman's face' (II, iii, 136)). She remarks that even lions are capable of pity, that even ravens are not drawn only to their own offspring – that in this regard all beings are capable of being at one with another. Like Tamora earlier, Lavinia argues that boundaries of alliance need not do what they do for Brutus and Sicinius: mark off what is included and excluded, what Roman, what Goth, as what ought to be protected and what we are free to destroy. Twice Tamora responds with a demand for silence ('I will not hear her speak, away with her!' (l. 137); 'I know not what it means, away with her!' (l. 157)). But Lavinia goes on and on; the only solution, Chiron realises, is to end dialogue, to cut off communication: 'I'll stop your mouth' (l.185). I'll sever your hands. I'll cut out your tongue.

Through such grotesque, pre-emptive violence and such insistent refusal to comprehend (or even listen), these Goths register real worry about the force of Lavinia's language. Centred around how open argu-ment might affect their plans, their anxieties gesture toward Habermas almost parodically; they refuse to enter into argument because if they did they would expose themselves to outcomes of compromise and possible persuasion. They have to insist on and eventually enforce Lavinia's silence, as dialogue promises to take them outside themselves, to make Tamora know 'what it means', to produce the intersubjective scenario that could undermine their violent designs.

Tamora and her sons are like Titus; they only attempt rectification by way of subtracting subjects or subtracting from them. The necessary failure of such a subject-centric calculus becomes most glaringly apparent in III, i, when Tamora's lover, Aaron, convinces Titus that violence can bring an end to violence – that if he chops off his own hand, his sons Quintus and Martius will be returned to him. Titus warms to the idea immediately ('Lend me thy hand, and I will give thee mine' (III, i, 187)), only to have that hand (along with the heads of the sons he had hoped to save) sent back to him: 'Here are the heads of thy two noble sons,' a messenger tells him, 'And here's thy hand, in scorn to thee sent back' (ll. 236–7). In this twisted, if predictable, scenario, Titus is presented with the part of himself he has allowed outside himself, the part he hoped would make him literally 'one with the other' yet permit him to remain who he is. Not what Habermas has in mind. If the joining of hands can indicate consent, compromise or connection – can indicate some fusion of perspectives – Titus believes that he might 'communicate' peace through the delivery of an actual hand disseered from the self.[69] Thus his gesture is met only with further distortion – with an offering of severed heads, the hand given back.

Such scenes complicate Shakespeare's conception of open selfhood as well as his relationship to republicanism. The scenes are quite different from their Coriolanian counterparts, where the openness embraced is more visceral and more uncompromising. Longing, in *Titus*, for the saving power of interaction and intersubjectivity, Shakespeare gestures forward to Habermas, but he also develops the thought of Cicero. Cicero urges that we respect the boundary between friend and enemy as Coriolanus does not; but he also thinks that boundaries between selves can be crossed – particularly in language – for good. As I point out in my final chapter, Ciceronian eloquence, nearly magical in its power, can effect an identification between an orator and a hostile audience, and can be the 'soulbending sovereign of all things'. Cicero believes that words 'can not only support the sinking and bend the upstanding, but, like a good and brave commander, can even make a prisoner a resisting antagonist', the antagonist that Lavinia would become were she permitted to continue talking.[70]

Lavinia and Tamora argue with those who oppose them in hopes of an intersubjective encounter. In assuming that to achieve genuine intersubjectivity one ought first to enter into an imaginary version of it, Cicero expands on this aspiration. To be effective – to move and per-suade his hearer – a speaker must create an internalised, projective sort of intersubjectivity, evoking the same emotions in himself that he wants to evoke in another. Praising the rhetorical capacities of Crassus in *De Oratore*, Antonius remarks that he seems 'to be not merely inflaming the arbitrator, but actually on fire' himself (333). He assumes the position of his hearer; he must be, as in Habermasian scenarios, at once himself and one with another.[71] If Tamora asks Titus to leave, for a moment, his position as a soldier and inhabit her position as a parent, and if Lavinia asks Tamora to leave her position as a Goth, Cicero implies that the way to get Titus to Tamora's position (and Tamora to Lavinia's) is to move beyond a rigid attachment to their own positions and also to inhabit the subjective state of their addressees – to feel how that state, and one's own state along with it, ought to be altered.

The movement tends to reconcile. In their anxiety about Lavinia's pleas, Tamora, Chiron and Demetrius seem to know so. They know, too, that interaction, acknowledging as it does the fact of differential positions even as it effaces them, makes room for criticism – a fact quite strikingly evident in Cicero's friendship theory. As pointed out in Chapter 2, Cicero advocates total openness to the friend, embracing both the risks and the rewards that such openness entails. One aspect of friendship not discussed at length in Chapter 2, though, is that being open means being made vulnerable to rebuke. 'When you yourself are the adviser,' Cicero writes, 'use your influence, as a friend, to speak frankly, and even, if the occasion demands, severely. And if you are the recipient of equally stern advice, listen to it and act as you are advised.'[72] Ciceronian intersubjectivity, like its Habermasian counterpart, makes one of two, yet preserves two as two. In their appeals to fellowship in parenthood or womanhood, respectively, Tamora and Lavinia also imply rebuke – that their interlocutors are acting incorrectly; they, too, seek to be at once fused with and separate from the other.

Cicero, Shakespeare and Habermas imply that at times we ought to try to live out such a paradox as that which might forestall violence. All three suggest that interaction should open, complicate and even multiply our positions as subjects. Cicero attributes virtually no limit to what lan-guage can do in terms of linking one subject to another, and underscores the republican cast of such links in his claim that language helps bind selves within the republic. He credits the genesis of civil society itself to the efforts of a mythical orator;[73] for Cicero, 'bonding consists of reason and speech, which reconcile men to one another, through teaching, learning, communicating, debating and making judgements, and unite them in a kind of natural fellowship.'[74] Republicanism is, with reason, often understood in terms of militarism, but Cicero's investment in discursive exchange allows him to understand republican being differently: 'Let arms yield to the toga.'[75]

However much Livy himself celebrates martial valour, his *Ab Urbe Condita* also shows how Rome depends on precisely what Cicero counsels. Like the Shakespeare of *Titus Andronicus*, Livy not only highlights how intersubjectivity complicates subject positions without abolishing them – as Cicero does – but also shows how the complex positioning of selves can make violence hard to conceive. Consider the following episode from the first book of Livy's history, an episode (imaginary or not) from the reign of Romulus – one that occurred during a war between Romans and Sabines and that involved the mass rape and forced marriage of Sabine women within Rome. Despite the utter disregard given them, these women took to the battlefield:

> the Sabine women, whose wrong had given rise to war, with loosened hair and torn garments, their woman's timidity lost in a sense of their misfortune, dared to go amongst the flying missiles, and rushing in from the side, to part the hostile forces and disarm them of their anger, beseeching their fathers on this side, on that their husbands, that fathers-in-law and sons-in-law should not stain themselves with impious bloodshed, nor pollute with parricide the suppliants' children, grandsons to one party and sons to the other. 'If you regret,' they continued, 'the relationship that unites you, if you regret the marriage-tie, turn your anger against us; we are the cause of war, the cause of wounds, and even death to both our husbands and parents. It will be better for us to perish than to live, lacking either of you, as widows or as orphans.' It was a touching plea, not only to the rank and file, but to their leaders as well. A stillness fell on them, and a sudden hush. Then the leaders came forward to make a truce, and not only did they agree on peace, but they made one people out of two.[76]

The Sabine women argue that their present positioning is so excruciating that it ought to make intersubjectivity – and an end to war – inevitable. The war, they argue, deprives them of subject positions except by lack; they will be widows if the Sabines win, and they will be orphans if Romans do. They claim that they can be neither themselves, except as beings defined by loss, nor one with another (the fathers who have killed their husbands, or vice versa) so long as war goes on. It is not just that their loyalties are torn but that their very selves have been rent.

The Sabine women, we might say, lament the very undoing of identity that Coriolanus seeks out. This may be, in part, because they have had no choice in anything; and so now they choose to risk themselves completely, only toward an end other than Coriolanus's own. I have said that in the world of *Coriolanus*, to be friend to all – to both Romans and Volsces – is to be friend to none. In *Coriolanus*, to fit the self to multiple positions makes the self fit for elimination; the characters of that play cannot follow Coriolanus in his desire to explode the self in more salutary fashion. Livy's Sabine women do not share that desire either. All the same, they present an alternative to inflexibly bounded selfhood. Arms yield to the toga, and bitter opposition to intersubjectivity, when the Sabine women 'go amongst the flying missiles'.

Their plea is touching; at least for the time being, war ends. Livy describes the dissuasion of Coriolanus from sacking Rome in similar terms – 'since the swords of the men could not defend the City, the women should defend it with their prayers and tears' (347) – and when Shakespeare develops the episode, Volumnia echoes the Sabine women in claiming to be pulled apart by rival attachments. She wins Coriolanus to her position with an argument that he has dislodged her, his wife, Virgilia, and the young Martius from every tenable position:

> Alas, how can we for our country pray,
> Whereto we are bound, together with thy victory,
> Whereto are we bound? Alack, or we must lose
> The country, our dear nurse, or else thy person,
> Our comfort in the country.
> (V, iii, 107–11)

When Coriolanus relents, Volumnia attains a kind of intersubjectivity; she becomes one with Coriolanus yet remains a Roman woman. But unlike the instance of Romulus's war with the Sabines, Volumnia's act of persuasion fails to yield the happy ending that could have been had in *Titus*, had Tamora yielded to Lavinia or Titus to Tamora. Unlike his mother, Coriolanus loses ground on which to stand and is swiftly killed by the man who activates the trap door – Aufidius. Intersubjectivity, here, is not equally available. Had Tamora won over Titus as to her son or had Lavinia won over Tamora as to her honour, by contrast, there would have been an accord more true and less tragic – Titus as himself, a Roman, but also a parent and one with Tamora; Tamora as herself, a Goth, but also a woman and one with Lavinia. This would, no doubt, put Titus and Tamora at risk, leaving them open to their enemies. But Shakespeare suggests that sometimes the way to forestall violence is to open oneself to it. As daughters to Sabines and wives to Romans, this is what the Sabine women do.

Cicero, Livy and the Shakespeare of *Titus* accord real value to how we can be open to words and to intersubjectivity. Being open to them can aid the formation of republics and can help hold them together.

In my initial critical review I showed how the republican tradition and legacy, when discussed alongside Shakespeare, are often linked with the development of less sinister, proto-liberal forms of bounded selfhood – for instance, with negative freedoms and positive liberties that would protect and entitle the self. Hadfield, like Patterson in her account of *Coriolanus*, locates the republicanism of *Titus* in its advocacy of a mixed constitution, ideals of broadened political participation, and citizens whose voices count.[77] Whether or not this is precisely right – Oliver Arnold, for instance, has argued that it is not[78] – the play is certainly republican in another sense, in so far as it advocates facets of intersubjective openness that Cicero and Livy regard as critical to the Roman republic's existence. As with Spenser in the previous chapter, then, Shakespeare can be republican in a fashion that has less to do with bounded selfhood and more to do with having one's vantage unsettled by another's, with vulnerability that is virtuous.

Through Titus and Tamora's refusals, through the distorted and pointless attempts to communicate, Shakespeare implies that a world without tragedy would be one without well-bounded, calculating individuals. Subjects would be de-centred and interaction might accomplish just what Habermas and Cicero say that it can. But the form of interaction toward which *Titus* points is not so uniformly Habermasian. The piling on of communicative failure in the play forces us to consider whether intersubjectivity is often unavailable, whether moments exist when moving outside the self cannot occur; in these moments the other cannot or will not be known, and a 'fusion of horizons' is simply not an option. For all that the play urges communicative forms of openness – for all that it is proto-Habermasian or neo-Ciceronian – it also suggests that we need other, more total forms of openness in order to avert tragic outcomes. It invites readers to reflect, for instance, on what world we would have if, when intersubjectivity failed, a more complete openness took the place of violence, even if only momentarily.

To recall this section's opening example, what if Titus had just spared Alarbus? What if he had spared him not because Tamora had reasons understandable to Titus – reasons that allowed him to be one with Tamora yet remain himself – but had spared Alarbus for no understandable reason at all?[79] And what if Aufidius had spared Coriolanus for the same reason? What if he had exposed himself to such total risk, as Coriolanus does for his mother – when he knows that being persuaded by her may prove fatal? '[F]or your son – believe it, O believe it!,' Coriolanus tells Volumnia, '[m]ost dangerously you have with him prevailed' (V, iii, 187–8). She, I have said, restores an intersubjective self-conception that is satisfactory to her. Coriolanian selfhood, its openness more absolute, moves beyond intersubjectivity entirely. He neither merges with the other, now Roman, nor remains the Volsce that he has become. For Shakespeare, this is the play's most admirable action. Rome requires it for its existence. If *Coriolanus* needs *Titus*, then, *Titus* needs *Coriolanus*. If the last chapter focuses on overlooked affinities between republican and radical thought, Shakespeare helps us appreciate how the latter needs the former, and vice versa, in order for open selfhood to be liveable.

It is true that intersubjective and total openness depend on others to embrace them, something that Shakespeare's characters often refuse to do. Still, in Shakespeare's Rome the proper – or at least the praiseworthy – response is not to attempt to withdraw into well-bounded selfhood. Occluding interiority so as to manipulate others holds no promise of happiness; in *Coriolanus*, Brutus and Sicinius manage only to imperil themselves by doing so, and Aufidius is purely dastardly in his triumphant deceit. Refusing to be moved by others' words also does no good. To cite an example from another of Shakespeare's Romes, Metellus and Cassius plead with Caesar to reconsider the banishment of Metellus's brother. Instead Caesar boasts about how imperturbable he is. 'Be not fond', he says,

> To think that Caesar bears such rebel blood
> That will be thawed from the true quality
> With that which melteth fools – I mean sweet words,
> Low-crooked curtsies, and base spaniel fawning.
> . . .
> I could be well moved, if I were as you.
> If I could pray to move, prayers would move me.
> But I am as constant as the Northern Star,
> Of whose true fixed and resting quality
> There is no fellow in the firmament.
> (III, i, 43–6, 64–8)[80]

Caesar is murdered a few lines later. If he cannot be moved, he can be killed; if he is not subject to one sort of vulnerability he is to another, just as Macbeth – the example with which I began this book – can be killed, though he thinks he cannot.

For Shakespeare, bounded selfhood is a pernicious fiction, and openness, despite the abyss into which it can lead, ought to be embraced anyway. To refuse violence is to be open to violence, Coriolanus shows, but it is to his merit that he is won over by others – won over as Titus and Tamora ought to have been – and that he risks having been won over to his utmost peril. Unwanted violence is sure to follow upon the self-hardening so often made along with a resolutely bounded sense of self, and Shakespeare suggests that only when we are open – to intersubjectivity, perhaps even to violence – does non-violence become possible, even as peace is often denied and never assured.

Rejecting the offer of resolutely bounded selfhood as fundamentally empty, Shakespeare's plays answer Bersani's call for thought about a practice that is hard to think and maybe impossible to achieve fully (how to exist in pure openness); his plays also supply examples which confirm Habermas's thesis that violence often begins in spirals of distorted communication, of failed intersubjectivity. Beyond this, plays such as *Titus* and *Coriolanus* are useful in that they urge a reworking of the self's boundaries, a more inclusive sense of how we can be 'open subjects'.

I say this partly because radical theory, for all that I rely on it in these pages, largely resists such reworking. It does so, I think, by accepting a logic that opposes forms of selfhood so stridently that intersubjective openness and total openness come to look mutually exclusive when, as Shakespeare helps us see, they may in fact be two sides of the same coin. Not only is much radical theory opposed to politics with deep investments in firm personal boundaries – investment that, Chapter 2 shows, can be found in writings by figures such as Hannah Arendt and John Rawls. Not only is radical theory opposed to granting ultimate value to individual interests, to discrete, delineated selfhood, or to the 'respect' for boundaries which, according to Arendt, defines civic friendship. Even positions that Habermas sometimes takes, more flexible about boundedness – longing as he does for worlds where we might know ourselves to be one with another while remaining ourselves – even these positions become suspect.

For many of those that advocate 'self-undoing' on grounds of its political appeal, to ascribe *any* intrinsic value to discrete selfhood – or to subjects 'remaining' what they are – can come to look like a fundamentally conservative, even dangerous act. Within such a framework, 'communication' can become manipulation's instrument, for lodged within intersubjectivity are still-bounded selves that could lapse into the kind of self-hardening that ends in the violence which intersubjectivity was to end. And so the self must relinquish its integrity; in much radical theory and in *Coriolanus*, personal boundaries must serve only instrumental purposes or be eradicated altogether. Thus for Bataille, as I discuss in the previous chapter, boundaries are valuable only in so far as they make sustainable and repeatable the experience of ecstasy, of being shattered through and through.[81] Thus Bersani dreams, as I do above, of selves turned inside out, part of what he calls a 'universal and mobile communication of being'.[82] Thus Agamben longs for life as an 'absolutely exposed singularity', of life before or beyond constructs of containment.[83] Thus Nancy wants to believe that 'individuality' and 'community' are necessarily antithetical, that 'being-with' lacerates, is necessarily the end of well-bounded selves.[84]

Such desires are worth taking seriously. As I imply in my section on Habermas, though, his work can be used to show how thoroughgoing cynicism toward boundaries is distortion, is overstatement, is simply not so. But Habermas has practised his own form of distortion, rejecting radical positions as utopian, naïve and inconsistent – for example, in his treatment of Bataille[85] – overlooking the fact that utter self-exposure can be good, can signal an openness that is not unstudied. Such antagonistic positioning has brought thinking about the subject of non-violence to an impasse, and Shakespeare's first and last tragedies offer a way out. They refuse to oppose forms and degrees of openness, as though a choice had to be made – on the grounds that the more attuned we are to the complexity of our boundaries and the ways and degrees to which they can be opened, the more difficult it is to imagine unwanted violence. *Titus* and *Coriolanus* show that the risk undertaken in total openness requires a more limited, intersubjective complement, just as intersubjectivity requires the complement of an offer that is unconditional, our reaching out in the dark. So doing, these plays disclose some of the complexity and situational value of boundedness and unboundedness, and they show that the forms of openness can and should be thought together, lest our theories of the open subject come to look like Titus's offer of a hand – like offers that go too far and not far enough, that undo themselves by what is withheld and what held at bay.

Notes

1. As I will demonstrate in detail, this is the argument of Annabel Patterson's '"*Speak, speak!*": The Popular Voice and the Jacobean State', Chapter 6 of her *Shakespeare and the Popular Voice* (Oxford: Basil Blackwell, 1989), 120–53.
2. Among other places, these accounts can be found in Giorgio Agamben, *State of Exception*, trans. Kevin Attell (Chicago: University of Chicago Press, 2005); see also his meditation on the concentration camp, *Remnants of Auschwitz: The Witness and the Archive*, trans. Daniel Heller-Roazen (New York: Zone, 2002); and *Homo Sacer: Sovereign Power and Bare Life*, trans. Daniel Heller-Roazen (Stanford, CA: Stanford University Press, 1998), esp. 119–80.
3. For Agamben's most thorough account of how states produce bare life, see *Homo Sacer*, 71–115.

4. Quotations from the play follow Jonathan Crewe (ed.), *Coriolanus* (New York: Penguin, 1999).
5. *Sodometries: Renaissance Texts, Modern Sexualities* (Stanford, CA: Stanford University Press, 1992).
6. *Homos* (Cambridge, MA: Harvard University Press, 1995), especially the chapter 'The Gay Outlaw', 113–81.
7. For Jacob Burckhardt's account, see 'The Development of the Individual', in his *Civilization of the Renaissance in Italy*, trans. S. G. C. Middlemore (New York: Modern Library, 2002), 91–117.
8. The classic contemporary account of these possibilities in both the sixteenth and seventeenth centuries can be found in Greenblatt's *Renaissance Self-Fashioning*, 1–9, which is discussed in the introduction and the previous chapter. For a concise history that focuses on the rise of print in England, see Sharon Achinstein's *Milton and the Revolutionary Reader* (Princeton, NJ: Princeton University Press, 1994), esp. 3–14. On religious persecution and the attendant need for inwardness, see Alexandra Walsham's *Church Papists: Catholicism, Conformity and Confessional Polemic in Early Modern England* (Woodbridge: Royal Historical Society–Boydell, 1993). For a recent argument, also mentioned above, that places emphasis on how an open conception of self was still very much dominant, see Cynthia Marshall's *The Shattering of the Self: Violence Subjectivity, and Early Modern Texts* (Baltimore: Johns Hopkins University Press, 2002). Unlike her essay on *Coriolanus* (see n. 10 below), Marshall's account of early modern selfhood in this book shares much with my own.
9. For an exemplary account that focuses on humoral theory's emphasis on porous corporeality and its continued influence in early modernity, see Gail Kern Paster's *Humoring the Body: Emotions and the Shakespearean Stage* (Chicago: University of Chicago Press, 2004).
10. Janet Adelman, '"Anger's My Meat": Feeding, Dependency, and Aggression in *Coriolanus*', in David Bevington and Jay L. Halio (eds), *Shakespeare: Pattern of Excelling Nature* (Newark, DE: University of Delaware Press, 1978), 108–24; and Cynthia Marshall, 'Wound-man: *Coriolanus*, Gender, and the Theatrical Construction of Interiority', in Valerie Traub, M. Lindsay Kaplan and Dympna Callaghan (eds), *Feminist Readings of Early Modern Culture: Emerging Subjects* (Cambridge: Cambridge University Press, 1996), 93–118.
11. Arthur Riss, 'The Belly Politic: *Coriolanus* and the Revolt of Language', *English Literary History* 59 (1992), 53–75; and Michael D. Bristol, 'Lenten Butchery: Legitimation Crisis in *Coriolanus*', in Jean Howard and Marion F. O'Connor (eds), *Shakespeare Reproduced: The Text in History and Ideology* (New York: Methuen, 1987), 207–24. For an account of the gendered privatisation of the body, see Russell West-Pavlov, *Bodies and their Spaces: System, Crisis and Transformation in Early Modern Theatre* (Amsterdam: Rodopi, 2006), 127–44.
12. Leonard Tennenhouse, '*Coriolanus*: History and the Crisis of Semantic Order', in Clifford Davidson, C. J. Gianakaris and John H. Stroupe (eds), *Drama in the Renaissance: Comparative and Critical Essays* (New York: AMS, 1986), 217–35, esp. 227; and Stanley Cavell, *Disowning Knowledge: in Six Plays of Shakespeare* (Cambridge: Cambridge University Press,

1987), 165. On Coriolanus's supposedly closed-off linguistic life, see James L. Calderwood, '*Coriolanus*: Wordless Meanings and Meaningless Words', *Studies in English Literature, 1500–1900*, 6 (1966), 211–24; Carol Sicherman, '*Coriolanus*: The Failure of Words', *English Literary History* 39 (1972), 189–207; John Plotz, '*Coriolanus* and the Failure of Performatives', *English Literary History* 63 (1996), 809–32; and Cathy Shrank, 'Civility and the City in *Coriolanus*', *Shakespeare Quarterly* 54 (2003), 406–23.

13. For a very recent argument that Coriolanus seeks such self-authorship, one which claims that Coriolanus does so through plague metaphors which he uses to characterise others but by which he himself is finally character-ised, see '"A Kind of Nothing": Plague Time in Early Modern London', Chapter 6 of Ian Munro's *The Figure of the Crowd in Early Modern London: the City and Its Double* (New York: Palgrave Macmillan, 2005), 175–200.

14. See *Shakespeare and the Popular Voice*, esp. 125, where Patterson discusses how 'critics of all persuasions' agree that Coriolanus is positively Hobbesian; see also James Holstun, 'Tragic Superfluity in *Coriolanus*', *English Literary History* 50 (1983), 485–507, esp. 493, where he begins to describe how *Coriolanus* presents 'a monarchical threat to mixed republican stability'.

15. Adelman, Marshall and Cavell, for instance, think that the play turns away from discrete being altogether as an ideal, advocating forms of dependence (Adelman, 119–20), being a subject-in-process (Marshall, 'Wound-man', 111–14) and mutual incorporation by way of language (Cavell, 167) as the play's – if not Coriolanus's – key value.

16. See Holstun on the citizens' scepticism of Menenius's 'contemptuously inappropriate' (487) choice of metaphor, as well as his assertion that, with *Coriolanus*, Shakespeare 'moved out of the Tudor conception of the body politic and into the seventeenth-century critique of the body politic as an outmoded fiction' (492).

17. Patterson, *Shakespeare and the Popular Voice*, 133, 143.

18. Specifically, Patterson writes that 'Shakespeare had not only pierced the fable's hide, he permitted his plebeians to do so as well'; see *Shakespeare and the Popular Voice*, 135.

19. Patterson states that the citizens employ a language of rights, and in doing so invoke 'a view of the semantics of power that is not supposed to have been available in political theory, let alone common usage, until half a century later'; see *Shakespeare and the Popular Voice*, 142.

20. For Patterson's most polemical statement of what early modernists ought to be doing when conducting political readings of texts, see *Early Modern Liberalism* (Cambridge: Cambridge University Press, 1997), esp. 1–26.

21. Thomas Smith, *De Republica Anglorum: A Discourse on the Commonwealth of England* (Cambridge: Cambridge University Press, 1906), 20.

22. Jürgen Habermas, *The Structural Transformation of the Public Sphere: an Inquiry into a Category of Bourgeois Society*, trans. Thomas Burger with Frederick Lawrence (Cambridge, MA: MIT Press, 1989), esp. 1–88. Indeed, the early modern public sphere has become of such interest that a recent issue of *Criticism* was devoted to it. See Joseph Loewenstein

and Paul Stevens (eds), 'When Is a Public Sphere?', *Criticism* 46 (2004), 201–77.

23. Among the works most directly concerned with making such challenges are the title essay of Jean-Luc Nancy's *The Inoperative Community*, ed. Peter Connor, trans. Connor et al. (Minneapolis, MN: University of Minnesota Press, 1991), 1–42; and Nancy's 'Of Being Singular Plural', in *Being Singular Plural*, trans. Robert D. Richardson and Anne E. O'Bryant (Stanford, CA: Stanford University Press, 2000), 1–99; Leo Bersani's work, begun most famously in 'Is the Rectum a Grave?', *October* 43 (Winter 1987), 197–222; Giorgio Agamben's *Homo Sacer* and *State of Exception*; and Judith Butler's *Precarious Life: The Powers of Mourning and Violence* (New York: Verso, 2004), as well as her *Excitable Speech: A Politics of the Performative* (New York: Routledge, 1997).

24. For Butler's clearest statement of the correlation between the ascription of rights and the fiction of autonomy, see *Precarious Life*, 25–8.

25. For a passage in which Butler describes the likelihood of exploitation that stems from the insistence on individual and national boundaries, see the chapter 'Violence, Mourning, Politics', in *Precarious Life*, 19–49, esp. 39–49. For Bersani's most succinct statement of the danger of self-possession, 'to define all relations as property relations' (128), see *Homos*, 128–9.

26. Butler describes such violent self-hardening most directly when discussing recent US foreign policy. See especially *Precarious Life*, 29.

27. Agamben, *Homo Sacer*, 9.

28. *Homo Sacer*, 121–2, 127.

29. *Homo Sacer*, 122.

30. *State of Exception*, 7.

31. For Agamben's most recent statement of this position, see *State of Exception*, 1–31; and *Homo Sacer*, 119–88.

32. For one instance in which Butler concedes the value of rights, see *Precarious Life*, 24–6.

33. This is the impulse behind Nancy's *Being Singular Plural*, as well as *The Inoperative Community*, especially that book's title essay. As should become clear, this is also the impulse behind Bersani's *Homos* and many of the other works cited below.

34. See *Inoperative Community*, 3–19, and *Being Singular Plural*, 34–65, for Nancy's consideration of the antithetical relation between individuality and being-with.

35. Nancy, *Inoperative Community*, 3.

36. *Inoperative Community*, 15, 35.

37. *Inoperative Community*, 19.

38. Taking up Nancy's notion of the inoperative, Jacques Derrida too wants to imagine a 'minimal community' founded on *philia*, which is older than subjectivity. See *Politics of Friendship*, trans. George Collins (London: Verso, 1997), esp. 200, 155, 236. See also the previous chapter.

39. Bersani, *Homos*, 128.

40. *Homos*, 120.

41. From a more extreme perspective – and in hopes of distancing queer theory from the liberal perspective that would celebrate how queers have helped

build and nourish community – see Lee Edelman, *No Future: Queer Theory and the Death Drive* (Durham, NC: Duke University Press, 2004).

42. Bersani, *Homos*, 76.
43. For more on the possible non-relation of life and law, see Giorgio Agamben, *The Coming Community*, trans. Michael Hardt (Minneapolis, MN: University of Minnesota Press, 1993), 65.
44. Patterson, *Shakespeare and the Popular Voice*, 126, 127.
45. For Agamben's account of the *iustitium*, see *State of Exception*, 41–51.
46. See especially *Shakespeare and the Popular Voice*, 142–6, where, among other things, Patterson asserts that in portraying plebeian rationality, Shakespeare 'shows us that popular, food-centered protest could *work*' (143).
47. For a persuasive argument about how the citizens' voices may in fact be co-opted by the tribunes who represent them, see 'Worshipful Mutineers: From Demos to Electorate in *Coriolanus*', Chapter 5 of Oliver Arnold's *The Third Citizen: Shakespeare's Theater and the Early Modern House of Commons* (Baltimore: Johns Hopkins University Press, 2007), 179–214. I agree with Arnold that the tribunes do so, though as my review of Arnold's book suggests (forthcoming in *Criticism* 51:3), I disagree with the notion that the citizens ought to have held on to their voices and, thus, their identity. Their desire for autonomy, after all, is what enables them to desire the violence that Shakespeare presents as useless.
48. Patterson, *Shakespeare and the Popular Voice*, 133.
49. See *Shakespeare and the Popular Voice*, 140–2, where Patterson discusses the play's theorisation of 'common power'.
50. For a highly nuanced account that in part responds to the argument here, see Nichole E. Miller, 'Sacred Life and Sacrificial Economy: Coriolanus in No-Man's Land', *Criticism* 51:2 (2009), 263–310. Miller's argument carefully delineates the extent to which Coriolanus can be said to be made into bare life by a state of exception; locates Coriolanus's elsewhere in a grace that the play seems to both offer and withdraw; and suggests how the play may be neither pro- nor anti-republican. Miller and I have differing senses as to whether and to what extent the play offers a 'world elsewhere' but are in accord in most other respects.
51. Daniel Juan Gil has enabled parts of this argument by demonstrating how sexual ties in early modern texts are often built on the absence of functional social ties. See 'At the Limits of the Social World: Fear and Pride in *Troilus and Cressida*', *Shakespeare Quarterly* 52 (2001), 336–59; and 'Before Intimacy: Modernity and Emotion in the Early Modern Discourse of Sexuality', *English Literary History* 69 (2002), 861–87. The summation of Gil's thoughts on this topic can be found in *Before Intimacy: Asocial Sexuality in Early Modern England* (Minneapolis, MN: University of Minnesota Press, 2006).
52. Bersani, *Homos*, 76.
53. Bray, *Homosexuality in Renaissance England* (London: Gay Men's Press, 1982), 24.
54. Goldberg, *Sodometries*, 17.
55. *Sodometries*, 19.
56. Bray, *Homosexuality in Renaissance England*, 19.

57. Indeed, when the obviously sexual charge in relationships such as that between Coriolanus and Aufidius is remarked upon at all, it is often either to discard such relationships as pathological or to distance them from sodomy. For an early example of the former, see Emmett Wilson, Jr's 'Coriolanus: The Anxious Bridegroom', which describes the 'pathological mother–son relationship' that leads Coriolanus to distance himself from Volumnia ('the phallic mother'), only to submit to 'feminine, passive wishes to submit to a strong father' (Aufidius); see David Wheeler (ed.), *Coriolanus: Critical Essays* (New York: Garland, 1995), 93–110, esp. 93, 98, 108. For an analysis that seeks to save the relationship between Coriolanus and Aufidius from sodomitical associations, see Bruce R. Smith, who argues that their changing relation represents '[t]he transformation of brutal aggression into bonded love'; see *Homosexual Desire in Shakespeare's England: A Cultural Poetics* (Chicago: University of Chicago Press, 1991), 34.

58. According to Goldberg, Coriolanus wants to 'devour the world and digest its structures', wants 'to "live" in some realm that is not the biological'; the play, in his view, 'imagines an "inhuman" sexuality', production that is not social but antisocial or asocial. See *James I and the Politics of Literature* (Baltimore: Johns Hopkins University Press, 1983), 187; and *Shakespeare's Hand* (Minneapolis, MN: University of Minnesota Press, 2003), 185. Like many of the play's critics, Goldberg places an emphasis on Coriolanus's desire to be self-contained, while I have argued that Coriolanus finds the notion of discrete selfhood repugnant and that we must understand this if we are to understand his appeal.

   In what is at present an unpublished lecture – but part of which will appear in *ShakesQueer* (forthcoming from Duke University Press) – Madhavi Menon has also advanced an ingenious argument that connects *Coriolanus* with queer theory. Menon focuses on how the play might be understood in terms of the 'fag-hag', a figure that, in her reading, undoes notions of both identity and stable temporality. For Menon, it is Aufidius and Volumnia, not Coriolanus, who bring about this undoing, but in most respects her argument shares with the one advanced here.

59. Agamben, *The Coming Community*, 86–7.

60. *The Coming Community*, 85–7.

61. Bersani, *Homos*, 76.

62. The dream of bounded selfhood has been described in numerous recent studies of homoeroticism in early modern England. For two examples, see Shannon's *Sovereign Amity: Figures of Friendship in Shakespearean Contexts* (Chicago: University of Chicago Press, 2002), esp. 21–2 and 45–6; and Jeffrey Masten's *Textual Intercourse: Collaboration, Authorship, and Sexualities in Renaissance Drama* (Cambridge: Cambridge University Press, 1997). See n. 28 of the previous chapter for a consideration of Shannon.

63. Cicero, *De Senectute, De Amicitia, De Divinatione*, trans. William Falconer (Cambridge, MA: Harvard University Press, 1938), 155.

64. See James E. G. Zetzel (ed.), *On the Commonwealth and On the Laws* (New York: Cambridge University Press, 1999), 5.

65. Hadfield, unlike Patterson, troubles the equation of republicanism and proto-liberalism and mentions *Coriolanus* only briefly, claiming that

Shakespeare had an acute interest in the history and meaning of republican Rome and that the play offers a meticulous analysis of the electoral process (58).

66. See Giovanna Borradori (ed.), *Philosophy in a Time of Terror: Dialogues with Jürgen Habermas and Jacques Derrida* (Chicago: University of Chicago Press, 2003), 35.

67. See Habermas's discussion of Hegel in *The Philosophical Discourse of Modernity*, trans. Frederick Lawrence (Cambridge, MA: MIT Press, 1987), 30. Among other texts, see also 'The Entwinement of Myth and Enlightenment' and 'An Alternative Way out of the Philosophy of the Subject', both in *The Philosophical Discourse of Modernity*; and pp. 1–141 in *Reason and the Rationalization of Society*, vol. 1 of *The Theory of Communicative Action*, trans. Thomas McCarthy (Boston, MA: Beacon, 1984).

68. All references are to Russ McDonald (ed.), *Titus Andronicus* (New York: Penguin Putnam, 2000).

69. For a reading of hands in Titus in the context of consent that is less Habermasian and more classically liberal, see Sid Ray, '"Rape, I Fear, Was Root of Thy Annoy": The Politics of Consent in *Titus Andronicus*', *Shakespeare Quarterly* 49:1 (1999), 22–39.

70. Cicero, *De Oratore*, vol. 1, trans. E. W. Sutton (Cambridge, MA: Harvard University Press, 1948), 331, 333.

71. Though they have similar investments in the flexible, multiple positioning of the subject within discursive exchange, I want to emphasise here that Cicero and Habermas do not espouse identical theories of communication. For more on this, see Chapter 5.

72. See *On the Good Life*, trans. Michael Grant (New York: Penguin, 1971), 187, 201.

73. *De Inventione, De Optimo Genere Oratorum, Topica*, trans. H. M. Hubbell (Cambridge, MA: Harvard University Press, 1949), 7.

74. M. T. Griffin and E. M. Atkins (eds), *On Duties* (Cambridge: Cambridge University Press, 1991), 21.

75. *On Duties*, 31.

76. *Livy I: Books 1 and 2*, trans. B. O. Foster (Cambridge, MA: Harvard University Press, 1988), 47–9.

77. See 'Shakespeare and Republicanism: History and Cultural Materialism', *Textual Practice* 17:3 (2003), 461–83, esp. 473.

78. See '"Their Tribune and their Trust": Political Representation, Property, and Rape in *Titus Andronicus* and *The Rape of Lucrece*', Chapter 3 of Arnold's *The Third Citizen*, 101–39.

79. I discuss this possibility in another, related context, that of Derridean hospitality, in '"And here's thy hand": *Titus Andronicus* in a Time of Terror', forthcoming in a special issue of *Shakespeare Yearbook*, 'Shakespeare After 9/11', ed. Julia Lupton.

80. This refers to the Folger Shakespeare Library edition, ed. Barbara Mowat and Paul Werstine (New York: Washington Square, 1992).

81. See especially *Guilty*, trans. Bruce Boone (San Francisco, CA: Lapis, 1988), 28–9.

82. *Homos*, 129.

83. *The Coming Community*, 65.
84. See *The Inoperative Community* and *Being Singular Plural*, passim.
85. See 'Between Eroticism and General Economics: Georges Bataille', 211–37 of *The Philosophical Discourse of Modernity*. On the issue of self-undoing sovereignty and the sacred, for instance, Habermas writes that Bataille opposes the rational subject to the sovereign one such that he cannot even articulate his theory and remain coherent (235–6).

Chapter 4

'That Transubstantiall solacisme': Andrew Marvell, Linguistic Vulnerability and the Space of the Subject

Spenser and Shakespeare, I have argued, imagine social experiences wherein vulnerability can become a definite good. Their characters exist most intensely and admirably when the self's integrity becomes briefly unthinkable. While I have not dwelled much on the point, such exposure often occurs during discussion – when, for instance, Britomart and Amoret relate their hard adventures to each other, or when Aufidius tells his dream to his rival. In these moments, speech does not merely express their vulnerability but also creates it – communicates it in some literal sense. The next two chapters, on Andrew Marvell and John Milton, fasten more intently on creation of this kind. They detail how linguistic vulnerabilities have existed and may yet exist.

In the first part of this chapter I address the issue fairly narrowly, examining Marvell's attitude toward Catholicism and especially toward concepts of transubstantiation and transubstantial language. Describing ways that 'transubstantial' words could be spoken in early modernity, I show how the term could refer not simply to the transformation of bread into the body of Christ but to any utterance aimed at producing direct material effects on the bodies of the world.[1] Those bodies included human ones, and so believing in transubstantial language often meant living with an intense and expansive sense of the power that words have to penetrate, expand, erode and transform persons. Though believing this may seem atavistic, work by Judith Butler shows how linguistic vulnerability is very much still with us. Unintuitive as it may be, a 'magical' notion of language remains a topic for academic and legislative contestation, and so one aim throughout the chapter is to describe intersections between early modern and current conceptions of speech's power to shape.

In the first part of my treatment of Marvell, I show how he often favours a self-protective speaking subject that, for him, is distinctly Protestant. Marvell does so in the nightmarish portrayals of transubstantial sociality that appear as early as the 1640s (in 'Flecknoe: An English Priest at Rome'), as late as the 1670s (in *An Account of the Growth of Popery and Arbitrary Government*) and, occasionally, in 'Upon Appleton House', the poem that centrally concerns me. From this vantage, to be linguistically vulnerable leads to the eradication of all personal boundaries and the most painful, inhuman forms of exposure. Only strict anti-transubstantial discipline can secure a liveable, and in this case rigidly bounded, way of being in the world.

But Marvell's thinking about linguistic vulnerability was, I argue in the second part of my analysis, not always zero-sum. Although Marvell was often anti-Catholic, he was not always simply or straightforwardly so. Much criticism – for example, that of Annabel Patterson and David Norbrook – has claimed just this, arguing that Marvell's anti-Catholicism most often is simply anti-transubstantiality, a proto-liberal form of republicanism, a disgust not for Catholics as such but for language that could impede progress toward self-sovereignty by seducing bodies and enslaving minds. I, by contrast, will argue that the great value of 'Appleton House' resides in its embrace of transubstantiality itself. Marvell's country house poem does this by showing how the seductive, even transformative pleasures of language compromise personal boundaries but do not abolish them. Indeed, 'Appleton House' often actually aligns bounded selfhood with decidedly open forms of life, making self-enclosure and self-exposure a single process. The poem does so through its presentation of the Fairfaxes and the nuns; it also does so through its very speaker, who uses language that would transubstantiate him, who asks that Nun Appleton make his boundaries more secure and, in a paradoxical process, expose him utterly.

I use Marvell's presentation of positive linguistic vulnerabilities as a point of departure for the chapter's latter sections. Moving beyond the specific question of Marvell's Catholicism, I draw connections between the 'boundary politics' in 'Appleton House', classical antecedents such as Virgil and Lucan, and contemporary theories of space. These sections think more broadly about the status of vulnerability, both linguistic and otherwise, in Marvell's spatial theory; about the place that that theory has in traditions of thinking about the topic; and about the place Marvell thus has in the history of selfhood. I argue that in not only adumbrating the situational, context-dependent value of boundaries, but in questioning their very ontology – in questioning whether they ought to always, only, exist so as to separate – Marvell questions temporal separations as well. So doing, Marvell suggests an especially complex, accommodating way to understand the development and the legacy of early modern selfhood. This way undoes binaries that place bounded selfhood, republicanism and proto-modernity on one side, and vulnerability, royalism and regress on the other. Whereas some critics see Marvell's modernity in how he bequeaths boundedness, Marvell himself suggests a history of the self that would not insist that personal frontiers can be present only if transubstantiality is absent, a history which would not claim that becoming modern – or republican – and being invulnerable to words are one and the same.

Linguistic Vulnerability Early Modern and Modern

As Judith Butler has shown, discussions of linguistic vulnerability remain quite prominent, particularly around topics such as hate speech, pornography and gays in the military. Her book *Excitable Speech* addresses the questions that dominate the discussions: To what degree are our bodies and minds marked by a vulnerability to words? How, for instance, do racial slurs affect those addressed, and how do slurs compare to more obviously physical assaults? Could the two ever be equated, and if so, under what conditions? Could a declaration of homosexuality, to cite a second example, be considered a homosexual act, one capable of seducing and 'infecting' those within earshot? If the experience of linguistic vulnerability can be understood along the same lines as physical coercion – if speech acts can violate personal boundaries in the same way that other acts can – does government intervention ever become appropriate? Butler poses such questions to discern how possibilities for the verbal exposure of vulnerability might be best managed, and to consider whether these possibilities must always be resisted, or whether, instead, we ought at times to welcome them.

Previous chapters alluded to Butler's search, in *Precarious Life*, for ways to inhabit (rather than simply minimise) the vulnerability that seems characteristic of social existence. In its exploration of language, the aim of *Excitable Speech* is no different. Butler insists that whether or not we enjoy our susceptibility to words – and whatever laws we pass to discourage the unwanted exposure of that susceptibility – we must learn to manage it, for there is no way for life to be consistently otherwise. For her words play a direct, inevitable part in both cognitive and bodily processes of subject formation. She values rigid boundedness in limited contexts – for instance, as an enabling legal fiction to help protect citizens against undesirable violence – but she also contends that no extremity of self-discipline, no extent of state regulation, could ever fully inoculate us against linguistic openness.

Butler accepts this vulnerability as a lived fact of existence. She proceeds with an acute sense of how 'having been called an injurious name is embodied, how the words enter the limbs, craft the gesture, bend the spine', of 'how racial or gendered slurs live and thrive in and as the flesh of the addressee' (159). Butler is well aware of speech's injurious potential. And yet if another's words can deprive subjects of a sense of self-sovereignty, breaking down their defences in a way that is felt as directly physical, in her view linguistic vulnerability need not be only and utterly debilitating. She seeks to figure out how best to deploy, rather than most effectively thwart, the shaping capacity of language – to learn, for instance, how to appropriate wounding words for salutary purposes. Abandoning the strand of liberal theory which focuses on erecting and enforcing the set of personal boundaries that would uniformly guard against verbal onslaught, Butler is interested in work that searches for the best ways to inhabit the necessary imperfection of all attempts at self-fortification, to embrace how we can be at once bounded, enclosed beings and open ones, exposed and altered by words. From within this experience, Butler believes, we might find the language that could help shape desirable forms of life.

In the seventeenth century, analogous questions about linguistic vulnerability often clustered around the concept of transubstantiation and its popular permutations. Starting with the quite determinate relationship between blessing and bread, wherein the latter becomes the body of Christ when a priest says it does, the concept referred out to a wide range of practices that, if still associated with the old religion, went well beyond transubstantiation as defined by Catholic doctrine. Keith Thomas details how such doctrine generated a vast corpus of popular, parasitic beliefs which attributed direct, 'magical' material effects to any number of speech acts, ones aimed at exploiting the permeable boundaries of objects and also of human subjects.[2] For some of those who, like Butler, embraced linguistic vulnerability as a lived fact of existence, that the world and its people were vulnerable to words was reason for optimism; speech could trouble personal boundaries not only to inflict injury but also to enact therapy. It could be used, for instance, as the pleasurable 'pipes' that join desiring subjects and desired objects – as speech does in Walter Montague's *The Shepherd's Paradise*, which featured Charles I's notoriously Catholic wife, Henrietta Maria. Bellesa, played by Henrietta Maria, and her suitor, Basilino, engage in a series of dialogues over the course of the masque, at the end of which Basilino articulates a transubstantial theory of speech. Love involves

> twoe hearts soe equall in it, as they
> Are measured by one another; they are the vessells wherein
> It is refin'd & heated, mutually by each others Eyes, and

Joyn'd by Pipes as subtile as our thoughts, by wch it
Runnes soe fast from one into another, as the exchange
& the returne, are but one instant . . .[3]

In Basilino's perspective, exchange and return, desire and its fulfilment, occur at once. Lovers' hearts submit to no objective measure; subjects, meaningless on their own, gather their meaning entirely relationally, the words spoken by each to the other the transubstantial pipes that join them in perfect interpenetration. Basilino enjoys discussion so much, in fact, that he fantasises about having their dialogues all over again, '[t]he repetition of wch would ease / me more, then the remove of all my other greifes' (74). This, as Bellesa puts it, is 'desire / refin'd into the purity of union' (74), one for which the first aim of conversation is for spoken words to affect things directly and therapeutically, soldering subjects to objects, present to future.

In another (if not erotic) form of therapy, embracing transubstantial language also could mean believing that words could cure an array of spiritual and physical maladies. According to two Elizabethan pamphleteers, for example, many believed that 'good words and prayers [could] restore them again to their perfect health.'[4] The most scandalously therapeutic use of transubstantial language, however, came from the mouths of Catholic martyrs. As Arthur Marotti explains, martyrs often employed the gestures and words of ceremony and devotion in order to convert the very 'place and paraphernalia of execution' into joyous space, and to change themselves from sinners into saints. John Bodey, for example, supposedly referred to the hurdle on which he was dragged to execution as a 'sweet bed' and the halter around his neck as a 'blessed chain', which he then kissed.[5]

Within the Protestant imaginary, by contrast, the prospect of linguistically vulnerable subjects and objects often was a nightmarish one, to be guarded against at all costs. A flood of pamphleteering at once warned readers of, and aimed to disprove, the transubstantial outlook; legislation required members of parliament to reject that outlook; and countless Catholics were imprisoned and executed, particularly as the accession of James II approached. Indeed, virtually every calamity or near-calamity of the seventeenth century, such as the Gunpowder Plot of 1605, the Irish Rebellion of 1641, and the Great Fire of 1666 were blamed, rightly or wrongly, directly or indirectly, on Catholics.[6] More than now, perhaps, linguistic vulnerability occupied a place in the foreground of the English social imaginary; and anti-transubstantial models gathered momentum during Marvell's time, influenced as it was by figures such as George Snell and Bishop Bramhall, and institutions like the Royal Society. According to these models, speech should not touch the furniture of the world or be spoken in hopes of having direct material effects.[7]

Language instead should aim to be persuasive, transparent and efficient – an aim, it turns out, not easily achieved. Locke and Hobbes, for example, both rejected transubstantial beliefs as simply mistaken, false relics of a dark past, but could hardly ignore the cultural power and potential danger of transubstantiality. For Locke, 'the end of speech' is the 'easiest and shortest way of communicating our notions'; words are signs of ideas, 'the thoughts of men's minds . . . conveyed from one to another' for critical examination.[8] From a Lockean standpoint, believing in transubstantiation means being insufficiently sceptical; to believe that words can act like things is to confuse one's categories. Although Locke will 'readily grant' 'that these opinions are false and absurd', he also worries that progress toward truth and the living of a 'good life' will be thwarted should language and world not be kept separate, should the English people fail to insist that words not violate the boundaries of things in the same way that things themselves can.[9]

In this respect, Locke resembles the more intolerant, absolutist Hobbes. For Hobbes, '[t]he words, *This is my Body*, are aequivalent to these, *This signifies, or represents my Body*' and 'to take it literally, is an abuse.' Those who take transubstantiation seriously refuse the distinctions that enable historical progress; the doctrine of transubstantiation belongs to an earlier era to which England must not return, when 'the Darknesse of the time [was] grown so great' that 'men discerned not the Bread that was given them to eat.'[10]

In his extended argument against transubstantiation, Jeremy Taylor lays bare the logic that holds anti-transubstantial frameworks together. Taylor, like others, declares absurd all heightened beliefs about what words can do to things – beliefs which 'entered upon the world in the most barbarous, most ignorant, and most vitious ages of the world', which are akin to belief in 'feeding a man with music' or 'quenching his thirst with a diagram', and which make men behave as 'beasts, and not reasonable creatures'.[11]

The refusal to divide words from things, Taylor claims, ends not only in refusing to divide present from past but also in refusing to see distinct bodies for what they are. Taylor writes that 'that which makes a body' 'is, extension, limitation by lines, and superficies and material measures', and that '[t]he first notion and conception of things teaches all men, that what is circumscribed and measured by his proper place is there and no where else' (211). This idea, that bodies are discrete and delineated, and that boundaries are marks of separation rather than contact or overlap (as they are in *The Shepherd's Paradise*), extends even to Christ, who 'moved finitely by dimensions, and changes of places . . . Christs body even after the resurrection is circumscribed as it was before' (216). Those who accept transubstantiation ignore the well-ordered, geometrical arrangement of bodies in space by believing both that the body of Christ might be fragmented – might, of a Sunday, appear in a thousand places at once – and that the parts of Christ's body might be concentrated into a single point. Bodies are '*partum extra partem*, one part without the other'; 'in a body there cannot be an indistinction of parts' and to believe in transubstantiation is to believe, wrongly, that bodies can be 'bounded and not bounded', 'contained and not contained' (226). Those who believe in transubstantiation tamper with the notion of bodily integrity and make boundaries confused, impure, alterable.

Such worries over what spatial boundaries are and what words can do to them may seem at some distance from the current political moment. They become more recognisable, though, when transubstantial practice extends beyond the blessing of bread. Consider, for instance, how language has been understood to have a magical, hyper-sexualising potential. Today policymakers worry that 'out' homosexual soldiers threaten, by the very declaration of homosexuality, to infect and unman their straight counterparts, to convert them from military discipline to reckless sensuality.[12] In seventeenth-century England, analogously, Catholic priests and other speakers of transubstantial language were often thought to threaten the undoing of otherwise productive, Protestant citizens; they threatened to convert the English people back to the old religion, to the carnal, undisciplined and unbounded selfhood with which that religion was so frequently linked. According to Henry Care, were the English people seduced by Catholic words and infected by transubstantial beliefs, they would be stripped of property and self-propriety alike. Made vulnerable to words, there would be no turning back; never to 'hear again the joyful sounds of Liberty and Property', they would be 'forced to fly destitute of bread and harbour . . . [their] wives prostituted to the lust of every savage bog-trotter . . . [their] daughters ravished by goatish monks' – all while having their own bowels ripped out.[13]

Marvell and the Anti-Catholic Imaginary

Over the course of his career, Andrew Marvell occupies multiple, complex positions with respect to controversies over Protestantism, Catholicism and vulnerability, linguistic and otherwise. Despite his brief conversion to the old religion in the late 1630s, at times Marvell is staunchly anti-Catholic. He is so as soon as the late 1640s, when he is thought to have written 'Flecknoe, an English Priest at Rome'. The poem is based on Marvell's encounters with the priest Richard Flecknoe, represented as ridiculous and insufferable, a speaker of poetry at once unintelligible and injurious. The speaker describes

> how I, silent, turned my burning ear
> Towards the verse; and when that could not hear,
> Held him the other; and unchanged yet,
> Asked him still for more, and prayed him to repeat:
> Till the tyrant, weary to persecute,
> Left off, and tried to allure me with his lute.
>
> (31–6)[14]

Flecknoe's (likely Latin) onslaught communicates nothing, and Marvell supplies clear, if comical, links between opacity and Catholic tyranny. Going beyond, say, the reading of mass to someone who knows no Latin, Flecknoe sears the speaker's ears with incomprehensible words.[15] He can speak verse, but cannot converse in a way that is transparent or even meaningful.

Instead, Flecknoe's speech works like a blowtorch. When self-addressed, that speech serves a malnourishing purpose, even as he thinks it does just the opposite – much like Taylor's Catholic who thinks that music can serve as food and that diagrams quench thirst; as though Flecknoe believes that his words could be added to his flesh, he 'circumscribes himself in rimes; / And swaddled in's own papers seven times, / Wears a close jacket of poetic buff, / With which he doth his third dimension stuff' (69–72). Misguided and diseased, Flecknoe stuffs his boundaries with words. Only his 'black habit' secures anything like stability for him; only it allows the priest to be something other than what he passes by: 'were he not in this black habit decked, / This half-transparent man would soon reflect / Each colour that he passed by, and be seen, / As the chameleon, yellow, blue, or green' (79–82).[16] Unlike someone with a more cultivated, disciplined and protected interior, Flecknoe would be a chameleon without the worn black habit, which lends him a thin, spurious coherence and keeps him from being utterly susceptible, an unthinking reflex of his surroundings.

The speaker portrays Flecknoe as afflicted with linguistic perversity, using speech that, failing to communicate meaning, is sent back to corporeal space.[17] The priest actually seems to want to use not just transubstantial words but also meaningful ones – after all, he becomes irate when the speaker cannot understand his blistering verse – but since he is Catholic he cannot, consigned instead to live transubstantial life. Marvell's poem fastens on Flecknoe's body and so doing levels a typically anti-Catholic charge: namely, and despite his wan embodiment, that the sensual and carnal are his words' true target. So when a listener can enjoy his verse, the listener is not the Protestant speaker, who Flecknoe tries to impress, but an Italian whose powers of persuasion are even less developed than Flecknoe's own, a person unreflectively stimulated by sound, not enlightened by meaning: he, 'because he understood / Not one word, thought and swore that they were good' (139–40). Flecknoe has come to know the unnamed Italian by writing love poetry for his use, and if Flecknoe has not yet succeeded in helping the Italian seduce his love object, he has, against his will, successfully seduced the Italian. Unable to direct his own will or words, the priest who almost lacks a body uses words that have only bodily appeal.

Earlier, when the speaker meets the Italian figure and the latter demands to see Flecknoe, the speaker will not make way on the narrow staircase leading to Flecknoe's apartment. In a mock suggestion that personal space be opened up, he instead parodies seductive language:

> I answered, 'He is here, Sir; but you see
> You cannot pass to him but thorough me.'
> He thought himself affronted, and replied,
> 'I whom the palace never has denied
> Will make the way here;' I said, 'Sir, you'll do
> Me a great favour, for I seek to go.'
> He gath'ring fury still made sign to draw;
> But himself there closed in a scabbard saw
> As narrow as his sword's; and I, that was
> Delightful, said, 'There can no body pass
> Except by penetration hither, where
> Two make a crowd, nor can three persons here
> Consist but in one substance.' Then, to fit
> Our peace, the priest said I too had some wit:
> To prov't, I said, 'the place doth us invite
> By its own narrowness, Sir, to unite.'
> (89–104)

The Italian misinterprets the speaker to be saying that he cannot climb the stairs to Flecknoe without a fight. Really he only says that the width of the staircase cannot accommodate them both without 'penetration' of one by the other. This leads to the speaker's unserious invitation for all three of them – Flecknoe and the two on the stairs – to unite in a sexualised Holy Trinity. Underlying the speaker's joke is his belief that, just as to equate language with flesh is a sign of unhealth, so the spiritual truth of the Trinity cannot be reproduced in material bodies without unhappy stabbing. Both, like believing in transubstantiation, would involve category mistakes; using essentially immaterial words for bodily sustenance is as ludicrous as attributing immaterial flexibility to rigid personal boundaries. Unable to imagine how to compromise those boundaries profitably without abandoning embodiment altogether, the speaker is a kind of anti-type to Coriolanus and to some of Spenser's characters. The speaker believes selves to be discrete and delineated, sheathed, bounded in the way that Jeremy Taylor describes lest unwanted violence ensue. For the speaker, the best escape – one foreclosed, until Flecknoe's intercession, by the Italian's incapacity to comprehend anything – would come through communicative language, the transparency that would make the staircase negotiable. Transparency would keep everyone separate and give them room to breathe again.

With an enfeebled subject at the poem's centre, the anti-Catholicism of 'Flecknoe' comes across comically. Later, in *An Account of the Growth of Popery and Arbitrary Government*, Marvell continues to voice trepidation about Catholics in terms quite similar to those applied to Flecknoe, only with a drastic tonal shift. What Flecknoe performed becomes the 'Transubstantiall solacisme', whereby a priest tries to use words to 'work in one moment a thousand Impossibilities' and 'change the very nature of things'.[18] But now – writing amid the machinations of Titus Oates's Popish Plot in the late 1670s – Marvell takes such solecism seriously, joining the joke of Flecknoe to Care's fantasy of propertied, civil subjects being shattered by Catholics. In a sentence that doubtlessly contributed to the persecution and killing of Catholics in the 1680s and beyond, Marvell's pamphlet opens with an ominous claim: '[t]here has now for divers Years, a design been carried on, to change the Lawful Government of England into an Absolute Tyranny, and to convert the established Protestant Religion into down-right Popery' – into a hellish inhumanity, one that Marvell worries 'will Infallibly Sweep the Table' of England (225). It is as though the English people have lost their ability to recognise Flecknoe's ridiculousness, as though his perverse way of being in the world genuinely threatens to become theirs. One Flecknoe is a joke; thousands of Flecknoes is not. Like Locke and Hobbes, the MP from Hull does not allow that bread can become Christ's body, or that the site of punishment can become a sweet abode simply because someone says that it can; but he does believe in the harm that linguistic vulnerability can cause. The 'facts' militating against transubstantiation are irrelevant if a sufficient percentage of the population is seduced by the notion of transubstantiality – if enough Catholic wives seduce their husbands, or enough Jesuits seduce young men and women, to the old religion.

Transubstantiality in 'Upon Appleton House'

Marvell more than once expresses an anti-Catholic outlook. But we can also view him as other than anti-Catholic, even when his treatments of Catholicism revolve around the themes of linguistic vulnerability that first arise in 'Flecknoe'. In a critical practice that has arguably become paradigmatic but that differs from this study, Annabel Patterson argues that Marvell's anti-Catholicism can and should be understood not as thoroughgoing hatred for Catholics per se but as mistrust of and doubt about the specific issue of transubstantial language. Marvell, for her, opposes such language mainly because it lends itself to tyrannical purposes – to moulding, seducing and controlling the English populace with unclear, coercive words.[19] While acknowledging Marvell's involvement in the persecution of Catholics, Patterson even treats his resistance to transubstantial language as integral to his essentially republican and proto-liberal frame of mind. The *Account*, she argues, is above all about 'constitutional principles and public institutions' at stake in the latter part of the seventeenth century; as part of a rights-based programme that she has labelled 'early modern liberalism', the pamphlet aims to make parliamentary affairs public, to specify and limit sovereign power over English citizens, and thus to provide citizens with opportunities for developing a more bounded, empowered and autonomous sense of themselves.[20]

According to accounts such as Patterson's – which typically focus on Marvell's parliamentary aspirations and career, and so typically treat *The Account, The Rehearsal Transpros'd* and the poems with explicitly political concerns – Marvell favours countering words that would coerce with those that could help English subjects better protect themselves.[21] In this reading, Marvell gives privilege to developing rational self-discipline and critical distance, finding the interpretive vantage from which one would remain unmoved by the seductions of empty rhetoric and the charms of false ritual. Early modernists such as Patterson contend that Marvell treats linguistic vulnerability as an unnecessary, undesirable feature of human life, and that he is admirable for having done so. Belief in transubstantial language limits self-sovereignty and disables judgement, hampering one's ability to demand, bear or exercise rights.

For roughly the last decade, Patterson's strategy for reading Marvell as other than anti-Catholic has, by and large, carried the day. Her strategy has its applicability, since Marvell does sometimes articulate proto-liberal positions that attach value to protected, bounded ways of being in the world. But approaches such as hers, particularly when personal boundaries are insisted on inflexibly, need to be placed in a wider, more accommodating field, one that moves beyond the particular Protestant imaginary within which linguistic vulnerability exists always only as an object of distrust. One way to view Marvell as other than anti-Catholic, and to recuperate him for the current political moment, has been to read his anti-Catholicism as a cover for his desire to minimise the vulnerability that transubstantial words would exploit. Another way, I hope to show, involves attending to those moments when Marvell embraces that vulnerability – when he, like Butler, searches for ways to live out the imperfect closure of personal boundaries.

Though 'Appleton House' is full of such moments, the poem merits little consideration for Patterson and her fellow travellers. It claims only a tiny fraction of her voluminous output, for example, and occupies under five pages of David Norbrook's fifty-five page treatment of Marvell's republicanism in *Writing the English Republic*. Patterson and Norbrook admire one feature of 'Appleton House': the comparatively brief portrayal of Marvell's pupil, Maria Fairfax. Unlike her uncritical ancestor (Isabel Thwaites, who is seduced by a nun), Maria can resist the words addressed to her by the suitors that would strip her of self-control. Also, she can use language to her advantage. Recuperating the portrayal of Maria as a 'counter-pattern' to the lesbian nuns, Norbrook writes that she is 'a woman distinguished by her skill in language . . . which, we are led to understand, would arm her against the kinds of temptations Isabella Thwaites had been unable to resist' (289).[22] Unlike Flecknoe, Maria uses words for the right purpose – not for seducing the bodies of others or for sustaining her own body, but for cordoning her body off. For Patterson, Maria figures the power over others that can come from strict self-discipline; '[s]haming the poet-tutor out of his self-indulgent laziness', Patterson writes, 'she acts like a military commander reviewing her slack troops.'[23]

In some respects, Maria's capacity for self-closure is doubtlessly admirable; in stanza 90's description, it wards off the unwanted coercions of suitors, protecting her from undesirable kinds of trespass:

> Blest nymph! that could so soon prevent
> Those trains by youth against thee meant:
> Tears (watery shot that pierce the mind);
> And signs (Love's cannon charged with wind);
> True praise (that breaks through all defence);
> And feigned complying innocence;
> But knowing where this ambush lay,
> She 'scaped the safe, but roughest way.
>
> (713–20)

Because of stanzas such as this, I will – as I have throughout – not be suggesting that the attitude expressed in 'Appleton House' is or ought to be one that regards vulnerability as completely and uniformly appealing. The poem suggests that in some contexts – for instance, when Maria perceives a duplicitous or malign intent – she ought to do her best to keep words from hurting her. Suitors' words should not always make her blush; she ought not always to take them fully into her and so be taken in by them. To be open, equally and uncritically, to everything outside the self would make consent meaningless, and in this sense, perhaps, we can be glad that Maria can protect herself. This point – about the value of boundedness – is one to which I will return in the chapter's latter sections.

In the importance they attach to personal boundaries, though, Norbrook and Patterson – and especially the latter – do more than express admiration for Maria's canniness. For both, Marvell devotes large expanses of the poem to what he never would have written, had he maintained a properly proto-liberal frame of mind: twenty-five stanzas that describe how Isabel Thwaites is seduced in the convent that once occupied the Appleton estate, and thirty-five more that portray the speaker luxuriating in markedly transubstantial interactions with the estate's environment. Norbrook, accordingly, acknowledges the difficulty in reading most of the poem as voicing progressive, rational-critical republican attitudes;[24] 'deep in the woods of the Fairfax estate', Patterson similarly opines, 'the ivy licks [the speaker] into reactionary beliefs and sensual relaxation just as . . . the nuns' smooth tongues had seduced' Thwaites.[25] In one sentence, 60 of the poem's 97 stanzas are summarily dismissed. From this perspective, the poem's halfhearted opposition between 'Catholic' and 'Protestant' subject positions – those which, respectively, exhibit and guard against linguistic vulnerability – deserves critical distaste.[26] Even more: when Patterson writes that '[t]he rhetoric, the sensuality, [and] the self-indulgence of the "Suttle Nunns" who practise idolatry and goodness knows what else readily invite both stigmatization and destruction,' it is oddly unclear whether the invitation is extended by Marvell or also by Patterson herself.[27] Given her claim that 'the Protestant / Catholic dialectic has been less than serious,' it is unclear how such a ready invitation could be understood to issue only or even primarily from the poem.[28]

Presumably Patterson does not intend such ambiguity, but its presence illuminates a danger in wishing that Marvell would insist on boundedness aggressively and uncompromisingly.[29] For even as Patterson works to clear Marvell of anti-Catholic bigotry, she produces discourse compatible with Henry Care's anti-Catholic fantasies. In both his anti-Catholic imaginary and her critical one, the hyper-sexualising potential of seductive language makes the question of personal boundaries zero-sum. Once the papal word gains entrance into the Protestant heart, there is no turning back; self-dispossession takes root, eroding the subject from the inside. In such a world, maintaining the fortress of self requires militant self-discipline, and military measures against those who might breach the castle walls.

In previous chapters, I invoked the insight – in the work of Butler, Bersani and Agamben – that keeping a too scrupulous watch over personal boundaries can lead to self-defensive attacks on those understood to threaten those boundaries. In the remark that the behaviours of the nuns 'readily invite both stigmatization and destruction', made without distance from the invitation, Patterson's account of 'Appleton House' bears that insight out.[30] Her approach thus seems limited as a discussion of how Marvell's relationship to Catholicism can open on to a discussion of his – and our – relationship to vulnerability. I agree that the poem unseriously opposes bounded and unbounded forms of selfhood that it associates with Protestantism and Catholicism; but, like some criticism by Rosalie Colie, Dorothy Stephens and Jonathan Crewe, I also think that the poem's instructive value resides in precisely its unseriousness,[31] a point I would like to explore through Marvell's portrayals of the cloister, the speaker and the Fairfaxes themselves.

From the very beginning of the poem, which depicts the relation of Fairfax to his estate, Marvell plays with the notion of what boundaries can be, imagining self-enclosure not as an escape from, but rather as a pleasurable version of, self-exposure. This is so even when the opposite appears true: for example, when the speaker remarks that houses should be neither inordinately large, nor uncomfortably small, and instead should serve as a proportionate expression of individual dimensions: 'No creature loves an empty space; / Their bodies measure out their place' (15–16). The comment seems to draw from a composed, reasonable Protestantism to be contrasted with wanton Catholic excess, but when the speaker goes on to describe the 'admirable lines' by which Fairfax measures out his place, he describes those lines quite strangely: they are ones 'By which, ungirt and unconstrained, / Things greater are in lesser contained' (43–4). Unlike the pristine self-containment that Patterson and Norbrook find in Maria, the Fairfax manor offers boundaries that are neither constraining, nor unmoving, nor perfectly proportionate to Fairfax – boundaries that, in being ungirt, are not barriers in any fixed or inflexible sense. Self-containment is instead given dynamism. In stanza 4 we see that the drawing of orderly boundaries at Nun Appleton does not arrange subjects and objects into discrete, separable elements:

> all things are composed here
> Like Nature, orderly and near:
> In which we the dimensions find
> Of that more sober age and mind,
> When larger-sized men did stoop
> To enter at a narrow loop;
> As practicing, in doors so strait,
> To strain themselves through heaven's gate.

The order of a 'more sober age' is not that of complete, comfortable enclosure, but that of intense and, it turns out, delightful excrucation. Returning to Thomas Fairfax himself within his manor in stanza 7, the speaker shows excrucation at work. With Fairfax inside,

> the laden house does sweat,
> And scarce endures the Master great:
> But where he comes the swelling hall
> Stirs, and the square grows spherical;
> More by his magnitude distressed,
> Than he is by its straitness pressed:
> And too officiously it slights
> That in itself which him delights.

The Fairfacian body measures out its place without the kind of boundary-drawing that would insist on clear demarcation of inside and outside. In 'Flecknoe' the integrity of personal boundaries cannot be compromised without painful, unpleasant penetration; here Marvell shows just the opposite. For Fairfax, inhabiting Nun Appleton is a process of pressing and being pressed, a process that is most pleasurable when it is most tense and when Fairfax and the home ostensibly outside him enter into indistinction. (It comes as a disappointment when the house quickly swells so as to preserve its owner's personal space.)

Marvell portrays Maria Fairfax similarly. Despite the degree to which she is protective, she not only gives Appleton its sweetness ('To her the meadow sweetness owes' (692)) but also partakes of it. On the grounds, 'The viscous air, wheres'e'er she fly, / Follows and sucks her azure dye' (673–4); she is presented with and treads upon the luxurious carpeting of the landscape that owes its beauty to her (stanzas 87 and 88). Patterson draws a sharp distinction between the speaker's pleasurable passivity and vulnerability and Maria's militant-Protestant discipline, but in the lines just quoted Maria herself seems imperfectly enclosed. We can even find ambiguity in the scene that supposedly shames the speaker out of his passivity:

But now away my hooks, my quills,
And angles, idle utensils.
The young Maria walks tonight:
Hide trifling youth thy pleasures slight.
'Twere shame that such judicious eyes
Should with such toys a man surprise
                              (649–54)

A straightforward reading would suggest that the speaker wants to conceal his toys before Maria sees him playing with them. But the lines also leave open the possibility that it is Maria who may surprise him with 'toys', that her judicious gaze works as a further, heightened form of toying – one in which his slight pleasures pale in comparison to the pleasurable effect of her look. In this case, he needs to prepare for the charge that her gaze contains. We do not know whether Maria simply puts an end to the speaker's sensual relaxation or is another source of it, if she not only has imperfect personal boundaries but also helps to imperfect his.

Such complexity – invitingly evident here and, I will show, elsewhere – thwarts familiar Protestant/Catholic binaries. Maria can be read straightforwardly only by overlooking such complexity or by dismissing it as unimportant; and only then can she be completely contrasted with the speaker and the nuns who might, in turn, be wholeheartedly ironised or dismissed. The poem's complex meditation on boundedness merits our attention, in the above scenes but also others, especially those involving Isabel Thwaites and the poem's speaker. These scenes more fully develop what the scenes just discussed only gesture toward: what living out the imperfection of personal boundaries might be like, particularly when that imperfection is linguistically, transubstantially felt.

Consider the scene in which Thwaites gets 'sucked' in by a nun's 'smooth tongue' (200). Marvell devotes a dozen stanzas to this nun's description of the cloister's pleasures, presenting transubstantial language that works as it did in its popular, constructive permutations; discourse is 'holy leisure', a form of therapy. For the nuns, masters of language excite affect, and unlike Maria's suitors, these seducers do so appealingly:

'Here we, in shining armour white,
Like virgin Amazons do fight.
And our chaste lamps we hourly trim,
Lest the great Bridegroom find them dim.
Our orient breaths perfumed are
With incense of incessant prayer
And holy-water of our tears

Most strangely our complexion clears.
. . .
Not tears of grief; but such as those
With which calm pleasure overflows . . .'
                    (105–14)

Unlike the ancestral Fairfax, who later fights so as to destroy the
nunnery, the nuns fight for a yield of mutual satisfaction. They don
white armour only to expose each other as Amazons; the purpose of
the personal frontiers that they impose is the pleasure that comes from
their temporary removal. In a striking formulation, the emotion which
'overflows' afterward bespeaks a kind of calm. Like Maria, the nuns
close the cloister's gates on men, but they can afford to embrace their
susceptibility to one another's prayerful words, can expose themselves
to a salubrious form of open being.

Norbrook writes that '[t]he satire of the lesbian nuns hits at the female
Catholic patronage of Henrietta Maria, while Fairfax's daughter Maria
offers a counter-pattern' (289); and the speaker does, after all, say of the
cloister that ''Twas no religious house' until Fairfax invaded it (ln. 280).
But the rest of the poem asks us to question such swift judgement. How
can we draw a firm distinction, for example, between the nuns (in relation to each other) and Maria (in relation to Nun Appleton)? Isabel is
sucked in; Maria, as I have mentioned, is sucked from: 'The viscous air,
wheres'e'er she fly, / Follows and sucks her azure dye' (673–74). In both
situations, boundaries are of instrumental importance; in both cases,
they exist only temporarily, warding off undesirable violence while enabling more genial experience.

If such vulnerability seems finally a sign of weakness, it is not, or not
entirely. If it seems simply to facilitate Fairfax's takeover and reformation of Isabel, a revenant Catholicism remains within her. We can
observe this in the 34th stanza, after the young Fairfax has evidently
waved the fly-like nuns away:

            the glad youth away her bears,
And to the nuns bequeaths her tears:
Who guiltily their prize bemoan,
Like gypsies that a child had stolen.
Thenceforth (as when the enchantment ends,
The castle vanishes or rends)
The wasting cloister with the rest
Was in one instant dispossessed.
                    (265–72)

To see only the nuns' weakness in these lines requires that we overlook their temporal and causal discrepancies. The first, between the

transitional or ongoing meaning of 'thenceforth' and the cloister's sup-posedly instantaneous dispossession, suggests that its vanquishing does not effect its vanishing, or does so only literally (which, in the history of the actual Appleton estate, incidentally was not the case). Such confusion suggests that Fairfax actually always has to combat the cloister's allure, from the moment of his entry onward. With this in mind, the stanza's first four lines assume new valences. The nuns are like 'gypsies that a child had stolen', and whereas myth initially would suggest that they have stolen Isabel, reversible syntax, a staple in Marvell's style, holds out the contrary possibility, that Isabel has stolen the nuns – that they remain with Isabel and so also with Fairfax, and not just this one, but through the generations. Lest we forget, the poem describes Maria herself as still a Thwaites, still tinged with the transubstantial; the poem ends still waiting 'Till fate her worthily translates, / And find a Fairfax for our Thwaites' (747–8).

William, the ancestral Fairfax, destroys the walls of the wasting cloister so as to build stronger, more rigid borders – around the grounds, Isabel herself and the Fairfaxes who are to follow. Yet Marvell does not accord complete victory to him, to the figure 'whose offspring fierce / Shall fight through all the universe' (241–42). William Fairfax complains about the nuns as those '[w]ho though in prison yet enchant! / Death only can such thieves make fast, / As rob though in the dungeon cast' (206–8). However bitterly, Fairfax recognises that not just the physical contours of space but also the quality of interaction contribute, directly, to the making of that space. It is as if the nuns could break prison bars with recourse not to a court but merely to the cannons of their lungs (255). Everyone is vulnerable, but so is everything, so vulnerability cannot simply be a sign of weakness. The ancestral Fairfax acknowledges the transubstantial capacity of speech to transform the space in which they live, how 'like themselves they alter all' (215). He finds reason for violence in this; Marvell himself, on the other hand, cannot bring to completion the fantasy, borrowed from romance, in which the nunnery would just vanish. Instead he returns to the verbal efficacy of speakers denied the proprietary force that Fairfax has; he has regard for the words that unmake rigid boundaries and that make a world in which their lives are worth living – an ephemeral world, certainly, yet one which cannot simply be waved away.

The nuns' practice also persists in the speaker himself. Fairfax's bitter valences vanish; and when he is again absent from the poem, the speaker uses transubstantial language. He finds himself inside a different cloister, a wood knit by darkness like the gloom surrounding the nunnery, yet – also like the nunnery – 'passable and thin' inside. This enclosure, like all enclosures in 'Appleton House', offers the opposite of detachment and withdrawal. In stanzas 71 and 72, the speaker confers among the birds and trees, suddenly in a world where impossible conversations occur:

> Thus I, easy philosopher,
> Among the birds and trees confer.
> And little now to make me wants
> Or of the fowls, or of the plants:
> Give me but wings as they, and I
> Straight floating on the air shall fly:
> Or turn me but, and you shall see
> I was but an inverted tree.
> . . .
> Already I begin to call
> In their most learned original:
> And where I language want, my signs
> The bird upon the bough divines . . .
>   (561–72)

Speaking to the other means desiring something other than clear distinctions. It means effacing separation, by way of easy philosophy; to speak to the other – the nun, the bird – is, in an act of nearly comically creative absorption, to become almost identical with it. To speak so is to lose any sense of discrete being. According to the *OED*, in the seventeenth century, to 'confer' in its intransitive sense can mean to 'confer with'; it can mean 'to converse', 'to talk together'. Conferring can be of a piece with the Lockean view of speech as the communication of thought between discrete beings. In its transitive (and, the *OED* tells us, now obsolete) sense, though, 'confer' could also mean 'to bring together' or even 'to add together'.[32] For the speaker of 'Appleton House' to confer 'among' the birds and trees is both to communicate with them and, in doing so, to be added to them, man and world made indistinct. Language does not manage the relationship between self and not-self, subject and object, but is that through which one starts to become the other. To label this a 'relationship' would be to understate the connection's intensity. Speaking in the learned originals of animals transubstantiates the self, makes of it a wingless bird, a tree without leaves; inside his cloister, words add to the speaker's nature, change him into altered versions of things.

Marvell returns to this pattern of enclosure and exposure in stanzas 76–77, the second of which consists of the speaker, now the 'great prelate of the grove', addressing Appleton's environs:

> How safe, methinks, and strong, behind
> These trees have I encamped my mind:

Where beauty, aiming at the heart,
Bends in some tree its useless dart;
And where the world no certain shot
Can make, or me it toucheth not.
But I on it securely play.
And gall its horsemen all the day.
. . .
Bind me, ye woodbines, in your twines,
Curl me about, ye gadding vines,
And, oh, so close your circles lace,
That I may never leave this place:
But lest your fetters prove too weak,
Ere I your silken bondage break,
Do you, O brambles, chain me too,
And, courteous briars, nail me through.
                    (601–16)

These stanzas elaborate on the scene in which the nuns enclose themselves to undo themselves. For the speaker, similarly, being bounded
– adding a border of verdure – does not guard against being nailed
through but instead makes it easier, makes better the pleasure of being
pierced; and being nailed through – not being kept apart – is the content
of his secure encampment. To play on the world is not to act on it from
afar; he speaks to Appleton with the hope that by accessing its openness
to his words, his own openness will, magically, be utterly exposed. He
wants his words to act on things so that things might then act on him;
he uses words, that is, as those in the cloister do, to abandon rather than
solidify a discrete, unsusceptible sense of himself. His secure play on the
world affords a paradoxical freedom: not the freedom exercised by an
autonomous self but the one that arrives from outside, that frees the self
from self-protective constructs of containment.

Describing interactions that reshape and transubstantiate selves, I
have wanted to question why we should wish that Marvell had con-
structed a poem whose words were always otherwise, that he had imagined a world where boundaries were more certain. Once, as the speaker
abandons the scene of a flood, he claims to wish just this: he says that
he will '[l]et others tell the paradox, / How eels now bellow in the ox'
(461, 473–4). And yet instead of closing himself off from such paradox,
he inhabits it; the paradox he forswears is the one he elaborates again
and again. The thousand impossibilities of transubstantial language that
Jeremy Taylor rejects and that Marvell excoriates in the *Account* are the
same impossibilities that 'Appleton House' enacts; when Isabel speaks
– when eels bellow in the ox – we see what advocates of early modern
liberalism reject, see the innocuous intensity of alterable, imperfectly
bounded selfhood that is the subject of paranoid Protestant nightmares.

Unlike nature as figured in 'An Horatian Ode' or as the speaker of 'Flecknoe' imagines it, the world of 'Appleton House' does allow of penetration, lets one subject live and speak from inside another. In such a world Isabel could enjoy being sucked in by a nun's tongue without anxiety about unwanted invasion. Effacing the separation between subjects and objects, language and world – indeed, turning communication into effacement's instrument – transubstantial words create therapeutic space.

'Appleton House', Spatial Politics and the History of the Speaking Subject

Still to be explained are the consequences, for *Open Subjects*, of Marvell's attitude toward vulnerability in 'Appleton House'. Thus far I have described how Marvell explores the imperfection of personal boundaries, often through possibilities offered by transubstantial language, in ways portrayed not as sinister but as salutary. 'Appleton House' places the self's boundedness and openness, its enclosure and exposure, into dynamic, mutually sustaining interrelation. 'Appleton House' thus might be said to answer Butler's call mentioned earlier – the call to think about the complex contours of selfhood, about ways to inhabit, rather than simply minimise, a vulnerable existence. To describe how the poem does so, I want to spend the balance of this chapter engaged in comparatively broad thoughts: about the politics of space implied by Marvell's questioning of fixed boundaries; about the consequences of his spatial thinking for his thinking about temporality; and, finally, about how both provide insight into how early modernists can and do write histories of selfhood.

For the critics with whom I have taken issue, the spatial and historical politics that underwrite their work leads them to dismiss much of 'Appleton House'. I have suggested that for critics such as Patterson and Norbrook, questions about Marvell's Protestantism versus his Catholicism are also questions about a proto-liberal republicanism to be contrasted with his occasional royalism. For Patterson and Norbrook, bounded and unbounded ways of being are, or at least ought to be, opposed to each other and can be mapped on to Protestant/Catholic, Republican/Royalist and progressive/regressive binaries.

Such mapping relies on certain assumptions about space and time. We have seen how, in their reading, Maria's linguistic discipline creates a space of negative freedom – of protection against – that bears traces of the rights-bearing liberal subject; and this conception of personal boundaries is underwritten by a more general politics of space that, as Thomas L. Dumm points out, assigns a pure, sacred quality to boundaries and to the self's interior space. Political work, accordingly, ought to render personal space as inviolable as possible, ought – like the Declaration of Rights that Patterson celebrates – to make the inviolability of personal frontiers seem universal and natural.[33] As is implied in material quoted above, Patterson and Norbrook's conception of the space of a proto-liberal republican subject – as protected, discrete and clearly delineated – corresponds to a progressive conception of liberal time, one that ought to jettison unbounded forms of life. The open being offered in the nunnery should be rejected in part for violating the personal space that should be sacred and in part because that violation leads to royalism and regress – because it seduces the subject into 'sensual relaxation and reactionary beliefs'.[34] Forms of selfhood that do not emphasise negative freedom and positive liberty ought to be abandoned on grounds of their atavism.

For those writing a history of the subject, failure to adopt this successive approach is equally atavistic. If a critic's assumptions are not recognisably liberal, Norbrook implies, they tend to be retrograde; 'it bears emphasizing', he writes, 'how many modern critiques of republicanism [as proto-liberal] are still coloured by a fusion of modern attacks on the Enlightenment with the stock themes of older royalist propaganda' (21). The suggestion here is that if one critiques liberalism, one tends to do so in backward-looking fashion. Patterson herself goes further, writing that when literary critics question liberal theory, they put in its place a suspect sort of cynicism. Patterson finds her defence 'particularly necessary in the academy, where it is customary to build new reputations by sneering at earlier idealisms and accomplishments as philosophically blinkered or politically oversimplified'.[35] If one wants to critique the 'idealisms and accomplishments' of early modern liberalism, it is likely to be in a destructive, self-serving fashion, not in order to recuperate supplementary aspects of Renaissance selfhood. Just as their liberal conceptions of selfhood highlight the distinction between one subject and another, then, so the history of the early modern subject ought to be that of a struggle by which bounded selfhood clearly distinguishes itself from, and triumphs over, its unbounded opposite.[36] To fail to write or wish for such a history is politically unpalatable and perverse.

The failure of 'Appleton House', according to this logic, resides in the insufficient distinction between figures like Maria and Isabel, emblematic as they are of liberal and transubstantial forms of life. Marvell fails to choose protected personal space and the securing of that space across a history in which the figures of Nun Appleton follow each other in clear succession. The poet instead flirts with unprotected, blurred, unbounded spaces that exist in a languorous, wandering time, a spatiotemporal axis turned adrift.

This very flirtation, though, may be the poem's most attractive aspect. To illustrate how this is – to explain the spatial and temporal consequences of how Marvell thinks vulnerability through – I must broaden my conceptual and contextual background. So far, with the exception of some recourse to Butler, I have focused on Marvell's contemporary context and on how he deploys the concept of transubstantial language to think about constructs of boundedness, limiting discussion mostly to the domain of early modern religious discourse. In this section I would like to keep the religious in mind but also move beyond it, placing Marvell in a wider field to examine his relationship to 'boundary politics' both spatial and temporal and to discuss the bearing that that has on political thought. I will thus consider Marvell's relationship not just to his present, but also more thoroughly to ours – especially in the fields of geography and spatial theory – as well as to his classical antecedents. So doing, I hope to present how we might look to Marvell (not to mention his antecedents) for help with our present and future.

For Norbrook, our best relationship to Marvell ought to mirror his best relationship to classical forebears. One valuable aspect of Protestantism, from this viewpoint, is its link to an English republicanism that secures bounded selfhood, and so classical republican figures such as Lucan, whom Norbrook takes to advocate such selfhood, are recuperable. Horace, Virgil and Ovid, by contrast, are for the most part retrograde and monarchist, of most use under radical revision by English republicans.[37] But I want to take seriously their ideas about space as well as Marvell's affinities with them.[38] Such affinities, I will show, hardly make Marvell retrograde or merely monarchist, but rather draw him into productive discussion with contemporary theorists of spatial and temporal boundaries. I will even show how his interest in the erosion of boundaries, though not obviously republican, is none the less compatible with classical republican thinking, including Lucan's own – a fact that helps re-orient our perspective on some of the binaries discussed above.

To be sure, Ovid, Virgil and Horace, like Patterson and Norbrook, all register awareness both that firm boundaries can serve innocuous and useful purposes and that imperfect enclosure can open paths to disaster. So often, spatial boundaries – those demarcating both places and persons – are far too fragile, too easily undone for awful ends. In Ovid, the openness of bodies can lead to tragedy. There is, famously, Tereus's rape and mutilation of Philomela in book 6 of the *Metamorphoses*.[39]

There is Daphne's story in book 1 (470–567), her flight from Apollo, her only recourse a prayer for transformation; she must become a laurel tree to achieve boundedness, and even then she remains subject to fragmentation at Apollo's hands. In this, Ovid displays acute awareness – awareness perhaps attenuated in Marvell's own fantasy of being made arboreal – that negative vulnerabilities, even after total transformation, sometimes cannot be escaped.

For many classical figures, open boundaries can accompany cataclysmic events and even hasten the breakdown of the world. In the *Aeneid*, for instance, Virgil presents the outcome of the Trojan War as hinging on a gate's momentary opening; Trojans take in the wooden horse, on Sinon's false word, only to be taken apart by Greeks.[40] Virgil remarks on Caesar's demise, and its effect on the world, in tones similar to those of Henry Care and the vehement anti-Catholicism discussed above. Some rivers stop while others spontaneously overflow; tears fall from the eyes of statues, and animals start to speak.[41] In *Odes* I, 2 Horace speaks ruefully of what Marvell speaks of comically in 'Appleton House', of how 'terror-stricken does swam in the overwhelming flood.'[42] And when the world is punished in the first book of the *Metamorphoses*, it is by undoing divisions, making land and sea indistinguishable at Neptune's behest, the reduction of the world to 'an ocean without any coastline' (279–92). In stanza 59 of 'Appleton House', similarly, rain makes the meadow into a sea; '[t]he river in itself is drowned, / And isles th'astonished cattle round' (471–2). Despite his levity, the speaker, like his classical antecedents, seeks sanctuary in the wood; he looks for forms of exposure that are less total.

Boundaries render the world liveable, and thinking about space without them is not easy. For all his investment in undoing, Marvell himself reaches a threshold that he cannot occupy forever; periodically he must withdraw from the spatial paradoxes he himself elaborates. Michel de Certeau writes that 'there is no spatiality that is not organized by the determination of frontiers,' '[f]rom the distinction that separates a subject from its exteriority to the distinctions that localize objects, from the home (constituted on the basis of the wall) to the journey (constituted on the basis of the wall) to the journey (constituted on the basis of a geographical elsewhere)'.[43] However complex the determination and construction of frontiers may be, de Certeau suggests, they are, intractably, part of how we make the world sensical and manage to exist within it. For Ovid, similarly, the world needs divisions because in their absence the elements lose their shape and creation becomes chaos; thus earth is severed from sky and sea parted from land.[44]

Once boundaries are in place, maintaining them requires work. Virgil, advising on care for the land in the *Georgics*, supplies a lengthy list of the difficulties that permeable, porous boundaries create for farming and gardening. Grapevines need hedges to keep away beasts, and soil needs sticky clay; otherwise weeds rise out and pests enter in.[45] Cultivating natural boundaries demands serious discipline, work that never ends; otherwise 'all things speed toward the worse and slipping away fall back.'[46] In the social domain presented in the *Aeneid*, Virgil evinces a similar need to keep gates bolted shut and to keep Aeneas's antagonist, Turnus, out (indeed, Trojans almost come to ruin by accidentally locking Turnus in) (ix.40–5, 728–30). We have seen how for Marvell, physical partitions – as the portrayal of the nunnery in 'Appleton House' shows – hold up no more easily; the nuns' tremendous efforts to keep Fairfax outside their walls only succeed for so long. In so far as Marvell admires their efforts here, he favours erecting fences around selves not only, say, by way of the legal abstractions that Butler endorses, but even by way of territoriality as defined by Edward Soja, by way of 'the production and reproduction of spatial enclosures that not only concentrate interaction . . . but also intensify and enforce its boundedness'.[47]

Earlier in this chapter and book, I discussed how insistence on boundaries can be used to mobilise violence, as, for example, when Brutus and Sicinius invoke the safety of citizens, and the need to protect their boundaries as well as those of Rome, in order to weed Coriolanus out. As Soja knows and as Zygmunt Bauman writes, 'the urgency and ferocity of the boundary-drawing and boundary-defining drive' can produce a nightmare version of what Virgil advocates in the *Georgics* and what Marvell says of the well-ordered grounds at the end of 'Appleton House'. Bauman calls this the '"gardening" state', wherein society becomes 'an object of designing, cultivating, and weed poisoning', and thus, can include and endorse intense violence.[48] I too have attended to problems that can arise when we draw boundaries. But drawing them, as Marvell and his classical antecedents show, is not always so sinister; garden states do not inevitably threaten to become gardening states. In the case of the nuns, territoriality presents no such danger; in a position of weakness, territoriality is absolutely necessary to their protection.

In his wish to obliterate barriers, Virgil's Turnus resembles not simply the ancestral Fairfax but also all that is dangerous about Coriolanus as I describe him in the last chapter. Turnus disregards boundaries completely, wants to turn others (if not himself) inside out; aside from the pathetic reversal in which he pleads with Aeneas, Turnus's last action is to make a boulder, used as a boundary marker, into a weapon. Earlier, he mocks the Trojan belief in separation's protective power:

Their trust in the rampart between us
Trenches that may slow us down, the thin line between life and destruction,
Give reassurance. But didn't they see Troy's fortifications
Crafted by Neptune's hand sink down as the fires devoured them?

(ix.142–5)

Turnus might be said to speak for Virgil, Horace, Ovid and Marvell alike when he remarks on how easy and how very erroneous it is to place much trust in the ramparts between people.[49] But if what I have said about these poets is true, what Turnus misses – and what they do not – is that although barriers can be broken, life nevertheless depends on them.[50]

And yet, for them, life also depends on the erosion and sometimes even the erasure of those barriers. Virgil, Ovid and Horace's investment in bounded spaces and selves is far from absolute. That physical and social demarcations cannot be upheld uncompromisingly or once and for all is not, for these figures, always only regrettable. This begins at the simplest level. For all that soil needs solidity, Virgil remarks, it must be porous and permeable; it must breathe vapours out and drink moisture in (ii.217–25). In Virgil social boundaries must also sometimes be open. We might remember that on the island of the Cyclopes, Trojans are saved by the same openness that undid them earlier. They escape to safety when Aeneas chooses to take in the Greek Achaemenides – and to be taken in by the latter's warning about Polyphemus – rather than regard Achaemenides as a second Sinon.[51] The founding of Rome depends upon this openness.

The health of bodies demands the same. To rid sheep of ulcers, Virgil remarks, knives are necessary;[52] in Ovid, exposing vulnerability so as to strengthen the exposed obtains in human bodies too – for instance, when Medea cuts the throat of Jason's father, Aeson, in order to replenish him, to turn his white hair black.[53] Indeed, being saved in Ovid, like being condemned, almost always entails changed boundaries.[54] If it does not entail being sliced open, it entails being transformed into something other, the replacement of one set of personal frontiers with another: Anius's daughters changed into doves after they are imprisoned (xiii.667–74); Phaethon's sisters made arboreal to end their mourning (ii.340–66); Perimele transformed into an island after her father pushes her off a cliff (viii.591–610). Boundaries of self must be lost in order to be regained, to make life more liveable, to go on at all. As does Marvell in his fantasies of becoming avian and arboreal, Ovid makes us wonder whether self-identity is compatible with transformation. Ovid even makes us wonder whether remaining what we are can actually require that we give ourselves, or be given, over to transformation that is beyond our control – just as stanzas 76–7 of 'Appleton House' ask us to consider the value of freedom that comes from the outside, that our 'secure play' on the world derives from, depends on, and in some measure even consists in, that world acting on us.

In seeing the good both in boundaries and in their absence, Virgil, Ovid and Marvell work under assumptions that, according to Doreen Massey, many contemporary theorists of space lack. 'The question', Massey writes, 'cannot be whether demarcation (boundary building) is simply good or bad . . . The issue is not bounded or unbounded in itself; not a simple opposition between spatial openness and spatial closure. Not spatial fetishism.'[55] In their own refusals of this fetishism, Virgil, Ovid and Marvell ask readers to separate the good forms of boundedness and unboundedness from the pernicious ones. In this, they anticipate Massey's call that our arguments about space be posed not absolutely but in terms of the relations that construct physical and social spaces as open or closed (165–6).

One such relation, on which I focused in my treatment of transubstantiality and to which I want to return, is specifically linguistic. That matter might be vulnerable to words was not, of course, a possibility that first emerges with the concept of transubstantiation; and Marvell's antecedents, like Marvell himself, display alternating investment in and worry about that vulnerability. Dido's fate in the *Aeneid*, to be sure, would have been happier had Cupid's arrow not pierced her heart and allowed Aeneas's words to become fixed there (iv.1–5). Dido had been like Maria Fairfax in her enclosure against words, her steadfast and successful resistance to suitors' pleas; only by losing this ability can she arrive at tragedy (iv.35–8).

Here words are too powerful, but elsewhere, indeed even for Dido, words are not powerful enough: for instance, when Aeneas is able to resist her desperate request that he remain at Carthage (iv.437–49).[56] In book 5 of the *Metamorphoses*, to cite another example, Emathion is too old to fight (in the battle over Andromeda) and so, like the nuns (in the battle over Isabella), 'words had to serve him for weapons.' He curses and denounces the fighting, kneeling by an altar just before Chromis decapitates him – after which 'a half-living tongue continued to utter its curses until all life was exhausted and finally lost in the flames' (v.101–6).

But the material power that words have over objects and subjects is not always futile, as in Emathion's case, or sinister, as in Dido's unwitting seduction (or both futile and sinister, as they are later in 'Flecknoe' and in anti-Catholic polemic). In the fourth *Georgic*, for instance, Virgil describes how Orpheus, mourning Eurydice, for seven months

'unfolded this his tale, charming tigers and drawing oaks with his song'
(iv.507–10). In the eighth eclogue, Alphesiboeus reminds us that it
is 'with song [that] the cold snake in the meadows is burst asunder';
'[s]ongs', he claims, can not only draw Daphnis home but 'can even
draw the moon down from heaven,' moving bodies from their proper
places in a way that Jeremy Taylor would claim words never could (lines
69–71). In the *Metamorphoses*, similarly, we encounter figures such as
the singer Canens who, Ovid remarks, could 'move the trees and rocks';
'she'd calm the fiercest of beasts, she would slow the course of the
longest rivers and halt the birds on the wing with her musical singing'
(xiv.337–40). Horace, to cite a final example, believes that when a
righteous man sings he can relinquish his bow and arrow; when he sings
a wolf flees from him.[57] Words do what Maria does upon her appearance on the grounds at Nun Appleton: make things motionless. Words
draw the world forth in sympathy and they drive harm away; they have
destructive force and effect the transformations that are the subject of
Marvell's dreams.

In *The Production of Space*, Henri Lefebvre advances an argument
that has been pursued by nearly all of the geographers and theorists of
space mentioned here: namely, that human space is not pre-given – an
emptiness waiting to be filled – but is rather a product, comprised of
relations between physical, mental and social elements. Lefebvre thus
suggests that spatial theorists ought to work to uncover 'as-yet concealed
relations between space and language'.[58] Marvell and his forebears help
do so by inflating the material effects of words. Virgil's notion of using
words to slow down rivers or draw the moon down from heaven, like
Marvell's fantasy of becoming almost identical with birds by conferring
with them, is either metaphorical or caricatural of Lefebvre's idea and
may, in either case, seem impossibly or unhelpfully fanciful. Before dismissing such fancy, though, we might bear two things in mind.

First, we might remember Gaston Bachelard's claim that 'in prolonging
exaggeration, we may have the good fortune to avoid the habits of *reduction*' and thus that we 'should follow the poet to the ultimate extremity
of his images'.[59] Attending to the fanciful, at the very least, offers an
antidote to spatial assumptions that are undergirded by the 'reinforced
geometrism, in which limits are barriers' – in which boundaries are or
ought to be fixed and space is or ought to be inert, complete rather than
under construction (215). The imaginative experiments of Marvell and
his antecedents keep us from accepting space as given in this way.

Second, we might take seriously Lefebvre's claim that the way we talk
about space goes into its production. 'If space is a product', Lefebvre
writes, 'our knowledge of it must be expected to reproduce and expound

the process of production'; thus space 'needs not only to be subjected to analytic scrutiny . . . but also to be *engendered* by and within theoretical understanding' (37). Since the perceived, conceived and lived are inextricable, Lefebvre suggests, the way we think and talk about space affects space as it is experienced. It seems productively unsettling, then, to heighten our sense of the force that words might have to make, unmake and remake worlds and the selves that move within them.

Critics like Norbrook and Patterson would align this refusal to choose closure over openness with the retrograde, monarchist impulses that Virgil, Horace and Ovid display. I hope to have implied, however, that to make this sort of claim one would not only have to practise spatial fetishism – closure as progressive, openness as regressive – but would also have to declare retrograde theorists of space such as Massey. One would even have to label Norbrook's republican exemplar, Lucan, as himself insufficiently invested in bounded existence. We can observe this, for instance, in book IX of the *Pharsalia*, which details Cato's passage through the Libyan desert with the republic's remaining defenders and which explores virtues and vices of both closed and open space, especially when the space is bodily.

Lucan clearly admires the Stoic fortitude of Cato – his fearlessness and his practised imperviousness to the outside-of-self, his wish to pass, with preternatural discipline, through the 'barren plains' and 'parched zone' (ix.382).[60] But the dream of unlocking self from world proves impossibly difficult. Here, as elsewhere in the poem, we are given a lengthy catalogue of the body's vulnerability, in this case to venom. And the solution, when Cato's men are most in need, cannot come from better self-enclosure; instead they are saved by the Marmaric Psyllans, who survive not by setting themselves off from, but by adapting themselves to, their snake-infested environment:

> the nature of their terrain
> requires them to live unharmed, despite snakes all around.
> They profit from having made their home in the midst of poison:
> They have arranged a truce with death.
>
> (ix.895–8)

Because of their long exposure, Psyllans have become 'immune to the serpents' savage bite' (ix.892).

As the speaker of 'Appleton House' would like his atmosphere to be, their atmosphere is as susceptible to them – and especially to their words – as they are to it; coming to the aid of Cato and his men, Psyllans are capable of 'driving adders away with spells and incantations' (ix.914). Their words can even save infected men from death: 'Often, the toxin squirted into the blackening marrow is flushed out by incantations alone' (ix.930–1). In the following chapter I focus on how linguistic vulnerability is at the centre of the rhetorical theory of Cicero, a figure who bulks large throughout this book. Even in the case of Lucan, however, we see that the survival of republicans, and of republican culture, depends as much on openness – in this case, to curative words – as it does on closure. We will see that for Milton, as for Lucan, such openness is of special importance when republicans are without actual republics.

'Appleton House' offers a conception of boundaries that shares not just with Virgil, Horace and Ovid but with contemporary spatial theorists and even Lucan himself; so doing, the poem helps us see that we cannot simply or easily set these figures in political opposition. Virgil and Horace, we might bear in mind, for a time were themselves republicans, and the fact that Ovid was not hardly drains his thinking of political interest. The link between Lucan and 'Appleton House', of course, does not quite make the latter a republican poem, but to lament this would be to miss much of what the poem has to offer. To be sure, certain of its episodes – those involving the invasion of the nunnery and Maria's suitors spring to mind – are concerned with a central problem of republican thought: how to escape the dangers of tyranny and the tyrant's arbitrary will. At moments, these episodes accord with one tradition of republican selfhood discussed in this book, the tradition that privileges bounded selfhood; others accord with the alternative tradition that I trace throughout, which privileges unboundedness. The tension between these traditions is a major focus of *Open Subjects* and can surely be found in 'Appleton House'. But whereas other chapters examine degrees to which Renaissance texts belong to the one tradition of republican thought or the second, my aim here has been a bit different. Above all, 'Appleton House' allows us to see what we gain when we view Marvell from outside the binary perspective that places republicanism, bounded selfhood and proto-modernity on one side, and pre-modernity, unbounded selfhood and royalism on the other. One aim here has been to describe what comes into view, what possibilities texts make available to us, when we do not make these equations and allow modern selfhood to emerge in flexible fashion.

On this score, this section has so far shown that Marvell and his antecedents help us see how boundaries are neutral as structures, their value context-dependent, and how we might thus sort out valuable and pernicious forms of boundedness and unboundedness rather than reject one form of life in favour of the other. With this insight in place, they also help add layers of complexity to our understanding of how boundaries operate.

For example, Marvell and his antecedents show how enclosure so often depends on exposure, and exposure on enclosure, how the two need not always be antagonistic. We can see this in remarks as seemingly unremarkable as those that Virgil offers about bee-keeping. One must find a protected place for the task and, to keep honey unfrozen in winter, make the hive's entrance very narrow; and yet the end of such careful enclosure comes in summer, when bees can be seen 'just freed from the hive, floating towards the starry sky through the clear summer air'.[61] Protection against the elements derives its worth largely from what it allows: the subsequent opening up to those elements. Horace for his part goes further, making enclosure and exposure into a single process in *Odes* I,9, 'Winter Without Bids Us Make Merry Within,' which seems a kind of precursor to Marvell's portrayal of the nunnery. Escape from the outside does not mean that we continue seeking protection once inside. Shelter against winter in fact inflames the desire for pleasure among those enclosed; Horace writes of 'the merry tell-tale laugh of a maiden hiding in farthest corner, and the forfeit snatched from her arm or finger that but feigns resistance' (21–4). Here, as for the nuns, shelter is an occasion for undoing, safety an occasion for abandon; the imposition of one set of boundaries allows for the erosion of another.

In his descriptions of space and place – the former being where we are 'open and free' but also 'exposed and vulnerable' and the latter being where we feel enclosed and secure – Yi-Fu Tuan makes a similar point. 'Human beings require both space and place. Human lives', Tuan writes, 'are a dialectical movement between shelter and venture.'[62] In *Odes* I,9 or when the nuns promise affective overflow within the nunnery's walls, enclosure and exposure can be so thoroughly intertwined that shelter provides occasion for venture, unbounded space and bounded place become blended, and the dialectical movement that Tuan describes occurs at once.[63]

For this reason, thinking about the flexibility of Marvellian boundaries also means attributing a complex and variable ontology to those boundaries. On this point, Marvell might be said to supplement Michel Foucault's writings on another vulnerable space, the 'heterotopia', two interrelated aspects of which are of interest here. First is the notion that heterotopias – which Foucault contrasts with well-bounded, normalised, utopic space – are spaces of desacralisation.[64] In contrast to sacralised space, which uses boundaries to minimise vulnerability, boundaries in heterotopic space are more dynamic; they serve to question, rather than simply solidify, separations that govern what is included in and excluded from a given space.[65] If this makes the space of heterotopia a space of 'transgression', Foucault emphasises that transgression need not eradicate boundaries but can also change them into something other than barriers – into structures that do something other than separate. For Foucault transgression can occur inside boundaries themselves, taking root within the lines of supposedly sharp, rigid breaks, dilating them into more flexible, accommodating spaces. 'Transgression', he writes,

> does not seek to oppose one thing to another . . . Transgression is neither violence in a divided world (in an ethical world) nor a victory over limits (in a dialectical or revolutionary world); and, exactly for this reason, its role is to measure the excessive distance that it opens at the heart of the limit and to trace the flashing line that causes the limit to arise . . . Perhaps it is simply an affirmation of division; but only insofar as division is not understood to mean a cutting gesture, or the establishment of a separation or the measuring of a distance, only retaining that in it which may designate the existence of a difference.[66]

Though Foucault does not develop the theme in his work on hetero-topia, one heterotopic, transgressive space can take shape around the boundaries of the subject itself.[67] And though Butler does not develop the idea herself, her work on linguistic vulnerability could be said to establish the space of the subject as heterotopic space, to encourage experience like that of Marvell's speaker in 'Appleton House'. Consider, once more, stanza 77:

> Bind me, ye woodbines, in your twines,
> Curl me about, ye gadding vines,
> And, oh, so close your circles lace,
> That I may never leave this place:
> But lest your fetters prove too weak,
> Ere I your silken bondage break,
> Do you, O brambles, chain me too,
> And, courteous briars, nail me through.

The speaker asks to be bounded, but flexibly and penetrably so; indeed, he is penetrated even as he is portrayed as using words to become more securely bounded. So doing, he throws the very ontology of personal boundaries into question. Interactions in the poem, especially when transubstantial words are spoken, thus show how the space of the subject is heterotopic no matter how closed off it might seem. But – and this is perhaps the most important point – the poem, like Foucaultian transgression, does not abolish boundaries altogether. It calls them into question not to eliminate them and to escape into a pure, utopic open-ness but to rethink what they can be. At various points, I have been cataloguing how the politics of space in 'Appleton House' consists in questioning, without rejecting, the basic, intuitive point that personal boundaries exist solely to demarcate and protect a neutral space of negative freedom. Marvell's poem does this in part by suggesting that they need not effect sharp separations, that boundaries can become inseparable from, and dynamically related to, what they contain and seem to exclude, and thus that boundaries can be bonds, not inert walls but spaces of accretion and erosion – of ceaseless activity.

The possible payoff, spatially speaking, is this: if the purpose of personal boundaries changes, then how we relate to them, in speech and otherwise, changes in turn. 'Appleton House' prompts a series of questions about how these changes might take place, and in so doing extends Butler's call for thinking through the self's imperfect enclosure: What if boundaries existed not just to keep things apart but to bind them together better – if we, like Lord Fairfax, inhabited the pleasurable friction that comes from one set of boundaries thrust into indistinction with another? And what if words were, as they are for Marvell's speaker when he asks for his body's surface to be made verdant, the medium through which to experience, rather than ward off, such indistinction? What if we took our address to someone or something, as the speaker takes his address to the birds and trees of Nun Appleton, as inaugurating an intense sharing and exposure, one that maintains a degree of difference but that also transubstantiates, that aims to make us almost identical with our addressees? In other words, what if, whenever possible, the words addressed by us and to us were embraced for their seductive capacity – for how they ask us to give in, to be won over as Isabel Thwaites is? What if these things – and not the crystallised enclosure that a more severe discipline would effect – were understood to be the most (if not the only) important things that we could do, and have done to us, with words?

Perhaps this would produce a naiveté. Radical theory, we have seen, is often accused of as much. Still, it would be a naiveté without innocence, in this sense one not unlike Butler's – one that would not forget the protections we sometimes need, but that would remember our equally pressing need to use our selves, and our boundaries, otherwise.[68]

'Appleton House' shows how unbounded and bounded forms of life need not be opposed as they are in 'Flecknoe'. One form need not be replaced by the other. This in turn raises questions about what sort of history of the subject Marvell presents in his country house poem and about what sort of future the poem might point toward – which brings me to my second point of interest regarding heterotopia. Foucault notes that the disruption of spatial boundaries as separations is often accompanied by similar temporal disruptions – that heterotopia often correlates with heterochronia. He writes that 'the heterotopia begins to function fully when men are in a kind of absolute break with their traditional time,' and that this happens when time loses its transitory dimension, when various ostensibly discrete times accumulate within a single space and, literally, 'take place'.[69]

'Appleton House' operates according to heterochronia of just this sort. Above I argued, for instance, that neither the nunnery nor transubstantial practice is eliminated – that Isabel Thwaites's Catholicism is not simply replaced by a well-bounded Marian Protestantism. Rather, Isabel in some important respect borders on and persists in Maria. Temporality at Appleton, in other words, accretes, lacking the sharp successions and clear developments whose absence Patterson laments. The poem's unfixed temporal boundaries are mirrored in the speaker's construction, in stanza 73, of a history composed of tree leaves:

> Out of these scattered sibyl's leaves
> Strange prophecies my fancy weaves:
> And in one history consumes,
> Like Mexique paintings, all the plumes.
> What Rome, Greece, Palestine ere said
> I in this light mosaic read.
> Thrice happy he who, not mistook,
> Hath read in Nature's mystic book.
>   (577–84)

This is not a history of the opposition, and subsequent replacement, of one discrete element with another, not a 'Protestant/Catholic dialectic' that could have been more serious. This history calls the boundaries of succession into question. If the leaves that make up the speaker's construction are events, those events, like plumes on 'Mexique paintings', are juxtaposed and even overlapping, arranged as elements that are non-identical but in touch with each other, in some way coexistent. Similarly, the speaker's futural 'prophecies' and his history composed of all pasts and of all speaking subjects – of all the world's fallen leaves – are understood to occupy the same space. We cannot find the emerging history of the liberal subject or its reversal, cannot trace in the poem an opposition of unboundedness to boundedness and a call for the former to be replaced by the latter, or vice versa. In contrast to the violent successions that the speaker describes in the poem's penultimate stanza – and that have made of the outside world only a 'rude heap' – it is such an accommodating temporality, such a happy ordering of history, that is embraced in 'Appleton House'.

In my first chapter, I argued that whereas Habermasian early modernists oppose enclosed and open forms of selfhood as progressive and modern on the one hand and retrograde and pre-modern on the other,

Habermas himself exhibits a more nuanced attitude toward modernity, showing how it would be a mistake for one model of speech and one way of being in the world to succeed another cleanly. By drawing connections between (without collapsing) classical, early modern and contemporary concerns over linguistic vulnerability, I have wanted to suggest that there are other ways of being modern than simply being a well-bounded liberal subject, and thus that there are ways to write a history of the subject which would accord with Habermas's later thinking about modernity and Foucault's thinking about heterotopia. While those invested in proto-liberal English republicanism advocate a history of struggle and triumph, my aim has been to suggest a history that is not linear but heterochronic, driven by both discontinuity and continuity, distinction and indistinction – a history that thereby refuses to valorise one form of life and denigrate another. Out of such refusals, we can see how poems such as 'Appleton House' offer a usable past in the history of vulnerability, one that is also a possible present and future.

Notes

1. As will become increasingly clear, I take my warrant for a broad use of the term in part from Catherine Gallagher and Stephen Greenblatt's argument that since linguistic ideas – from most religious to most seemingly secular – very often revolve around the issue of transubstantiation, speaking of the transubstantial word in a less than doctrinally Catholic sense was a common practice. See *Practicing New Historicism* (Chicago: University of Chicago Press, 2000), esp. 141. For some accounts of the various ways in which transubstantiation has signified as a theory of language over the last three centuries, see the essays collected in Douglas Burnham and Enrico Giaccherini (eds), *The Poetics of Transubstantiation: From Theology to Metaphor* (Burlington, VT: Ashgate, 2005). For the most comprehensive account of transubstantial language in early modernity, see Arthur F. Marotti's *Religious Ideology and Cultural Fantasy* (Notre Dame, IN: University of Notre Dame Press, 2005), esp. Chapter 3, 'Manuscript Transmission and the Catholic Martyrdom Account', 66–94. For an account of the materiality of language that can be distinguished from transubstantial ones – because more restricted and mediated in terms of the material effect that words can have – see Richard Kroll's *The Material Word* (Baltimore: Johns Hopkins University Press, 1991).
2. *Religion and the Decline of Magic: Studies in Popular Beliefs in Sixteenth and Seventeenth Century England* (New York: Oxford University Press, 1971), 36, 46.
3. *The Shepherd's Paradise* (Oxford: Oxford University Press, 1997), 73.
4. See John Deacon, *A summarie ansvvere to al the material points in any of Master Darel his bookes More especiallie to that one booke of his, intituled,*

the Doctrine of the possession and dispossession of demoniaks out of the word of God, 1601, 212.

5. *Religious Ideology and Cultural Fantasy*, 84.
6. See J. P. Kenyon, *The Popish Plot* (Harmondsworth: Penguin, 1974), esp. 'The Catholic Problem', 1–36.
7. See R. F. Jones, *The Triumph of the English Language: A Survey of Opinions Concerning the Vernacular from the Introduction of Printing to the Restoration* (Stanford, CA: Stanford University Press, 1953), and esp. Chapter 10, 'The Useful Language', 293–323.
8. A. D. Woozley (ed.), *An Essay Concerning Human Understanding* (New York: Meridian, 1964), 294, 256.
9. 'A Letter Concerning Toleration', in David Wootton (ed.), *Political Writings of John Locke* (New York: Penguin, 1993), 420.
10. Richard Tuck (ed.), *Leviathan* (Cambridge: Cambridge University Press, 1996), 441, 423.
11. See *The real presence and spirituall of Christ in the blessed sacrament proved against the doctrine of transubstantiation*, 1653, A4, 206, 229.
12. See Chapter 3 of Butler's *Excitable Speech*, 'Contagious Word: Paranoia and "Homosexuality" in the Military', 103–26, for an extensive account of the logic of such anxiety.
13. Quoted in Warren Chernaik and Martin Dzelzainis (eds), *Marvell and Liberty* (New York: St Martin's, 1999), 313.
14. Nigel Smith (ed.), *The Poems of Andrew Marvell* (Harlow: Pearson Education, 2003). All quotations of Marvell's poetry are from this edition.
15. See Edward J. Reilly for an article that focuses closely on how Flecknoe's language resembles Latin. 'Marvell's "Fleckno," Anti-Catholicism, and the Pun as Metaphor', in *John Donne Journal* 2:2 (1983), 51–62, esp. 55.
16. Reading the poem alongside emblem books, Joan Hartwig makes a similar argument, pointing out the chameleon's association with both flatterers as well as lovers who change at the will of the beloved. See 'Marvell's Metamorphic "Fleckno"', in *Studies in English Literature, 1500–1900*, 36 (1996): 171–212, esp. 192.
17. Warren Chernaik argues that the poem's satiric weight resides primarily in something not unlike this perversity, 'the imaginative creation of a disordered universe where poems are worn as clothing and diseases displayed as badges of honor'. *The Poet's Time: Politics and Religion in the Work of Andrew Marvell* (Cambridge: Cambridge University Press, 1982), 166–7.
18. Annabel Patterson, Nicholas von Maltzahn and N. H. Keeble (eds), *The Prose Works of Andrew Marvell*, 2 vols (New Haven, CT: Yale University Press, 2003), 2: 229.
19. As will become clear, this is certainly the case in Patterson's reading of 'Appleton House'; it is also the case in her description of *The Account*, especially when she describes Louis XIV's sinister, seductive romance with Charles II in *Marvell: The Writer in Public Life* (Harlow: Pearson Education, 2000), 149–50.
20. See *Marvell: The Writer in Public Life*, 143, 146. The earliest statement of this position appears in her *Marvell and the Civic Crown* (Princeton, NJ: Princeton University Press, 1978), but for the more comprehensive and foundational statement, see her *Early Modern Liberalism* (Cambridge:

Cambridge University Press, 1997), esp. 1–26 and Chapter 6, 'Secret History', 183–231.

21. Aside from Norbrook, who I discuss further in the body of the chapter, some of the clearest markers of the paradigmatic nature of Patterson's view within Marvell studies can be found in the recent collection *Marvell and Liberty*, which includes numerous arguments similar to Patterson's, including those of Dzelzainis and M. L. Donnelly, which take up Catholicism in particular. For another account of not just the rights, but also the responsibility of individuals to think, and to think together, in the wake of crumbling central authority, see Andrew Barnaby's argument in 'The Politics of Garden Spaces: Andrew Marvell and the Anxieties of Public Speech', in *Studies in Philology* 97:3 (2000), 331–61, esp. 333–5, 352, 356. Discussion of Marvell's liberalism in general itself reaches at least as far back as the bizarre debate between Cleanth Brooks and Douglas Bush. See Brooks, 'Marvell's Horatian Ode', and Bush, 'Marvell's Horatian Ode', in *Andrew Marvell*, ed. Michael Wilding (Nashville, TN: Aurora, 1970), 93–113, and 114–24; as well as Brooks, 'A Note on the Limits of "History" and the Limits of "Criticism"', *Sewanee Review* 61 (1953), 129–35.

22. John Rogers offers a more elaborate reading of Maria's liberalism in *The Matter of Revolution: Science, Poetry, and Politics in the Age of Milton* (Ithaca, NY: Cornell University Press, 1996), 84.

23. *Marvell: The Writer in Public Life*, 56.

24. *Writing the English Republic: Poetry, Rhetoric, and Politics, 1627–1660* (New York: Cambridge University Press, 1999), 288–9.

25. *Andrew Marvell* (Plymouth: Northcote House, 1994), 29.

26. This is not to say that no criticism finds this dialectic unserious. James Holstun, for example, has argued that the nuns are ultimately (if also lamentably) unthreatening to the poem's 'self-interested Protestant *aufhebung*'. '"Will you Rent our Ancient Love Asunder?": Lesbian Elegy in Donne, Marvell and Milton', *English Literary History* 54 (1987), 835–67, esp. 851–2.

27. *Marvell: The Writer in Public Life*, 52.

28. *Andrew Marvell*, 30.

29. For some recent historical accounts which demonstrate how the complexity of Protestant and Catholic identities makes it difficult to disentangle the two easily, see John Bossy, *The English Catholic Community 1570–1850* (New York: Oxford University Press, 1976); Alexandra Walsham, *Church Papists: Catholicism, Conformity and Confessional Polemic in Early Modern England* (Woodbridge: Royal Historical Society–Boydell, 1993); and Lucy E. C. Wooding, *Rethinking Catholicism in Reformation England* (Oxford: Clarendon, 2000). For a reading of Marvell's refusal of the Protestant/Catholic binary in another context, see Laura Lunger Knoppers, 'The Antichrist, the Babilon, the Great Dragon: Oliver Cromwell, Andrew Marvell, and the Apocalyptic Monstrous', 93–123, in Knoppers and Joan B. Landes (eds), *Monstrous Bodies/Political Monstrosities in Early Modern Europe* (Ithaca, NY: Cornell University Press, 2004), esp. 122–3.

30. *Marvell: The Writer in Public Life*, 52.

31. In her classic study of what she calls the 'madly multiple' poem, Colie describes how anything like an assured position (anti-Catholic, pro-Maria

or otherwise) is difficult to stake out. See *'My Ecchoing Song': Andrew Marvell's Poetry of Criticism* (Princeton, NJ: Princeton University Press, 1970).

More recently, Stephens and Crewe have also attached politicised value to how the narrator's sympathies do not reside entirely with the proto-liberal dream of law that would secure personal boundaries. Stephens suggests that for Marvell 'an orderly harmony is not only impossible but not necessarily even preferable,' and that 'we find our most fitting home in the ridiculous, in something that is paradoxically quite disparate from ourselves'; Stephens notes – rightly, I think – that what the poem enjoys most of all is certainly not 'unpretentious self-sufficiency and self-governance'. Like Stephens, I agree that the poem enjoys the ridiculous, but unlike her I would like to focus my discussion of such enjoyment around the transubstantial word. Moreover, while Stephens sets up an opposition between figures who have personal boundaries and those who are vulnerable, those who are active and who are passive, Maria and the speaker, I will argue that even these opposi-tions are difficult to sustain. See *The Limits of Eroticism in Post-Petrarchan Narrative: Conditional Pleasure from Spenser to Marvell* (Cambridge: Cambridge University Press, 1998), esp. 205, 196, 203, 206.

Focusing on the poetics of enclosure in largely secular terms, Crewe argues that, through the speaker's self-portrayal, 'Appleton House' exposes and undoes 'a widespread cultural fantasy of the supposedly autonomous, originary masculine subject'. I certainly agree that there are no autonomous masculine subjects to be found in Marvell's country house poem, but it should become clear that I would also argue that what Crewe identifies as the speaker's attempts at regaining self-possession are actually ways of experimenting with how self-enclosure and self-exposure can go hand in hand. See 'The Garden State: Marvell's Poetics of Enclosure', in Thomas Healy (ed.), *Andrew Marvell* (New York: Longman, 1998), 57, 68–70. This article is reprinted from Richard Burt (ed.), *Enclosure Acts: Sexuality, Property and Culture in Early Modern England* (Ithaca, NY: Cornell University Press, 1994), 270–89.

32. *OED Online*, Oxford University Press, 2007.
33. See 'Freedom and Space', 29–68, in *Michel Foucault and the Politics of Freedom* (New York: Rowman & Littlefield, 2002).
34. *Marvell: The Writer in Public Life*, 52, and *Andrew Marvell*, 30.
35. *Early Modern Liberalism*, 2–3.
36. It is clear, in the introduction to *Early Modern Liberalism*, that Patterson writes a Whig history over which we can find clear temporal progres-sion from, say, the demand for rights, to the elaboration of those rights and, finally, to the enforcement of them. In *Writing the English Republic*, Norbrook by contrast treats the Interregnum as a kind of high point of the exercise (if not the recognition) of negative freedom and positive liberty prior to modernity's decline (see, for instance, his claim on p. 13 that the early modern public sphere was far more enabling than the bourgeois one that would follow).
37. In his recuperation of Lucan, Norbrook advocates setting aside something that we are 'constantly told' of: 'the importance for early modern poetry of . . . Horace and Virgil'. We would do well to disregard this because both of

them, 'with whatever qualifications and subtexts, ultimately celebrated the reign of Augustus' (24–5).

38. Patterson herself is attuned to the political ambiguity of Virgil, not just in terms of how he is appropriated but in terms of the Virgilian texts themselves. See *Pastoral and Ideology: Virgil to Valery* (Berkeley, CA: University of California Press, 1988).
39. Ovid, *Metamorphoses*, trans. David Raeburn (New York: Penguin, 2004), vi.412–674.
40. See book 2 of the *Aeneid*, trans. Frederick Ahl (Oxford: Oxford University Press, 2007).
41. Virgil, *Eclogues, Georgics, Aeneid I-VI*, trans. H. Rushton Fairclough (Cambridge, MA: Harvard University Press, 1999), *Georgics* i.466–97.
42. See *Horace: the Odes and Epodes*, trans. C. E. Bennett (Cambridge, MA: Harvard University Press, 1988), I.ii.5–12.
43. *The Practice of Everyday Life*, trans. Steven Rendall (Berkeley, CA: University of California Press, 1984), 123.
44. *Metamorphoses* i.4–25.
45. *Georgics* ii.371–5, i.176–86.
46. *Georgics* i.199–203.
47. *Postmodern Geographies: The Reassertion of Space in Critical Social Theory* (New York: Verso, 1989), 150.
48. *Modernity and the Holocaust* (Ithaca, NY: Cornell University Press, 1991), 13, 34.
49. To be sure, even though they see danger in exposure and ascribe value to boundaries of various kinds, Virgil, Ovid and Horace all register awareness that, no matter how scrupulous those efforts are, they remain incomplete. Consider, for instance, *Odes* III, 16. There Horace describes how Acrisius, told that his daughter Danae will have a child who will kill him, imprisons her behind oak doors in a bronze tower, surrounded by guard dogs. But no space in the lived world can be enclosed once and for all. Thus Zeus manages, in the form of golden rain, to impregnate Danae with her father's killer, Perseus. Consider, similarly, Atlas's attempt, in book 4 of the *Metamorphoses*, to keep all strangers, Perseus among them, outside the boundaries marking off what is his, his orchard surrounded by thick walls, guarded by a gigantic dragon. Perseus, making nightmarish Atlas's dream of fixity, violates those boundaries by pulling out Medusa's head; from afar he transforms Atlas into a mountain (iv.645–62).
50. On the impermanence – but also the importance – of boundary-drawing, see Patrick McGreevy, 'Attending to the Void: Geography and Madness', in Paul C. Adams, Steven Hoelscher and Karen E. Till (eds), *Textures of Place: Exploring Humanist Geographies* (Minneapolis, MN: University of Minnesota Press, 2001), 246–56.
51. *Aeneid*, iii.588–685.
52. *Georgics* iii.452–6.
53. *Metamorphoses* vi.284–93.
54. See pp. 1–17 of Marina Warner's *Fantastic Metamorphoses, Other Worlds: Ways of Telling the Self* (Oxford: Oxford University Press, 2002) for a thorough description of the myriad causes and consequences of Ovidian metamorphosis.

55. *for space* (London: Sage, 2005), 165.
56. Indeed, time and again in the *Aeneid* words fail to have sufficient effect, for good and ill. Polyphemus uses his voice to make ocean waves, but Aeneas escapes anyway (iii.670–85); and Anxur, 'spouting / Big talk, believing that words beget force' (x.545–8), has his forearm summarily lopped off.
57. *Odes* I.ix.9–12.
58. *The Production of Space*, trans. Donald Nicholson-Smith (Malden, MA: Blackwell, 1991), 17.
59. *The Poetics of Space*, trans. Maria Jolas (Boston, MA: Beacon, 1969), 219–20.
60. All references are to Lucan, *Pharsalia*, trans. Jane Wilson Joyce (Ithaca, NY: Cornell University Press, 1993).
61. *Georgics* iv.51–61.
62. *Space and Place: The Perspective of Experience* (Minneapolis, MN: University of Minnesota Press, 1977), 54.
63. For a lucid description of the assumptions that allow for the opposition of space and place, see Massey, *for space*, esp. 6.
64. Like personal space in 'Appleton House' and its antecedents, and in contrast to the ideally absolute, inviolable closure characteristic of sacralised or normalised space, heterotopias presuppose 'a system of opening and closing that isolates them and makes them penetrable at the same time'; they deploy notions of boundaries but remain open and vulnerable. See 'Different Spaces', in James D. Faubion (ed.), *Essential Works of Foucault*, vol. 2: *Aesthetics, Method, and Epistemology*, trans. Robert Hurley et al. (New York: New Press, 1998), 183.
65. As the term suggests and in contrast to contained, normalised, self-identical space, heterotopias juxtapose and combine incompatible elements; they are 'different spaces, these other places, a kind of contestation, both mythical and real, of the space in which we live' (179).
66. See 'A Preface to Transgression', also in volume 2 of the *Essential Works*, 74.
67. Dumm does just this, explicitly in 'Freedom and Space', and implicitly in his *united states* (Ithaca, NY: Cornell University Press, 1994), especially in Chapter 4, 'Rodney King, or the New Enclosures', and Chapter 6, 'Joyce Brown, or Democracy and Homelessness'.
68. For another account of 'naiveté without innocence', a phrase I borrow from Joseph Litvak, see his *Strange Gourmets: Sophistication, Theory, and the Novel* (Durham, NC: Duke University Press, 1997), esp. 112–50.
69. 'Different Spaces', 182.

Habermas Goes to Hell: Pleasure, Public Reason and the Republicanism of *Paradise Lost*

Introduction

In this final chapter I am concerned with what counts, for Milton and for us, as the legitimate use of public reason. I build on the previous chapter by exploring a vulnerability covered there: our capacity for being affected, altered and even taken in by words, especially when they offer pleasure. I ask whether this capacity can be part of a discipline that ought to be called critical; and I conclude that Milton helps answer this question in the affirmative.

As I see *Paradise Lost* taking part in a discussion that extends from the classical period to the present, I place the epic not only in its own context but also alongside the work of figures such as Plato, Cicero, Habermas, Foucault and Michael Warner. Setting out with the criticism of Miltonists such as David Norbrook and Sharon Achinstein, I show how Milton has been linked with the set of Habermasian practices aimed at curbing the self's susceptibility to words and with a public way of life defined by strict, uncompromising discipline – one focused on sifting through valid and invalid rhetorical appeals, generating uncoerced consensus and fabricating durable futures. Such discipline becomes synonymous with a well-fortified critical distance from which public selves are impervious to pleasure.

Corresponding to this conception of Milton's publics, I argue, is a conception of his republicanism. Most studies – both within literary studies and in the work of historians such as Blair Worden, Quentin Skinner and Jonathan Scott – locate Milton's republicanism in ideals that link civic virtue with bounded selfhood, the public exercise of positive liberties with the maintenance of negative freedoms. These studies, in other words, presuppose the value of a *res publica* that cultivates bounded, discrete, essentially autonomous actors – a space within which judicious individuals could, as in Habermasian public sphere theory, employ a reason unclouded by irrational passion and so remain unmoved by the offer of coercive, temporary pleasure. In doing so, ideal Miltonic selves could strengthen the structure and legal architecture of the republics of which they would be part and by which their boundaries as citizens might be guaranteed.

While such readings find their warrant in Milton's writings, they are by no means exhaustive, especially when it comes to *Paradise Lost*. His portrayals of Paradise and Pandemonium, for instance, find value in joining rational disputes and sensual caresses; in the therapeutic pleasures of public argument; in the enjoyable, transformed world made by vulnerable subjects within the space of conversation; and, finally, in republican selfhood that does not depend on the republic's support. Early on, a Foucaultian context will be of most use to me, since Foucault, unlike Habermas, advocates publics that couple pleasure and critique. Such coupling, largely ignored in contemporary public sphere theory, offers a provocative linkage of rational discipline with what Milton calls rational delight, a delight explored in his depictions of the first couple and the fallen angels. Considering in both cases what it means to constitute a 'public', Milton shows sympathy for interaction defined by an indistinction between ostensibly public and ostensibly private spaces and behaviours – coffeehouses and gardens, the giving of reasons and the taking of pleasures – whose separation permits Habermasian forms of modern, public selfhood to emerge. To discuss the connection between this form of public being and an alternative form of republicanism in which Milton shows interest, I draw not just on Foucault but also, in what makes for an unlikely grouping, on the oratorical treatises of Cicero. Parting from Platonic tradition by endorsing public pleasure and salutary sociability that take place after the republic's collapse, Cicero's treatises highlight the reality, felt intensely by Milton, that to be republican often meant to live without a republic and so meant turning to interactive therapeutics for what a more strict discipline could never offer. And here resides an important but neglected component of Milton's insights into reason's place in public life as well as in histories of public and 'republican' selfhood. If figures like Michael Walzer are right to claim that current political thinking often, erroneously, sets principled rationality and passionate intensity at necessary loggerheads,[1] and if – as I argue – even quite radical public sphere theorists such as Warner still tend to think critique and pleasure apart,[2] my reading of *Paradise Lost* suggests that current theorising about public reason and the republican legacy would do well to look more closely at texts of early modernity, when 'public' reason and 'private' passions, including pleasure, were deeply, regularly and openly regarded as intertwined.[3] This is so, I point out, even in spaces such as the coffeehouse, which, despite its association with the public sphere's structural overhaul, was full of the same pleasures depicted by Milton. Since Milton's publics, his republicanism and his embrace of rational delight are themselves intertwined, study of his epic suggests that public and republican selves themselves need not – and ought not – undergo the transformation that would harden them against pleasurable, transformative words.

Public Reason in Current Studies of Milton and Early Modern England

Milton has often been understood to have affinities with Habermas. Shortly after *The Structural Transformation of the Public Sphere* appeared in English translation, for example, Donald Guss claimed that both Habermas and Milton put forth debate as a way to assume responsibility for change, subject all topics to open scrutiny, and undertake the search, always ongoing, for voluntary agreement.[4] Around the same time, David Zaret explicitly revised Habermasian chronology by virtue of the printing public emergent in the seventeenth century (rather than the eighteenth) and invoked *Areopagitica* in order to do so, arguing that Milton's tract 'holds that sound decisions in politics would be the result of a free and open exchange' and voices hope that the English people can develop the critical discipline requisite to do so.[5]

Since the early 1990s, interest in making connections between Habermasian publics and those of Milton's period has bloomed, often by deepening the emphases just mentioned – highlighting how the dispersal of authority within early modern publics generated the need for dutiful individuals to interpret with rational-critical discernment, to build reasoned, uncoerced consensus.[6] Connections between Habermas and Milton in particular have proliferated similarly, venturing beyond the prose tracts to the poems, including *Paradise Lost*. Completed after the Restoration, when Milton was forced for a time to go into hiding as a possible traitor, the poem was composed in part under conditions of renewed censorship; none the less, it has been read as a figural reflection of the open, rational-critical discussion and disciplined selfhood that Milton has been understood to advocate in the heady days of revolution. Norbrook, a central proponent of this sort of work, claims that we find the period's proto-Habermasian intellectual energy not just in *Areopagitica* but in *Paradise Lost*'s various experiments – including those conducted by God himself – aimed at reviving public spirit, at opening society in general and enlightened rational debate in particular, to ever greater degrees. The agreement between God and Adam, for Norbrook, typifies the poem's – and the early modern public sphere's – 'extraordinarily open universe', in which 'huge vertical distances are bridged by free horizontal communication'. To keep the notion of unco-erced agreement in play, this bridging enables, demands and supplies the training ground for the individual cultivation of distance and criti-cal acumen.[7] Achinstein, similarly, argues that Milton, throughout his career, developed a notion of a 'revolutionary' reader 'fit to withstand coercion by political rhetoric'; for Achinstein, the multiplication in early modernity of divergent (often propagandistic) opinion offers practice in the detection of empty emotional appeals.[8]

Norbrook and Achinstein, that is, regard *Paradise Lost* as consistent with the dominant tone of *Areopagitica*, in which Milton longs for an English citizen who is a 'good refiner', a 'scout into the regions of sin and falsity' – who, when presented with a bold book, excels at the 'scanning of error' and is apt 'to keep waking', 'to stand in watch', to read the book of the world with 'undazl'd eyes'.[9] For them, *Paradise Lost* would also accord with most of *Paradise Regained*, with Jesus as the ideal subject, for whom Satan's empty rhetoric is as 'surging waves against a solid rock' (4.18), and who, with only a few exceptions, offers Satan responses that are markedly pacific (he responds 'temperately' (2.378), 'patiently' (2.432), 'calmly' (3.43), 'unmoved' (4.109)).[10] Guarding the boundaries of judgement, for Norbrook and Achinstein, both fosters individual autonomy in its own right and renders selves worthy of the protections and entitlements promised by a republican polity. The republican self is thus well bounded, active but impervious.

Such arguments can be construed (and are often explicitly advanced) in reaction to some very prominent critics who see reason's place in Miltonic subject formation as decisively coercive. Here I have in mind critics like Stanley Fish, who de-links Milton from investment in public sociability as such, and like Francis Barker, who, drawing on Foucault's *Discipline and Punish* in order to critique Milton, sees the pamphlet-eer's publics and republicanism as emblematic of a shift from sovereign to disciplinary power. For Barker, the critical discipline advocated in *Areopagitica* inaugurates a modernity during which a bounded subject emerges within a new (yet still coercive) regime of truth – one that grants the subject only the most limited form of 'freedom'.[11] In this chapter I also think about Milton in terms of Foucault, but not so as to turn our attention again to the subjection involved in early modern subject for-mation; instead, by drawing connections between Milton and some of the later writings of Foucault, ones more sympathetic to public reason than those that Barker draws on, I will offer a view in which Miltonic reason does not further a strictly bounded existence, either in the form of autonomy or in the form of a straightjacketing subjection.

To be sure, I would not deny either that Milton is sometimes intolerant and coercive in ways that Foucault, throughout his career, would call symptomatic – as Milton undoubtedly is in, say, his views toward Catholics – or that the poet is sometimes an advocate of hard-earned consensus achieved through the exercise of uncompromising critical discipline. Milton can be both of these things, occasionally at once, as he is in *Areopagitica*. Still, much of the energy and vitality of *Paradise Lost* cannot be adequately accounted for by either of the views just presented. I agree with critics such as Norbrook, Guss and Achinstein in so far as they show that despite his disappointment with the revolution, Cromwell and the Restoration, Milton 'never gave up on the people of England' (as Achinstein puts it) or on public reason (14). And given the influence, within literary studies, of earlier Foucaultian theories of the subjected subject, I also share the desire of Norbrook and others to describe politically productive, 'anti anti-enlightenment' pictures of reason in the early modern public sphere – especially given the degree to which current publics remain largely exclusive in structure and impoverished in practice.

I want, however, to present a supplementary idea as to what it can mean for us to find attractive public actors in Milton. While Habermasians find in *Paradise Lost* a need to employ critical discipline in the service of a larger consensus and a stronger polity that would in turn strengthen its citizens, I will show how such discipline – in later Foucaultian theory and in Milton's poem – is used otherwise: to produce more directly therapeutic and pleasurable effects, even when this means giving up the distance and affective invulnerability that Habermasians place at the core of critical discipline. Though I will show this in some detail, I want to highlight, at the outset, one entailment of my argument: that I, in line with some recent criticism, present Milton as not clearly, uniformly or ultimately opposed to moments when Adam, Eve or the fallen angels give themselves over to arguments that offer pleasure.[12] For both Fish and most Habermasian critics, Milton abhors these moments as naïve and undisciplined even when he seems to admire them. Rather than explain away the speaker's apparent sympathies, I will contend that they are serious and meaningful; and while I recognise that his sympathies are not unalloyed (are they ever?), I will not attempt to reconcile them with opposing sympathies in Milton, whether they be Habermasian, Platonic, Puritan or otherwise.[13] I thus hope that the chapter's latter sections will justify their admittedly partial focus.

Public Reason in Habermas and Foucault

As is well known, Habermas and Foucault disagree about public reason in several respects.[14] One of their most basic disagreements has to do with whether critical discipline exists, first and foremost, for the purpose of reaching agreements that are uncoerced, that result from searching for shared interests while also respecting individuals as bounded, discrete beings.[15] For Habermas, such agreements – arrived at in an open, status-disregarding, egalitarian public sphere that critiques and aims to affect the legislative domain – are a major promise of enlightenment.[16] Habermas may seem naïve or utopian in this. But since he recognises that the promise of cooperative intersubjectivity is only partially fulfilled and likely to remain so, a certain vigilance – involving the detection and refusal of coercive appeals to status or emotion – plays a crucial role in approximating communicative utopia. Habermas writes that those who 'act judiciously' do not 'give in to their affects'; they just do not permit the exposure of linguistic vulnerability, whether or not that vulnerability would be felt as pleasurable.[17]

Foucault, by contrast, tends to downplay consensus and legislative influence as goals of public reason, partly because he believes that power and truth are circularly linked.[18] Because he places emphasis on the coercion and exclusion involved in generating consensus, Foucault eschews the brand of discipline that would claim to minimise force by minimising our affective susceptibility to words. Foucault's investment is instead in counter-discourse, deliberate appeals to affect, and the more disagreeable, subversive forms of Cynic *parrhesia*.[19] Often, being disagreeable is, straightforwardly, unpleasant, and means seeking to expose the vulnerability of one's interlocutor.[20] But being oppositional can also entail a self-exposure – an exploitation of vulnerability that is neither unpleasant nor uncritical – since one way to speak counter-discourse is to question a conceptual divide crucial to Habermasian theory: that between public and private, often construed more specifically as one between critique and pleasure.[21] For Habermas, enlightenment depends on the emergence of a public sphere – in salons, coffeehouses and print culture more generally – understood to be largely distinct from, even if still overlapping with, the private sphere.[22] He accordingly makes little room for pleasure within the space and time of public critique. It remains for him a topic that could be discussed as part of a shared horizon but that poses a danger to critical discipline; it involves 'giving in to affect' and injudicious action, and is thus left largely private.

In Chapter 1, I discuss how in certain of his later works – for example, *The Philosophical Discourse of Modernity* – Habermas acknowledges that such distinction-making is too stringent. He comes to admire 'the productivity and explosive power of basic aesthetic experiences' of 'a subjectivity liberated from the imperatives of purposive activity' – experiences that are present in avant-garde art and that he considers a gain of enlightenment. Habermas even urges us to 'conceive of rational practice as reason concretized' in, among other things, the body. But these thoughts are not very fully developed. They remain on the periphery of his theories of communicative action, and so Habermas never emphasises the 'explosive power' of aesthetic experience – let alone of argumentative pleasure – as a possible goal or component of public critique.[23]

When Foucault describes Diogenes engaging in 'scandalous behavior' – exposing himself in the agora, masturbating and offering a rationale – we see a (perhaps shockingly) more flexible discipline. Scandalous behaviour, for Foucault, is an aspect of *parrhesia* that wrenches public life precisely by including pleasure as part of critical experience – by performing in public a supposedly private act. Diogenes's action and rationale reveal the arbitrarily drawn boundaries of the public domain and of the selves inside it; when he goes out and masturbates it is on the grounds that, since eating, which satisfies a bodily need, is allowed in the agora, masturbation ought to be, too.[24] In insisting that bodily satisfaction already exists, and belongs utterly, out in the open, the public use of reason coincides with and is enabled by the public use of pleasure.

Foucault's recuperation of reason here not only emphasises pleasurable, rather than affect-free, critical discipline but also displays how rational delight can have world-making force. Indeed, for Foucault pleasure can transform space both by troubling its boundaries physically, as Diogenes does, but also by simply imagining space as otherwise than it is. Consider the essay, 'What is Enlightenment?' There, Foucault's recuperation of Kant differs from Habermas's in part by focusing on Kant's almost entirely negative definition of Aufklärung as an '*Ausgang*, an "exit," a "way out"', by which he means a grasping of the world as it is only to 'transfigure' it imaginatively.[25] Doing so makes for pleasurably speculative, rather than obviously purposive, critique, speaking not so we can win consensus as to a plan of action, but so we can imagine worlds not inflexibly structured by the divisions and antagonisms to which we feel bound. The 'value of the present', Foucault writes, 'is indissociable from a desperate eagerness to imagine it . . . otherwise than it is, and to transform it . . . [in] an exercise in which extreme attention to what is real is confronted with the practice of a liberty that simultaneously respects this reality and violates it' (305, 311). This form of liberty is far different from the sort that the Habermasian self, unlocked from the world that he critiques, would exercise in order to compel lasting legislative change. Foucaultian violation can simply consist in doing what painters do, making natural things more than natural, beautiful things more than beautiful; in terms of critique it can mean not changing government but practising 'the art of not being governed so much';[26] in terms of enlightened public reason generally, it can mean imagining a more habitable world and creating one within the bounds of interaction, fabricating escapes within the world in which selves are inescapably lodged.

The creative function that Foucault ascribes to language in 'What is Enlightenment?' helps clarify a fundamental difference between his thought and that of Habermas. In fact, it even distinguishes Foucault from a more radical theorist such as Michael Warner, who also finds a transformative, world-making capacity in public pleasure. If we return to Diogenes exposed in the agora, we see that he is aware of the imposed distinction between acceptable public and private behaviours, between argument in the agora and masturbatory pleasure. But by imagining that public life could be otherwise – that it is certainly possible for him to perform the scandalous act that ostensibly has no place in public – he violates, transforms and goes beyond his world within the space of sociability. In this world-making respect, his practice is precisely the kind ruled out by Habermasian critical practice; for Habermas, Diogenes's behaviour would imply an underdeveloped, pre-modern worldview, one which does not draw the distinctions necessary for critique even to exist – distinctions between objective, social and subjective worlds, between words and worlds, health and truth, and so on.[27] Though his theories of intersubjectivity aim to de-centre and destabilise the self, when it comes to Habermas's account of public life, the birth of critical discipline none the less coincides with the birth of critical distance. Diogenes operates under other assumptions, using critique to realise the 'otherwise' of pleasurable public being, immediately if also only temporarily, until the guards take him away. He creates a pleasurable world even as he exposes himself; he generates the enjoyment that Habermasian selves leave outside the space of argument. For Habermas, giving in to affect exposes one's insufficiency as a public actor; in his account of Diogenes, by contrast, Foucault shows how self-exposure can be more than sufficient as a rational, critical act. Ejaculating in the agora, making his point by giving in to pleasure, Diogenes changes the space outside himself not despite losing self-control but because of it, because he has made himself vulnerable.

Warner supplements Habermasian frameworks in a fashion similar to Foucault, but with a crucial distinction. In a series of important essays, most of which are collected in *Publics and Counterpublics*, Warner advocates opening publics to almost any act, not simply those that 'scrutinize, ask, reject, opine, judge, and so on', since publics need not be informed by a hierarchy with rational-critical reflection at the top and elements such as play, pleasure, theatricality and affect either marginalised or excluded. In this, Warner and Foucault resemble each other. But whereas Diogenes can perform (masturbation) and make arguments (about its place in public) as part of one practice, Warner claims that critical conversation, regardless of kind, obscures the poetic capacity of interaction to transform public space.[28] In Warner's view, no matter how oppositional or disagreeable one's position is, to remain within the critical model is dangerous, because to do so is to enter the temporality of legislative politics, to relinquish hope for the immediate transformation of space, and to adapt to what Warner believes are the future-minded restrictions of all rational-critical discourse. Along with Lauren Berlant, Warner has thus advocated 'sex in public' on grounds of its salutary world-making force.[29]

This challenge to normative public boundaries has been energising and revelatory within the fields of both theory and literary studies. In thinking rational-critical and pleasurable, transformative practices apart, however, Warner arguably reinforces one Habermasian assumption even as he repudiates others. Like Habermas, Warner's conceptual machinery pairs critical discipline with critical distance, and thus operates by assuming a distinction between (if not a hierarchical ordering of) the principled exercise of reason and the passionate experience of pleasure. Warner discusses acts centred on embodied sociability, affect and play alongside acts of rational-critical judgement, but scarcely considers whether they could be discussed together – whether acts of argumentation and acts of world-making affective expression can take place at once. Warner ends the essay 'Publics and Counterpublics' with the claim alluded to in the last paragraph: that once alternative publics enter the sphere of public argument, they 'enter the temporality of politics and adapt themselves to the performatives of rational-critical discourse' (88–9). 'For many publics', Warner writes, 'to do so is to cede the original hope of transforming, not just policy, but the space of public life itself'; were it not for his (unexplained) qualification '[f]or many publics', one could infer not just that Warner sees serious tension between rational-critical and affective, playful behaviours, but even that he regards these behaviours as mutually exclusive (89).

Habermas limits his theorisations by suggesting that critical discipline ought to be exercised in public only so as to foster self-control and thus produce uncoerced agreements. Warner reveals this limit in his valorisation of public sex; but like Habermas he also, perhaps inadvertently, sanitises critical discipline and aligns it with distance. I hope to have suggested that Foucault's work supplies a forceful reminder of how, when employed in service of pleasure rather than policy, such discipline can plunge selves into dynamic relation with the spaces they inhabit and can briefly reconfigure. In arguing, Diogenes cannot make a law that would allow him to pleasure himself publicly and that would keep the guards away; but by masturbating in the open anyhow, he does anything but accept the given view of the agora as a sanitised space. In imagining the world otherwise, similarly, the Foucaultian critic may not always have direct influence on the legislative sphere, but he can have an intimate effect on the sphere of his actual existence. For Foucault, public reason need not adapt itself to legislative temporalities at the expense of world-making ones. Instead, critique can become an end in itself, offering local and temporary, but also transformative and therapeutic forms of release. This point may strike us as commonsensical; but the point, for whatever reason, is rare in contemporary public sphere theory.

Rational Delight; or, Paradise

As will become clear, I have included the foregoing theoretical discussion because it can serve as a useful interpretive lens for *Paradise Lost*. But it also provides important justification for turning to texts of early modernity in order to rethink the contours of contemporary publics. Robert Cockcroft has shown, recently and at length, that pathos in general (and pleasure in particular) play an important part in the tradition of rhetorical theory extending from Aristotle to Thomas Wilson, Philip Sidney and beyond.[30] Cockcroft's work implies that traditions of early modern openness are multiple – that they are not limited to Christian intercession, prayer and confession but extend as well to the domain of rational debate. As Cockcroft and others have also demonstrated, reason and passions, including pleasure, are regularly regarded as part of a single complex in the Renaissance, a fact that has generated interest in the public dimensions of early modern affect.[31] That both red-blooded Habermasians and vanguard theorists like Warner overlook the 'single complex' possibility suggests to me that not just Foucaultian theory, but early modern literature can help further thinking about publics.

This point, I will be arguing, is borne out in Milton's portrayals of the fall of Adam and Eve and of Pandemonium, both of which explore the dynamics of rational debate, consensus and pleasure in complicated and surprising ways. In terms of vocabulary introduced so far, this will mean Eve acting like Diogenes in the agora, and the fallen angels imagining the *Ausgang*, using world-making language in a manner akin to Foucault's enlightened philosophers. I will thus chart how these episodes challenge the divides that inaugurate modernity and modern selfhood in Habermasian narratives. As I pointed out in my initial critical review, *Paradise Lost* has value for Habermasian readers for precisely the opposite reason – for displaying the value of the divides (between public and private, reason and passion, words and worlds, and so on) discussed in the previous section. Such readers thus see the episodes of interest here quite differently from me.

Consider, to begin, Norbrook's reading of the fall, which is part of a long and venerable critical practice.[32] While careful not to attribute Satan's seduction of Eve simply to her 'inferior female power of rationality', Norbrook focuses on how the garden's incomplete divisions between public and private – Eve's simultaneous inclusion in and exclusion from the space of Adam's discussions with Raphael – 'offer points that Satan can exploit', adding to the persuasiveness of his offer of power. The instructive value of the fall rests both in this Habermasian lesson – in how the garden offers neither an ideal public forum (one that would grant women full inclusion) – and in the inadequate exercise of critical discipline that ensues; Eve, followed by Adam, 'fails her test' in demonstrating 'practical prudence and an effective understanding of language'.[33] She fails to see through Satan's empty appeals, ones couched in faux-republican idiom; the episode, read by Norbrook as one of the poem's many experiments in just how open communication can be, calls for more discerning rational capacities, better training in the 'practical prudence' of a reason not swayed by passion.

In his emphasis on passing the test of critical discipline, Norbrook's work extends Achinstein's earlier efforts in *Milton and the Revolutionary Reader*. As suggested above, she reads *Paradise Lost* in the context of the public sphere's emergence and as an exercise that trains its readers in critical distance. Focusing on the debates in Hell, Achinstein argues that those debates – like the one leading up to the fall – are intended to help readers see through false arguments.[34] In Achinstein's account, readers are meant to experience the appeal of being taken in by empty rhetoric but also to develop the ability to separate themselves from the fallen angels;[35] Milton supplies readers with clues which show that in taking the debate in Hell seriously – in considering that they might adapt to Hell, improving it to resemble Heaven – the fallen angels engage in a thorough (and thoroughly debilitating) misreading of their plight, imprudently plunging themselves into a physical and mental perplexity.[36] Laura Lunger Knoppers, similarly, links the happiness in book

2 and the assent given to Satan's plan with an unreflective, uncritical 'politics of joy' that Milton would have associated with the Restoration and would have surely detested.[37]

It will be clear that readings offered by critics such as Norbrook, Achinstein and Knoppers are plausible; but so are others. Moreover, while the stories of the first couple and the fallen angels can be read as cautionary tales that point (if only by negation) to Habermasian ideals, episodes in the poem that are said to offer a positive valuation of those ideals are more problematic, eschewing as they do critical discipline that is pitched toward autonomy and uncoerced consensus. Consider, for example, Adam's talk with God, one, I mentioned above, that Norbrook reads as evidence of the poem's 'extraordinarily open universe' and that supplies training in how to tell true from false.[38]

During this talk, Adam surveys the world's creatures, realises that he alone has not been paired off and, objecting, asks what happiness, what rational enjoyment, he can find without a human partner. When God answers that Adam in fact is not alone – after all, animals 'also know, and reason not contemptibly' – Adam questions whether the difference between a human sovereign and his brute subjects can be bracketed, since '[a]mong unequals what society / Can sort, what harmony or true delight?' (8.364–84). The first man, God reminds him, fails to appreciate that the very fact of the debate he is right now in reflects 'infinite descents', a bracketing of status difference infinitely greater than that which he laments (410). In this respect, God's argument is an astonishing one; reason enables disregard not simply for immense but for inconceivable difference, in which one party is omniscient and the other completely ignorant, one infinitely powerful and the other utterly powerless. God, that is, seems to assert the achievability of Habermasian ideals and lend credence to Norbrook's claim that one can find an extraordinarily open universe in Milton's epic.

Reason here might even be said to create a space for an egalitarian, open debate in which Adam, by dint of the force of the better argument, persuades God to abandon his own position in favour of Adam's – except, of course, that God ends the debate by effacing its status as debate:

> I, ere thou spak'st,
> Knew it not good for man to be alone,
> And . . .
> Intended thee, for trial only brought,
> To see how thou couldst judge of fit and meet
> (444–8)

Adam, we discover, has not persuaded God that he ought to have Eve after all but simply arrives at the position which God has always held, and which, moreover, emphasises rather than denies the importance of difference; in order to pass his trial Adam has been made to argue in favour of an unbridgeable difference between himself and the 'brute', to prove that he knows his superiority over that brute, who, in contrast to God's initial claim, is indeed 'unmeet' for Adam. To pass muster, he must give weight to difference in a 'debate' that itself instantiates this very weight, with God misleading Adam all along; the former devises the 'debate' as a kind of exercise, cultivating critical discipline in Adam by surreptitiously leading him along a predetermined path.[39] Without question, Norbrook is aware that there is 'an uncomfortable residue of manipulation' at play here, though this makes his point a couple pages earlier – that 'huge vertical distances between levels [in Milton's universe] are bridged by free horizontal communication' – a bit puzzling.[40] The point suggested by the debate seems to me rather different: that fostering critical discipline does not mean fostering individual autonomy, and that Milton may have other uses for critical discipline in mind. His portrayals of the first couple and the fallen angels detail these uses – even as these portrayals also, understandably, evince more awareness about the dangers of coercion than the exchange between Adam and God does.

Let us begin with the case of Adam and Eve. In clear ways, their fall results from excessive linguistic susceptibility and inadequate critical discipline, since both Adam and Eve fall by erroneously giving in to an argument. Despite her assertions that she can stand 'single' against devilish rhetoric, Eve shows herself, from the outset, to be emotionally vulnerable to Satan's appeals. When Satan first flatters her, '[i]nto the heart of Eve his words made way' (9.550); when he argues in favour of partaking of the Tree of Knowledge, 'his words replete with guile / Into her heart too easy entrance won' (9.733–4), and within the space of a single conversation Eve internalises and starts to parrot Satanic discourse. She wonders, briefly, how it is that a serpent can speak (9.551), but somehow cannot see through the anomaly. Without the sort of training that God imposes on Adam in book 8, she is incapable of making the distinctions needed not to fall. Given her earlier, insistent disagreement with Adam about whether they ought to work together, we might say that Eve is insufficiently Habermasian on two counts, seemingly ill-equipped either for reasoned consensus or for the exercise of strict critical discipline.

Adam's own 'training' proves equally inadequate; his supposedly superior power for making discriminations does not stop his own fall into affective susceptibility; soon after Eve explains what she has done, he also eats, for he cannot forgo Eve's 'sweet converse' (9.908). Listening to Eve, he is 'fondly overcome with female charm' even though he knows better (999). In these ways the story of the fall seems, straightforwardly, the story of reason's failure to master passion and to refuse the offer of pleasure. In terms of the above discussion, it is the story of the need for, and the exceedingly difficult project of developing, a properly sanitised discipline, one that would keep in mind Michael's injunction to 'Judge not what is best / By pleasure' (11.603–4). From this perspective, it seems reasonable to claim that the instructive value of the fall resides in its call for readers more fit than Adam and Eve, for the training that, Achinstein argues, *Paradise Lost* provides.

But this story is only part – and probably not the most important part – of the story of the fall. That Milton imagines moments of tragic affective susceptibility does not entail that he has a uniformly negative attitude toward such susceptibility. In part this is simply because being taken in by false arguments, in Milton's view, is occasionally, blamelessly, unavoidable – for instance, when Satan changes his appearance into that of a 'stripling cherub' (3.636) and tricks Uriel into thinking that his purpose in visiting Eden is simply to admire the first man: 'So spake the false dissembler unperceived, / For neither man nor angel can discern / Hypocrisy, the only evil that walks / Invisible, except to God alone' (3.681–4). If an angel cannot see through Satan's false appeals, the reader cannot help but wonder how this applies to Adam and Eve – whether there are limits to the truth-enabling and coercion-limiting functions of critical discipline. And while this possibility can raise the question of whether the first couple is really free to fall, it can also prompt consideration of alternative uses for the discipline in which Milton shows such interest.

Close scrutiny of Adam and Eve's interactions rewards this sort of consideration, because paradisal debate is at times defined by the openness to affect that gets Eve into trouble elsewhere. If her vulnerability leads to the fall, it also has an honoured place in some unfallen debate. When she withdraws from the discussion between Adam and Raphael in book 8, for example, it is for these reasons:

> went she not, as not with such discourse
> Delighted, or not capable her ear
> Of what was high: such pleasure she reserved,
> Adam relating, she sole auditress;
> Her husband the relater she preferred
> Before the angel, and of him to ask
> Chose rather; he, she knew would intermix
> Grateful digressions, and solve high dispute

With conjugal caresses, from his lip
Not words alone pleased her.

(48–57)

Earlier, the narrator explains how God 'framed / All things to man's delightful use' (4.691–2), and for Eve, 'all things' has included and ought to include arguments.[41] If Milton suggests that a more sanitised, distanced brand of critical discipline could have prevented the fall, he also suggests that such discipline would preserve, in slightly altered form, what it temporarily swears off: the possibility for giving in to the appeals of one's partner in debate, yielding what is unacceptable from a Habermasian point of view, yielding a consensus in exchange for a caress.

In the debate that precipitates the fall in book 9, Adam insists on the opposite: that debate and pleasure be kept separate. He tells Eve that conversation with her is joined to and *flows from* reason without quite falling within the domain of the rational; sociability is understood to sustain the self no less than food and to occur with, but also potentially without, words. God created labour not so as to deny

Refreshment, whether food, or talk between,
Food of the mind, or this sweet intercourse
Of looks and smiles, for smiles from reason flow,
To brute denied, and are of love the food,
Love, not the lowest end of human life.
For not to irksome toil, but to delight
He made us, and delight to reason joined.

(9.237–43)

Talk is '[f]ood of the mind', a 'sweet intercourse' of looks and smiles. If God has joined 'delight to reason' and 'smiles from reason flow,' Adam thinks that Eve makes him a better man by engaging him in this word-less 'intercourse' of embodied expression; 'from the influence' of her 'looks' he receives '[a]ccess in every virtue', becomes wiser, stronger and more watchful (309–11). Adam, in short, now locates their value to each other elsewhere than in rational, critical debate. And as he attempts to convince Eve that they should occupy the same position rather than sep-arate ones, he creates a situation in which he and Eve can either argue or give pleasure to each other, but not both, and certainly not both at once.

Eve, for her part, does not seem to want to return Adam's smile in book 9. She wants to argue. But whereas earlier she wanted arguments ended with a kiss rather than a consensus, now, wanting a place in Paradise away from Adam, she puts an end to his kisses with an argu-ment. What has changed? Given the model of paradisal debate offered earlier, it is at least arguable that Eve's disagreeable stance here stems from Adam's (newfound) assumption of a sharp distinction between high disputes and conjugal caresses. Earlier he let them coexist, but now he suggests that rational discussion might be appropriate with Michael, or with Raphael, or even with God, but is inappropriate in his domestic relation to his wife.[42] Even though his stated desire has been for an equal, for one 'fit to participate / All rational delight', he assumes gender difference and separate spheres (8.390–1).

Given Adam's apparent shift in attitude, their debate can be read as one not just about dividing their labours but also as one about debate itself and about its place in the garden. Eve favours disagreement and argument, and she may not have been disagreeable in such tragic fashion, had Adam responded to her in a way that would acknowledge her as a legitimate argumentative partner – that would answer her desire to have disputes and caresses occur at once. Eve may disagree so insistently partly because the first man, adopting a narrow view of pleasurable domesticity, has begun to assume that all debate with his wife is vain, unpleasurable contestation. The first man, in other words, begins to resemble the husband in Milton's divorce tracts, in which marriage ought to be characterised by 'a reasonable agreement in the main matters of society' and in which to disagree with a spouse means to hate her – to violate the domestic sphere's role as 'delightful intermission' to the rest of life.[43] That Adam's conception of domestic debate (as essentially acrimonious) is a problem before Eve ever withdraws, however, suggests that Milton has introduced an element of self-critique.

This is half of Norbrook's point; Eve deserves inclusion in the garden's nascent public sphere and is excluded anyway. But if Norbrook's reading centres around who is excluded from full membership as this sphere starts to form in separation from the properly private – on the fact that Eve is left to her pleasures within their bower while Adam meets his argumentative partner Raphael 'in the door' (5.299) – my focus has been on what is excluded when Adam changes in relation to Eve, on how the very fact that a public/private divide has begun to arise helps to hasten the fall. Eve only draws a boundary between the two of them after Adam draws a boundary between debate and pleasure with her.

To appreciate the value of such a focus, we might consider the episode in the context of the foregoing discussion of Diogenes. While Adam now wants argument only outside the domestic sphere – with God or angels, but not with his wife – Eve in this moment is more like Diogenes; if by pleasuring himself in the agora he brings the private into the public, by arguing in the garden Eve does the reverse. She views her relation with

Adam as not only pleasurable but also critical. And just as Diogenes is backed by instances in which bodily satisfaction is allowed in public, so is Eve backed by instances in which serious dispute belongs in the bower. Her view is odd only if domestic bliss and critique, affective susceptibility and argument, are considered separable, which for her they are not.[44] In just this vein, the spaces in which Adam talks to Raphael and to Eve (obviously) are quite similar; a fact of which Adam, acting as though the same sphere should be shaped into two, seems oddly unaware.

As I have said, Norbrook suggests that the fall takes place because of the garden's imperfect distinction between public and private – both because Satan can exploit Eve's simultaneous inclusion in and exclusion from the domain of Adam's conversations with Raphael, and because Adam and Eve exhibit an insufficiently sanitised 'practical prudence'.[45] In this respect, his argument implies that the story of the garden is valuable in showing how the fall takes place: because the garden is insufficiently modern, insufficiently Habermasian. Even as he appreciates how Habermasian divisions between public and private do not always hold, or do so deleteriously, Norbrook valorises how those divisions, properly realised, might produce a public subject who is invulnerable to passion.[46] The greatest value of the first couple's story as I have described it rests somewhere else entirely: in how unfallen argument, as Eve describes it in book 8, occurs in a realm of indistinction, one neither properly public nor properly private in the senses that Habermas and Norbrook attach to those terms; and in how the fall is precipitated at least as much by Adam's attempt at a nascent formation of separate spheres – marked off for argument and for enjoyment – as by the imperfect separation of those spheres. In book 9, we might say, Adam seems not so much insufficiently Habermasian (in excluding Eve) as actually too Habermasian in assuming a separation between public and private at all. Milton himself, on the other hand, does with Paradise what Diogenes does with the agora; he shows how it has been and can be a hybrid space – in this case, one where seemingly public uses of reason can be brought into ostensibly domestic spaces for ostensibly domestic ends. Milton shows how unfallen subjects are hybrid ones, critically disciplined but affectively open, indeed disciplined to enjoy open being better, joined with the 'other self' in an intersubjectivity beyond Habermasian imaginings.

Pleasing Sorcery: Public Reason in Milton's Pandemonium

For Adam and Eve, to fall is for caresses and conversations to cleave apart, their components degraded into burning lust and mutual accusation. The question that remains is how to remedy the fallen condition – to decide whether, for instance, argument and enjoyment must be thought apart to prevent further calamity in a fallen world, or whether Milton suggests ways to restore the lost hybridity of Paradise. One reaction to a fall – one doubtlessly present in the long view that Michael lays in front of Adam before he is exiled from Paradise – is to create internal and external safeguards so as to prove worthy of redemption. But another reaction, of principal interest here and premised on the notion that to fall is, in some real way, to fall for good, involves generating remedies for the present.

In book 2, I want to claim, Milton does just this. To demonstrate how he does so, I want to shift my contextual vocabulary, giving Diogenes (and Foucault's treatment of him) a background presence and bringing forward a figure more thoroughly applicable to this part of the epic as well as more central to the tradition of republican thought of which Milton was part and with which this chapter ends. Certainly, Diogenes is not the only classical antecedent of relevance to *Paradise Lost*'s exploration of public reason, pleasure and critical discipline; and with respect to book 2, we might most clearly view the issue through the lens of the Roman republican Cicero, with whom Milton has strong affinities, who is cited time and again as an exemplary figure in the prose writings (*Of Education* among them),[47] and whose disagreements with Plato, in certain important respects, are a classical analogue to the Foucault–Habermas debate as just outlined and to the tensions in book 2 as I see them.[48]

In this strand of public sphere theory, Plato resembles Habermas. In *Gorgias*, Socrates denounces oratory (and public life generally) on the basis of its saturation in affect and unconcern for discerning the good; philosophy, on the other hand, aims at the cultivation of control, self-mastery and a virtuous spirit.[49] Aimed as it is at gratification and pleasure, oratory for Socrates is akin to pastry-baking; Socrates opines that were he himself to argue in court and lead a more public life, he would be utterly out of place – like a doctor, accused by pastry chefs, before a jury of children (22–3, 105–6). Rather than the public being populated by mature men who refuse the empty pleasures which words can give, Socrates imagines a public filled with boys who know no better than to give themselves over to pleasure – than to believe that living pleasantly means what the interlocutor Callicles says it means, 'having as much as possible flow in' and judging orators' words only by the delight that they yield (67). Socrates and Habermas are by no means equivalent. But like Habermas (or, say, most of *Areopagitica*), in *Gorgias* Socrates would prefer that public selves be vigilant in their refusal of interactive gratification; like Habermas, he links discipline with distance; like Habermas, he suggests that pleasurable publics are immature and malformed.

Cicero regards public pleasure in a manner more closely resembling Foucault (if, surely, far from identical to Diogenes). Although heavily influenced by Stoic ideals of apathy that would make the public self passion-free,[50] contemptuous of immoderation[51] and outright appalled by agoric masturbatory practice,[52] Cicero is not a thoroughgoing Stoic and does, like Diogenes, assume that rational pleasure belongs in public. In part this is because Cicero believes that orators depend on pleasure – on audiences opening up to it – in order to be persuasive. In a series of treatises (including *De Inventione*, the three books of *De Oratore*, *Brutus*, *Orator* and several others), he ties persuasion to pleasure and reason to passion on the grounds that body and mind are intimately linked. When he explicitly parts with Platonic thinking, Cicero writes that in 'separat[ing] the science of wise thinking from that of elegant speaking', Socrates produced 'the undoubtedly absurd and unprofitable and reprehensible' practice of 'having one set of professors to teach us to think and another to teach us to speak'.[53] Cicero assumes that one cannot 'without disaster' separate the passions and pleasures that Socrates associates with the body from the rational practice that he associates with the mind (21). Effective public argument must be addressed to the total individual, and so persuasion requires not only 'the winning over' and 'the instructing' but also 'the stirring' of one's audience.[54]

One sure way to stir an audience is to please it. For Cicero, 'it is a peculiarly satisfactory experience for a man to take pleasure in conversation and seek to excel at it,'[55] and the ideal speaker uses this peculiar linguistic satisfaction to his advantage. An orator's words, for example, will have ornament and charm,[56] and will offer pleasure in every aspect of presentation – in the words, ideas, metaphors and rhythms of speech; all, to a real extent, is *ad delectionem*,[57] pitched toward a verbal delight that can 'escape causing satiety' and continue without end.[58] There is in fact 'such a charm about the mere power' of words 'that no impression more delightful than this can be received by the ear or the intelligence of man.'[59]

Cicero strays from both Socratic and Habermasian lines of thought not only by embracing the pleasures of public argument, but also by imagining the ideal orator as deploying enjoyable words in power-laden and even somewhat coercive ways. Cicero asserts that it is 'the most marvellous gift upon earth ... to be able to employ one's powers of speech to rivet men's attention, so that their wills are subjected to one's own';[60] through a kind of deliberate distortion, those who are eloquent are 'capable of elevating and enhancing anything they want to say' (269). While this may seem an unpalatable public practice, it is less so when one keeps in mind that Cicero's orator must engage in self-manipulation so as to manipulate his audience; as noted in Chapter 3, he must be 'on fire with passion, and inspired by something very like frenzy', 'not merely inflaming the arbitrator, but actually on fire himself'.[61] Like Foucault, Cicero does not focus on limiting pleasurable or power-laden (or power-laden because pleasurable) aspects of interaction but rather seeks to enlist those aspects for virtuous, salutary purposes. Because Ciceronian eloquence has the power to transform speaker and hearer alike, it also resembles its Foucaultian counterpart in the assumption that words – to Cicero 'the governing force in every tranquil and free community' – are world-making and transformative (223). Eloquence can affect the very bearing of others, can 'support the sinking and bend the upstanding' (331–3). Even more: the potent word is the 'soulbending sovereign of all things', which renders the eloquent 'armed to perform the most necessary tasks in the world', able 'to transfigure a spiritless and misguided nation, to revive its sense of honour, to reclaim a whole people from its errors'.[62]

Cicero does not violate divides nearly as flagrantly as does Diogenes exposed in the agora. But by linking argument and pleasure in a more liveable and quotidian – yet no less intense or transformative – way, Cicero supplements Foucault in explaining the mechanics of how pleasure and public reason belong together. If in this Cicero is usefully unlike Foucault, I have suggested that in his descriptions of oratorical puissance and rational pleasure he is like Foucault, more flexible as to what reason can and should be used to do than are Socrates, Habermas and Michael Warner alike.

Book 2 of *Paradise Lost*, I will now show, displays a similar flexibility. As the fallen angels fabricate a world for themselves – Pandemonium – they also form a number of 'public' spaces. In portraying them, Milton finds worth in forms of public being different from those advocated in the passages from *Areopagitica* cited earlier but similar to those implied in less defensive (if less frequent) moments of that same tract – where to regulate printing means to 'regulat all recreations and pastimes, all that is delightfull to man', where 'the passions within us', 'the pleasures round about us' need not be resisted too strongly.[63] Jesus himself, he who will be 'fully tried / Through all temptation' (1.4–5), who in *Paradise Regained* will resist all of Satan's offers and arguments, similarly faults Stoics for condemning all pleasure (4.304–5). In book 2 of *Paradise Lost*, Milton attends to the question of whether pleasure has worth when it derives from arguments, in this case arguments powerful

enough to transform those within earshot. Milton's conclusion, I want
to argue, is fraught but is more in keeping with the concession that Jesus
makes than with what his resistance to Satan itself suggests. And the
conclusion has consequences for how we think about publics. While
Habermas commends the emergence of public spaces for the discrimi-
nating rational autonomy that they are thought to enable[64] (and that the
first couple supposedly have in short supply), Milton dwells in book 2
on how spaces like them offer the experience of a rational delight like
that of unfallen experience in Eden, only more potent, more like the
delight felt in Ciceronian publics. Jesus, Milton makes obvious, is right
to resist Satan's arguments and offers of pleasure. How the fallen angels
should regard infernal reason, though, is not nearly so straightforward,
for their lot differs from that of the Son; their rational delight is as close
to heaven as they can ever get, and it takes precedence over the vigilance
that would ward off coercive emotional appeals – even when such vigilance may seem both important and easily achievable.

   In book 2, the fallen angels argue over what to do with themselves now
that they have been damned. And as they argue, strangely enough, Hell
seems relatively free of the conditions that we typically attach to communicative coercion. Consider, first, Satan's not entirely invalid (if also
not entirely honest) claim about the meaninglessness of status differen-
tials in Hell: since 'where there is then no good / For which to strive, no
strife can grow up there / From faction; for none sure will claim in hell /
Precedence, none, whose portion is so small / Of present pain, that with
ambitious mind / Will covet more' (2.30–4). Satan acknowledges status
difference – he is, after all, sitting on a 'throne of royal state' – but also
points to the fact that that throne is 'a safe unenvied throne / Yielded
with full consent' and that marks of greater 'status' are essentially marks
of greater pain, mooting ambition in Pandemonium. Second, while the
debate is limited to a handful of speakers, that handful is far more than
in the poem's other debates. Access to the debate, similarly, is granted
far more broadly than anywhere else in the poem, to at least a 'thousand demigods on golden seats', all of whom arguably could have taken
part (1.796, 2.1, 23–4). Third, everyone seems in happy agreement.
Toward the end of the debate – after Moloch, Belial and Mammon make
arguments – Beelzebub outlines a 'bold design', to have one of their host
attempt to infiltrate the garden. Full assent is given to that design, and
Beelzebub then waits, to no avail, for a demigod to 'second, or oppose'
the proposed attempt, which suggests that the last word ends up being
the word acted on because the debate has exhausted itself internally
(387–9, 419). Satan seems right to say that hell is structured with an
'advantage' to 'union, and firm faith, and firm accord', since the secret

conclave comes closer than any debate in the poem to supplying conditions for the speech situation, ideal for Habermas, that achieves inter-subjectivity without the serious erosion of discrete individuals. Nothing in Pandemonium seems to thwart the unfettered exercise of critical discipline pitched toward a reasoned, uncoerced consensus. Habermas, as promised in my title, has gone to Hell.

Or has he? Satan opens the debate by saying that 'he who can advise, may speak' (2.42), and yet debate, after just a handful of speakers, has already come to an end, provoking a series of questions – the first of which, perhaps, being why 996 demigods decide to sit quietly in their golden seats. Has none of them noticed that Beelzebub's speech seems to have been scripted by Satan? That, in giving voice to 'devilish counsel, first devised / By Satan' (2.379–80), he makes Satan's offer of himself appear more selfless and martyr-like than it is; that Satan has hidden his motive – the maintenance of status difference, obtained through, and desired for the sake of, glory? That he alone will be free of the 'dark opprobrious den of shame' that is Hell? That, as a result, a debate among relative equals ends up looking as predetermined as the discussion between Adam and God, such that a potentially revolutionary shift from absolute monarchy to parliamentary Hell fails to get the rebel angels anywhere? Why, for that matter, do numberless millions of the fallen inside the hall of this infernal court throng like 'fairy elves' engaged in 'midnight revels' instead of challenging the boundary that separates them from the 'secret conclave' of debate – instead of objecting to the fact that they, who had 'seemed / In bigness to surpass the earth's giant sons', are now shrunken into shapes 'less than smallest dwarves' (1.774–98)? Can they not see that this is simply more of the 'bad influence' (5.694–96) that Satan infused into Beelzebub's breast and that ended in their fall from Heaven? How can they be so unwary – why does the debate not spark outrage but make joy sparkle in their eyes (2.387–8)? Why do they not they rise up, en masse, and demand to be heard?

When they hear the plan, the host of hell instead voices 'loud acclaim', and so from one vantage the production of public opinion here is injudicious (2.519–20). In giving in to their affects, the fallen angels fail to see that the debate is based on a serious exclusion of potential participants and arguments. One could explain the demigods' silence by the 'awful reverence' with which they regard Satan (2.478). The docility of those kept out of the secret conclave could be seen in terms of Milton's oft-cited insistence on the inability of most English subjects to negotiate the difficult interpretive demands placed on them and their tendency to be coerced by emotional royalist appeals. Achinstein and Knoppers, as I have shown, claim just this. Their readings are plausible enough – joy is felt fleetingly here, and soon enough the fallen angels will, for a time, be changed into snakes. Their vulnerability is of a rather negative sort in that it has been mobilised for Satan and Beelzebub's plans to destroy humanity. No one voices the possibility that what has been called common interest is not really common; there is only the most minimal argumentative antagonism, and the fallen angels seem utterly susceptible, lacking even the slightest degree of evaluative detachment. From this perspective, the debate in Hell looks backward to Plato's publics of children and the pastry chefs who please them, and forward to Habermas's description of the recent deformation of publics, where the primary activity available to the dwarfed majority is the occasional opportunity to register 'loud acclaim' in response to the 'herald's voice' or the opinion poll. And so perhaps Habermas has not gone to Hell after all.

And yet I find myself believing that he has. I say this not just because a seemingly ideal Habermasian speech situation has failed to produce ideal, coercion-free critical debate (because Milton has a difficult time picturing such a debate even under Pandemonium's near-perfect conditions – because what seemed like a Habermasian framework goes up in flames). More importantly, Habermas goes to Hell when the narrator admires the agreement reached at the debate's end, when Milton constructs a space for argument in which the kind of critical discipline that enables uncoerced consensus is just not very important. 'O shame to men!' the narrator exclaims. 'Devil with devil damned / Firm concord holds, men only disagree / Of creatures rational' (496–8). The concord attained by the fallen angels – and granted Milton's temporary approbation – has nothing to do with the unforced force of superior arguments. The result is instead closer to Cicero's ideal speech situation, in which the minds of the audience are not just instructed (about options for bettering their lot), or won over (as to the plan to infiltrate the garden), but also stirred, even manipulated (to a moment of joy).

Although he counsels manipulation, Cicero would still frown at one aspect of this moment, since Satan and Beelzebub lack virtue. Milton would do the same but voices admiration anyway. Why? On one level, the debate is about the means by which to achieve an agreed goal (to improve, or at least not worsen, their collective condition). In that respect, it may be worth lamenting that 'common interest' is determined by far fewer individuals than initially appeared possible, and that those who stay silent accept the determination unflinchingly. But the debate is also pragmatic in a second and perhaps more important sense in so far as it goes beyond the attempt to produce agreement about improving their lot at a future point; if only temporarily, it also achieves the actual goal – 'Joy' – that supposedly motivates the debate to begin with.

C. S. Lewis, anticipating Achinstein's argument in a way, writes that the 'door out of Hell is firmly locked', that the debate is an attempt to find an escape from pain, 'to find some door other than the only door that exists'.[65] What Lewis neglects is the possibility that the rebel angels misread their plight and give in to joy's appeal fortuitously, perhaps even deliberately. Whether because or in spite of Satan's intentions (a distinction rendered irrelevant here), just discussing how to find a door out of Hell actually creates one; however power-laden this gathering at Pandemonium's court is – however much Satan exploits the demigods' vulnerability to affect – the gathering none the less brings a pleasurable world into being. In doing so, the debate in Hell offers a form of public life that does not demand the tabling of all aims other than future-directed critique. The debate demonstrates the capacity of public reason, even in the form of a coercive, partially staged argument, to suspend these problems simply by arguing over worlds without them. The fallen angels attend closely to the reality of their situation and imagine how that situation might be otherwise, their existence defined by more than just pain. Like Cicero's ideal orator, Beelzebub and Satan raise up the afflicted, changing their community of agony into something more enjoyable. Put another way, they discuss the door that would be like Foucault's *Ausgang* – that would open on to a world that is elsewhere yet within their current world – and in being persuaded of that door's existence it, however briefly, comes to be, offering the fallen angels an escape. The debate in Hell only fails if critical distance is considered paramount and if the debate's performative, world-making dimensions are deemed unfit or irrelevant or without worth.

A Habermasian reading like Achinstein's regards the scenes in Hell in just this fashion. For her, the fallen angels, overtaken by pleasure, display the critical insufficiency that landed them in Hell's unhappy mansion to begin with.[66] In such a reading, Milton's attitude toward the fallen angels is like that of Jesus toward the unredeemed – to those 'captive tribes' 'who wrought their own captivity' (3.414–15), those who are 'thus degenerate, by themselves enslaved' (4.144) – in *Paradise Regained*. The reading also accords with some of the narrator's judgements – for example, his claim that Belial counsels 'ignoble ease' 'with words clothed in reason's garb' (226–7) and his evident disdain for certain kinds of performance.[67] In other writing, Milton does fantasise about stripping audiences of self-control – in the *Second Defence of the English People* he hopes that readers have been 'conquered at last' by his arguments and will 'acknowledge themselves my captives'.[68] But the narrator's comments in book II are like those made in texts such as *Areopagitica* and *The Tenure of Kings and Magistrates*, where he is wary of those, perhaps like these fallen angels, too willing to 'strait give themselves up' into the hands of another authority,[69] those who 'desert their own reason, and shutting their eyes ... think they see best with other mens'.[70]

Milton could not fully sympathise with the secret conclave. But to deny his sympathy entirely requires that we as readers mistake the fallen angels' situation for that of, say, the Revolution, when the possibility for change seemed not just supreme but limitless, when pleasure might appear a mere temptation or distraction that would lead to a Restoration; it requires that we see their situation as one in which the past and possible future are all that count. In discussing that future, Mammon raises the possibility that

> Our torments also may in length of time
> Become our elements, these piercing fires
> As soft as now severe, our temper changed
> Into their temper; which must needs remove
> The sensible of pain.
>
> (2.274–8)

Beelzebub's staged speech in favour of infiltrating Eden trumps Mammon's presumably unstaged one counselling peace, but in allowing his speech to be trumped – in giving himself over to the pleasure afforded by Satan's bold performance – Mammon, in no time, gets just what he wants. The critical discipline needed to see this as his best option is the only kind he requires. In Hell, what matters most is not which argument for an imagined future wins – which *Ausgang* the fallen angels attempt to make permanent – but whether those arguments produce pleasure in the present, whether they permit infernal torments to be felt as therapeutic elements. For Cicero, the orator's greatest capacity is to verbally transform the sphere of his, and his audience's, existence, and Milton does not discount this. This public sphere is not simply immature; this is not naïve pastry-baking.

For these reasons, Milton's portrayal of Hell seems less a catalogue of how to guard against affective appeals and more a reflection on situations – easy for a disappointed, Restoration Milton to envision – in which discipline pitched toward building transparency, accuracy and uncoerced agreement pales in comparison to that pitched toward a therapeutic yield of pleasure. Indeed, as the portrayal of Pandemonium unfolds, consensus and even persuasion vanish altogether, while pleasurable contestation continues on. As Satan leaves, each angel pursues 'where he may likeliest find / Truce to his restless thoughts, and entertain, / The irksome hours' (2.524–7). Some gather to speak 'sweet' discourse, reasoning 'high'

> Of providence, foreknowledge, will and fate,
> Fixed fate, free will, foreknowledge absolute,
> And found no end, in wandering mazes lost.
> Of good and evil much they argued then,
> Of happiness and final misery,
> Passion and apathy, and glory and shame,
> Vain wisdom all, and false philosophy:
> Yet with a pleasing sorcery could charm
> Pain for a while or anguish, and excite
> Fallacious hope, or arm the obdured breast
> With stubborn patience as with triple steel.
>   (2.559–69)

In the first five of the above lines reason cannot, no less than the poem itself does not, bring the terms involved into cohesive relation. The rebels talk about providence, foreknowledge, will and fate, terms that stand in tension, and rather than synthesise, ideas rigidify into blatant opposition; fate becomes fixed rather than mutable, will free rather than constrained, foreknowledge not partial but absolute. The more reasoning one does with these terms, the more one attempts to accommodate them to a principle of non-contradiction – to make the terms, like Habermasian selves, agree with one another – the more inevitable entrance into a wandering maze becomes.

Yet the possibility soon arises that the fallen angels may mean, in the end, for the terms not to come together – that a wandering brand of critical discipline has worth, if pleasure or comfort, instead of transparent understanding or agreement, is taken as one of rational sociability's legitimate ends. The rebels, who have been 'reasoning high', now 'argue'. 'Argument' in Milton's period can be understood not only as a process by which a series of statements are connected in order to establish a position and persuade an addressee, but also (like the paragraph of 'Argument' with which each book of the epic begins) as simply a summary or abstract of a subject matter, a specification of content. The 'argument' in these lines moves toward the latter sense, becomes the open-ended specification of content – the content of good, evil, happiness, misery, passion, apathy, glory, shame. Unlike in *Areopagitica*, reason here is anything but choosing, anything but arriving at consensus. Rational discourse in these moments is at once critical and speculative or fantasmatic; delighting in one another's company, the fallen angels proliferate argument without aiming to arrive at a single answer, losing themselves in labyrinths of their own design.

And the more complex the partitioning is – the more turns and shifts they build in – the better; outside the space of conversation, they are left only with 'fallacious hope', 'stubborn patience' for what has yet to arrive. Their conversation ought to go on as long as possible, since it is, after all, 'pleasing sorcery', mystification, the wilful transformation of the space that aims to damn them into uncertain, pleasurable terms. The very words, such as good and evil, by which God condemns the rebels are the ones by which they charm pain and anguish, arm themselves with patience, imagine their world otherwise. They give and receive the words that could wound only to experience their charm. Having relinquished their ability to make final discriminations and decisions, they render their existence more liveable. Even if this false philosophy excites hopes never to be fulfilled, the fallen angels use critical discourse to alleviate, if only for a moment, dominant power's hold over them, interactively bringing an alternate discursive world into being.

By making themselves vulnerable to words their world becomes just the same. If Hell is God's supply chest, the same 'dark materials' with which He might create new worlds belong also (if not equally) to them (2.916), and in wandering they achieve an imaginative *Ausgang*. Whereas Habermas believes that the willingness to give in to affect makes one unsuitable for public argument, for the fallen angels that willingness is precisely what makes those arguments worthwhile; likewise, whereas Achinstein sees but weakness in their susceptibility to each other's words – their 'failings in . . . apprehending the simple truth of God's eminence' – such susceptibility may also be their greatest source of strength, their truest escape from torment.[71]

To address what Milton might think of the fallen angels' rational, imaginative practice, we could note that, although what they do is just what Raphael advises Adam against doing, that advice is at best half-hearted. His injunction to '[d]ream not of other worlds' (8. 174–5)[72] is difficult to take seriously, because to become concerned with hidden matters – the very ones with which *Paradise Lost* concerns itself – and to dream of other worlds is not just what the fallen angels do; it is what Adam and Raphael do, too. Adam seems to agree that he should keep his eyes on things of practical use, but he none the less goes on to say how pleasant Raphael's convoluted, lengthy and very speculative response about heavenly bodies has been. Words, Adam claims, 'bring to their sweetness no satiety'. And the angel, for his part, agrees: 'for I attend, / Pleased with thy words no less than thou with mine' (8.179–216, 1–3, 11.247–8). Raphael, 'affable archangel', 'sociable spirit', himself disregards his injunction against dreaming of other worlds; instead, the angel's advice looks less like sincere position-taking than a way to lengthen his sweet discourse with Adam, just as the fallen angels argue about apathy as a way to please one another (7.41, 5.221).

This sort of speculative rationality resembles the 'mystical dance' of angels, which, like the movement of planets, has a design and aim – a discipline – just one that is not readily recognisable, and indeed that exhibits most design when it seems to exhibit no identifiable design at all, when it forms 'mazes intricate, / Eccentric, yet intervolved, yet regular / Then most when most irregular they seem' (5.622–4). This resembles the narrator's own practice as described at the beginning of books 3 – when he cannot help but 'wander where the muses haunt' – and 7 – when, 'Dismounted, on the Aleian field . . . / Erroneous there to wander and forlorn', Urania's company consoles him (3.26, 7.19–20). Conversation can make even the fallen angels' hill like earth itself, which after the creation of land 'seemed like to heaven, a seat where gods might dwell / Or wander with delight, and love to haunt her sacred shades' (7.328–9).

Because of such resemblances between Milton's practice and that of the fallen angels, I cannot help but imagine him tempted – indeed tempted to the point of sympathy – by their pleasing sorcery. In the *Second Defense*, Milton writes of his desire to withdraw from the given world, of '[h]ow many things there are . . . which I have no desire to see . . . how many things that I should be glad not to see, how few remain that I would like to see.'[73] Milton devotes the entire first book of his *History of Britain* to the obscure part of his country's past, 'like one who had set out on his way by night, and travail'd through a Region of smooth or idle Dreams'.[74] He registers very early on in his commonplace book that practised patience and indolence are not the same,[75] and while he sees how the fallen angels at times succumb to the latter, his situation under Charles II must have driven home the real value of the former – as it must have for Cicero himself after his exclusion from the Forum. Time and again in Cicero's writings we are told of how '[a] man's mind . . . is nourished by learning and reasoning,' and how 'he is led by a delight in seeing and hearing' – how, 'whenever we are free from necessary business and other concerns we are eager to see or to hear or to learn, considering that the discovery of obscure or wonderful things is necessary for a blessed life.'[76]

The turn from 'administration' to philosophy – and especially to rational pleasure – allows those engaged in discussion to escape their plight, to locate an *Ausgang*; how enjoyable it is, by spinning out conversation as long as possible, to forget the 'common misery', to exclude past and future alike within the interactive present[77] – to engage with one's interlocutor and to follow discourse, as Antonius does Crassus's in *De Oratore*, 'to the exclusion of everything else'.[78] Even for Cicero, so focused on how persuasion happens, this means allowing discussion to wander: 'We should have considered what to do when we were embarking,' he remarks at one point, with a mock-seriousness like that of Raphael, 'now we must certainly spread our sails to the wind, no matter where it will carry us.'[79] In youth Milton had 'tasted by no means superficially the sweetness of philosophy'[80] and in the youthful *Comus* he portrays brothers, who have lost their sister, consoling themselves with a philosophy whose powers they praise in very Ciceronian terms: 'How charming is divine Philosophy!' the younger of these brothers exclaims. 'Not harsh and crabbed as dull fools suppose, / But musical as is Apollo's lute, / And a perpetual feast of nectared sweets, / Where no crude surfeit reigns' (476–80).[81] I cannot help but imagine that Milton felt something similar while creating his Restoration epic. Cut off now from the cheerful ways of men, disappointed, hiding, experiencing the agony that Satan and Adam do when they express themselves while alone, with his poem he consoled himself, imagining a life around others. I cannot help but see him speaking the language of a critical discipline that wanders in pleasure, the one spoken by the fallen angels, a discipline that embraces vulnerability and whose accomplishment resides in its exercise, in the mere enunciation of enjoyable words. I cannot help but picture him taken in by the public life of Pandemonium.

Milton's Place in the History of Publics and Republics

I have been arguing that Milton respects even as he is wary of the pleasures of critical discipline. This means that his epic can be understood to occupy more than just a Habermasian place in theories of public selfhood, and I want to end by explaining some consequences of this for the place of *Paradise Lost* in the history of the public sphere and, consequently, of English republicanism. In my reading of Adam and Eve, I examined how unfallen debate can occur in a zone of indistinction, within which ostensibly 'public' and ostensibly 'private' behaviours coincide. There, I suggested that the structural transformation of the garden – the cleaving apart of reason and pleasure, and the cordoning off of each into a separate space – would be a lamentable event. In this sense Milton longs for forms of public life whose relationship to the past would not be defined by sharp breaks – and certainly not by the self's emergence, in public space, as a bounded actor who would declare affective vulnerability immature and leave it wholeheartedly behind. My procedure has been to position Milton with respect to Cicero and

Foucault on the one hand and Plato and Habermas on the other, so I am no doubt methodologically inclined not to see such sharp breaks in how public selves appear and operate. In this case at least, non-literary texts give some warrant to this inclination, since Milton's portrayal of pleasing sorcery in book 2 mirrors a recorded instance of the self in public that is just as complicated as the cases of that book and of Adam and Eve – an instance which shows how the alleged transformation of the public sphere in early modernity retains reason and pleasure within a single complex.

Specifically, the fallen angels' pleasing sorcery resembles what was said to take place in the English coffeehouse.[82] The first of these in England appeared in 1650, and much of what was said to have gone on there – in reports both negative and positive – seems largely unrelated to the brief account that Habermas offers, and more closely related to what the fallen angels do when they speak sweet discourse to improve the irksome hours.[83] First, just as the fallen angels do not arrive at an answer when they argue about fate, so consensus was not generally considered the aim in the coffeehouse; it was a place 'where men of differing judgments croud',[84] where various positions mingled without aiming for synthesis – where disagreement and speculative argument went on until the doors closed.[85] As one pamphleteer put it, '[i]nfinite are the Contests, irreconcileable the Differences here.'[86] Second, coffee-house interaction was characterised by its detractors as an unsupervised form of chatter[87] that could transform participants (in some cases, from men into women), and that had more to do with pleasure than with the search for truth through the exercise of affect-free critical discipline. Like the pleasing sorcery that charms the fallen angels, coffeehouse life, as one broadside had it, resembled the 'shifting Scenes' on an 'Inchanted Island' where 'who knows what magick may be a working.'[88] Just as these angels generate arguments so as to keep the conversation going, the effect of coffee was 'more than Magick';[89] coffeehouses were full of 'bottomless stories', 'joys built on vanity' that were 'worse than Hell of Brimstone'.[90] Another response, praising the coffeehouse for reasons similar to those for which it was condemned, claims that 'man is a sociable creature, and delights in company . . . Discourse is Pabulum Animi, cos Ingenij, The minds Dyet, and the great Whet-stone of Ingenuity.'[91]

Histories of the coffeehouse, including those that describe its pleasures, tend to place focus elsewhere, but both early Whig defenders and Tory opponents characterised it as a space populated by radically susceptible selves – ones who (again, like the fallen angels) gave voice, and gave in, to the pleasurable, creative crowding of differing judgements and arguments, to imagining the world otherwise than it was.[92] So while Achinstein focuses on how Milton carves a place for himself in a Habermasian history of public selfhood and advocates a 'fit reader' who would do none of these things,[93] when considered in the context of writings just cited, the pleasing sorcery of book 2 shows just the opposite: how the history of the public self has been and can be defined in part by vulnerability, how those who employ critical discipline can and should continue to give in to affect when new spaces for public argument arise.

Broader ramifications of this historical point come from looking at the consequences of Milton's thinking about public selves for his thinking about English republican ones. For Norbrook and Achinstein, as I have said, the cultivation of critical distance enables civic virtue as a form of positive liberty, an exercise of 'rights to' (in terms, for instance, of free speech and political participation); in turn, such cultivation also helps individuals secure negative freedoms or 'rights against' (say, the seizure of property or person). For them, critical distance and some (however incomplete) degree of popular sovereignty are the mutually reinforcing pair at the core of what makes Milton republican. In this sense, Miltonists who draw on Habermas resemble several prominent historians of seventeenth-century republicanism discussed elsewhere in this book,[94] including J. G. A. Pocock, Blair Worden, Quentin Skinner and Jonathan Scott – all of whom, like Zera Fink much earlier, link (usually checked) levels of popular sovereignty to a proper republican bearing, one defined by rational self-control set largely against passion and wholly against passivity.[95] Just as Achinstein claims that the verbal explosion of the early modern public sphere demanded critical vigilance, so do these accounts of the possible English republic claim that the mid-century governmental collapse, isolating the individual as never before, put him (as Pocock puts it) 'in possession of his conscience', with reason as his strongest weapon; he would have to 'consider which of the contending parties had done the least to bring about the breakdown and deserved to be entrusted with restoring the balance, and act as his resolution directed him'.[96] As is probably obvious, I would argue that like readings directed through a Habermasian lens, these readings are plausible but partial; they see Milton setting the exercise of reason against the experience of passion too insistently and set republican selfhood within a rather narrow frame, one more appropriate for a figure like James Harrington, for whom 'reason and passion are two things' unambiguously and uniformly opposed, as are 'two potent rivals . . . in continual suit'.[97]

But such treatments (like Norbrook's own)[98] also acknowledge the openness of republicanism as a conceptual structure.[99] For all that accounts just mentioned oppose the republican use of reason and the experience of passion more rigidly than would Cicero or Milton, then, all also are well aware that the republican moment was, in Norbrook's terms, 'a period of experiment',[100] not of knowing precisely what it meant to be republican but of imagining what it might mean. Regicide, Pocock reminds us, took place not in order to form a well-conceived republic; instead 'the several doctrines which may be called republican ... were articulated as men came to face the fact that the historic constitution had collapsed, and to formulate various moral, political and theoretical problems with which its collapse confronted them.'[101] For Cicero and Milton, two central figures in the history of republicanism, one such problem was how to use public reason after the collapse of the constitution and in the absence of any real balance between the one, the few and the many, and if both advocate openness to pleasure as one of reason's most salutary ends, then for them that rational pleasure – and the vulnerable selves opened up to it – are an important part of, even as they may be an impediment to, republican ways of being. As with his conception of the public sphere, then, we would struggle to find in Milton the emergence of a republicanism that leaves pleasure outside its boundaries.

The connection between the open quality of republican thought and of Milton's publics becomes stronger if we bear in mind that when Milton imagined what his affiliation meant to him, being republican and being without a republic went hand in hand. Mid-century English republicanism occurred very much in the imaginations of Milton, Harrington, Marchamont Nedham and others; it was not, or not for any sustained period, an English reality.[102] Even as Milton himself wrote *The Ready and Easy Way* – even as he voiced 'hopes of a speedy and immediate settlement forever in a firm and free commonwealth' – England was on the verge of the Restoration.[103] Writing the pamphlet was a republican act without any real chance of a republic, a thought experiment, a dream of a better and more durable world that was likely, Milton knew, to remain unreal. Still, simply imagining that this world could come to be, readily and easily, must have been some comfort, a use of reason that gladdened him. Perhaps the compensation was more than inconsiderable, given that such use of reason could ease even the fallen angels' anguish.

While Worden sees in these later years of Milton's life a withdrawal from politics,[104] Norbrook, Achinstein and I would not, would claim that Milton's republican politics persist. But we would have differing senses of what counts as 'politics'. They lean heavily on ways that Milton, though he lacked the political influence that he had in the 1640s or early 1650s, remains focused on changing the state – in, for instance, the actual programme of the *Ready and Easy Way*, or in wishing for the citizenry needed to carry that programme out. As suggested by the very titles of their books, public life for Norbrook and Achinstein is exciting partly for this reason, for its capacity to effect revolution and rewrite the English republic. The fallen angels' publics thus cannot be of much political interest; they are incapable of communication with God's sphere of true legislation. From such a perspective, the fallen angels are socially and politically enfeebled because they cannot create a lasting future for themselves, having lost a reliable horizon in the moment that they were swayed by Satan. This perspective, however, relies on a separation between speaking and making, and on subordinating the former to the latter – a subordination that, as Hannah Arendt points out, leads to the classification of all occupations centred on 'performance' as the lowest, least productive form of work, since playing a flute, or acting, or arguing for its own sake, are unpredictable and impermanent in their effects and cannot add to the fabrication of a lasting world occupied by stable, well-fortified individuals.[105] When changing the state is the primary goal of politics, speaking is only of instrumental worth, only in so far as it leads to the making defined as a decisively improved future for bounded selfhood: one with superior laws, better rights, increased freedom. For Norbrook and Achinstein, Milton's speech remains political – and republican – in its attempt to build this future.

With Norbrook and Achinstein, I have suggested that Milton does not retreat from politics; unlike them, I have also suggested that parts of his poem eschew legislative aims as the prime end of politics, and that at times he turns away from the public spheres that find their reason for being in helping steer the state with utmost vigilance. Milton was long sceptical about what law could be used to do,[106] and all the speaking that he and others did about a lasting English republic did not end in that republic's making; and so late in his career he effaced the separation, made speaking into a form of making. So doing, he links the fallen angels to a more modest, if perhaps more fanciful, tradition of thinking about publics and politics – one focused on the pleasures we take from giving reasons, one that makes worlds, and remakes selves, with words, a tradition lodged within what we call republican.

This is to say that not all moments are comparable to the headstrong moments of *Areopagitica* and *The Tenure of Kings and Magistrates*. Intrinsic to much of Milton's republican thinking is this awareness that true republican states were rare and fragile, their legal architecture likely to crumble under the blows of ambition and fortune. Ways to live among the ruins would have to be found.[107] For this reason, being republican often meant developing practices for living without, or even assuming the absence of, true republics – for finding consolation while under tyranny and on the margin, as Marcus Tullius Cicero banished from the Forum, as John Milton cut off from office. Like his publics, Milton's republicanism was often focused on the strenuous civic virtue and self-control that English subjects would have to employ to protect themselves as citizenry, to make real the republican commonwealth and somehow make it last; but as a republican he also dwelt on the rational delight felt by vulnerable selves within the publics which formed without the actual republic's precarious, then vanished existence.

Such delight saves Pandemonium, gives it structure and keeps it, however tenuously, from becoming Chaos. Giving up distance in favour of susceptibility and immanence – in favour of opening up to discussion's delights – the fallen angels' false philosophy appears as the imagined 'otherwise' of Foucaultian reason, the 'exclusion of everything else' that takes place in Cicero. The fallen angels find exits, ones which need not be dismissed simply because they are contingent on the space and time of interaction, simply because these are exits that can never open on to rooms in some concrete, definitively improved future backed by the force of law.[108] Rather, they reveal the degree of their world's constructedness and, thereby, afford the fallen angels the creation of a passing but liveable present. At the same time, their public reason – the republicanism of Pandemonium – might be said to offer a future as well, one always indefinite and impermanent but also always possible, a future in which such a present, and the presence of salutary vulnerability, can be had again.

Notes

1. See the title essay of his *Politics and Passion: Toward a More Egalitarian Liberalism* (New Haven, CT: Yale University Press, 2004), 110–30. For another exploration of this issue, see the essays collected in Jane Gallop (ed.), *Polemic: Critical and Uncritical* (New York: Routledge, 2004); and for accounts that examine the dynamics between political selves and passionate ones in the early modern period, see Victoria Kahn, Neil Saccamano and Daniela Coli (eds), *Politics and the Passions, 1500–1850* (Princeton, NJ: Princeton University Press, 2006).
2. As I will point out later on, this is the case in an article that Warner wrote with Lauren Berlant, 'Sex in Public', *Critical Inquiry* 24 (1998), 547–66; an interview with Annamarie Jagose, 'Queer World-Making', *Genders* 31 (2000); 'Publics and Counterpublics', *Public Culture* 14 (2002), 49–90; as well as Warner's book-length summation of his thinking on these topics, *Publics and Counterpublics* (New York: Zone, 2002).
3. John Staines, Michael Schoenfeldt and Anne Ferry all have noticed the conjunction of reason and affect or passion in Milton, each in a differ-

ent way. See Staines, 'Compassion in the Public Sphere of Milton and Charles', and Schoenfeldt, '"Commotion Strange": Passion in *Paradise Lost*', both of which are collected in Gail Kern Paster, Katherine Rower and Mary Floyd Wilson (eds), *Reading the Early Modern Passions: Essays in the Cultural History of Emotion* (Philadelphia, PA: University of Pennsylvania Press, 2004). See Ferry, 'Milton's Creation of Eve', in *Studies in English Literature, 1500–1900*, 28 (1988), 113–32. For a more general recent account of the dynamics of rhetoric and passion, from Plato and Aristotle to Sidney and Milton, see Robert Cockcroft, *Rhetorical Affect in Early Modern Writing* (New York: Palgrave MacMillan, 2003).

4. See 'Enlightenment as Process: Milton and Habermas', *PMLA* 106:5 (1991), 1156, 1158, 1165, 1167. A similar argument has been advanced by Victoria Kahn, who claims that Milton's republican thinking construes both biblical covenant and political contract as rational, open-ended and revocable. See 'The Metaphorical Contract in Milton's *Tenure of Kings and Magistrates*', in David Armitage, Armand Himy and Quentin Skinner (eds), *Milton and Republicanism* (Cambridge: Cambridge University Press, 1995), 82–105. In another article, Kahn explicitly connects Habermas to Renaissance humanism more generally. See 'Habermas, Machiavelli, and the Humanist Critique of Ideology', *PMLA* 105:3 (1990), 468.

5. 'Religion, Science, and Printing in the Public Spheres of England', in Craig Calhoun (ed.), *Habermas and the Public Sphere* (Cambridge, MA: MIT Press, 1992), 219. See also Zaret's *Origins of Democratic Culture* (Princeton, NJ: Princeton University Press, 2000). For a more recent example of this argument, see Matthew Jordan's *Milton and Modernity* (New York: Palgrave Macmillan, 2001).

6. For some of the most recent accounts of the early modern public sphere and its consequences for selfhood (accounts written from perspectives that overlap with those so far described to varying degrees), see Zaret's *Origins*, as well as Kevin Sharpe's *Reading Revolutions: The Politics of Reading in Early Modern England* (New Haven, CT: Yale University Press, 2000); Jennifer Anderson and Elizabeth Sauer (eds), *Books and Readers in Early Modern England: Material Studies* (Philadelphia, PA: University of Pennsylvania Press, 2002); Sharpe and Steven N. Zwicker (eds), *Reading, Society and Politics in Early Modern England* (Cambridge: Cambridge University Press, 2003); and Sauer, '*Paper-contestations*' and *Textual Communities in England, 1640–1675* (Toronto: University of Toronto Press, 2005).

7. *Writing the English Republic: Poetry, Rhetoric, and Politics, 1627–1660* (New York: Cambridge University Press, 1999), 485, 486–7. Jordan, similarly, draws a parallel between heavenly society and the worldview of the emergent seventeenth-century bourgeoisie, a view underpinned by the progressive 'experience and practice of a collectivist individualism . . . that effected an ongoing, dynamic integration of freedom and equality with differences of rank' (55). According to a critic like Annabel Patterson, we are justified in regarding Milton not merely as an English republican or a 'grand Whig' but as an enlightened early modern liberal. See *Early Modern Liberalism* (Cambridge: Cambridge University Press, 1997), esp. 62–89.

8. *Milton and the Revolutionary Reader* (Princeton, NJ: Princeton University Press, 1994), 25. This is also the argument in the chapter of Achinstein's book that I will treat below, and in Chapter 4 of that book, 'Reading in the Revolution: *Eikonoklastes* and the Battle of Perspectives'.

9. See Ernest Sirluck (ed.), *Complete Prose Works of John Milton*, vol. II (New Haven, CT: Yale University Press, 1959), 521, 516, 547, 558.

10. References are from Stephen Orgel and Jonathan Goldberg (eds), *The Major Works* (Oxford: Oxford University Press, 1991).

11. In *The Tremulous Private Body*, Barker argues that if *Areopagitica* marks an important moment in the emergence of the individual, the subject is still a subjected subject, the reflex of a larger system; Milton's proposal, far from being that anyone ought to be allowed to say anything, is simply that censorship ought to take place after rather than before publication. In both his early *Surprised by Sin* and his recent *How Milton Works*, Fish, though starting out from a somewhat different set of assumptions, arrives at a position ultimately akin to Barker's. Without relying on the historical shift that Barker traces, Fish argues simply for the primacy of Milton's religious proclivities, his emphasis on internal activity, its attendant exclusions and readerly inadequacies; the maintenance of a state of perpetual Christian watchfulness requires the reader, like Barker's 'modern' subject, to interiorise conflict rather than seek to resolve it in a public forum. See Barker, *The Tremulous Private Body: Essays on Subjection* (London: Methuen, 1984), esp. 31, 48. See Fish, *Surprised By Sin* (New York: St Martin's, 1967), esp. 4; and *How Milton Works* (Cambridge, MA: Belknap, 2001), esp. 31, 56–7.

12. See, for example, Henry Weinfield's 'Skepticism and Poetry in Milton's Infernal Conclave', in *Studies in English Literature, 1500–1900*, 45:1 (2005), esp. 206; and Peter Herman's *Destabilizing Milton: Paradise Lost and the Poetics of Incertitude* (New York: Palgrave Macmillan, 2005). Weinfield and Herman both refine William Empson's argument in *Milton's God* (London: Chatto & Windus, 1965).

For a typical reading of the fallen angels, see Achinstein, who argues that the perplexed wandering of the fallen angels is 'similar to Spenserian error but also to Milton's own concept of failed virtue' (213). See John Staines (n. 3, above) for a Habermasian framework that works hard to accommodate affect.

13. The difficulty in presenting a totalising view of Milton is a primary theme of Herman's *Destabilizing Milton*, especially in the compelling introductory sections; but acknowledgement of this difficulty can also be found in the work of Arthur Barker, John Rogers and Stephen M. Fallon. See Barker, *Milton and the Puritan Dilemma, 1641–1660* (Toronto: University of Toronto Press, 1990), esp. 217; Rogers, *The Matter of Revolution: Science, Poetry, and Politics in the Age of Milton* (Ithaca, NY: Cornell University Press, 1996), esp. 109; and Fallon, *Milton Among the Philosophers: Poetry and Materialism in Seventeenth-Century England* (Ithaca, NY: Cornell University Press, 1991).

14. It would be nearly impossible to summarise the articles and books that address this topic. For the classic collection of essays that frame and comment on the 'debate', see Michael Kelly (ed.), *Critique and Power:*

Recasting the Foucault/Habermas Debate (Cambridge, MA: MIT Press, 1994). For a brief overview of some of the issues currently at play in discussions of these theorists, see David Ingram, 'Foucault and Habermas', in Gary Gutting (ed.), *The Cambridge Companion to Foucault*, 2nd edn (Cambridge: Cambridge University Press, 2005).

15. Habermas thinks that critical discipline serves this purpose and that hope for agreement is at the foundation of debate's very existence. If the fact of debate implies that we do not agree, we only bother to debate and to exercise critical discipline so that we will. See *Reason and the Rationalization of Society*, vol. 1 of *The Theory of Communicative Action*, trans. Thomas McCarthy (Boston, MA: Beacon, 1984), 25.

16. See 'The Entwinement of Myth and Enlightenment: Horkheimer and Adorno', in *The Philosophical Discourse of Modernity*, trans. Frederick Lawrence (Cambridge, MA: MIT Press, 1987), esp. 111 and 129. See also his account of the rise and fall of the public sphere from the eighteenth to the twentieth centuries in *The Structural Transformation of the Public Sphere: an Inquiry into a Category of Bourgeois Society*, trans. Thomas Burger with Frederick Lawrence (Cambridge, MA: MIT Press, 1989). For the standard collection of essays that explore this theme, see Maurizio Passerin d'Entrèves and Seyla Benhabib (eds), *Habermas and the Unfinished Project of Modernity* (Cambridge, MA: MIT Press, 1997).

17. See *Reason and the Rationalization of Society*, esp. '"Rationality": A Preliminary Specification', 19, as well as 8–42 more generally. See also 'Discourse Ethics: Notes on a Program of Philosophical Justification', 43–115, in *Moral Consciousness and Communicative Action* (Cambridge, MA: MIT Press, 1990).

18. See, for example, 'Truth and Power', in *Power/Knowledge: Selected Interviews and Other Writings* (New York: Pantheon, 1980), 109–33.

19. See, among other texts, Joseph Pearson (ed.), *'Society Must Be Defended'* (New York: Picador, 2003), 70, and *Fearless Speech* (Los Angeles, CA: Semiotext(e), 2001), as well as Frederic Gros (ed.), *The Hermeneutics of the Subject: Lectures at the Collège de France, 1981–2* (New York: Palgrave Macmillan, 2005), esp. 371–412. See Nancy Fraser for perhaps the most prominent critique related to the Foucaultian critique invoked above, in 'Rethinking the Public Sphere: A Contribution to the Critique of Actually Existing Democracy', in *Social Text, No. 25/26* (1990), esp. 62–3.

20. Foucault describes this in his account of the 'provocative dialogue' that Diogenes engages in with Alexander; in their dialogue, the former infuriates the latter by disrupting his sense of himself, revealing that Alexander is not what he thought he was, that his rule has been hardly masterful. See *Fearless Speech*, 124–33. As critics have noted, this mode of interaction, while not a focal point in the following account of ways that Milton is not Habermasian, is unfamiliar neither to him nor to *Paradise Lost*. In an article written after *The Tremulous Private Body*, Barker attends to just this. See 'In the Wars of Truth', *Southern Review* 20 (1987), 119.

21. Habermas has famously argued that Foucault is a sceptic of enlightenment and of public reason. See *The Philosophical Discourse of Modernity*, 238–93. As should become clear, Foucault, particularly later in his career, is sceptical only of certain traditions of enlightened public reason.

22. *The Structural Transformation*, 27–30.
23. *The Philosophical Discourse of Modernity*, 113, 317.
24. *Fearless Speech*, 122.
25. 'What is Enlightenment?', in *Essential Works of Foucault, 1954–1984*, vol. 1: *Ethics: Subjectivity and Truth* (New York: New Press, 1997), 313.
26. See 'What is Critique?', in James Schmidt (ed.), *What is Enlightenment?: Eighteenth Century Answers and Twentieth Century Questions* (Berkeley, CA: University of California Press, 1996), 384.
27. See 'The Entwinement of Myth and Enlightenment', in *The Philosophical Discourse of Modernity*, as well as *Reason and the Rationalization of Society*, esp. 43–74, for more on this.
28. See 'Publics and Counterpublics', 89, and 82–9 for his full statement of the world-making properties of publics.
29. See 'Sex in Public' and, relatedly, 'Queer World-Making'.
30. See his *Rhetorical Affect in Early Modern Writing*, esp. 'Ideas of *pathos* from Plato to Milton', 40–73.
31. See Staines, Schoenfeldt and several of the essays collected in *Politics and the Passions*. A philosophical basis for the 'single complex' possibility can be found in the rejection of dualism on the part of Milton and others. Rogers's *The Matter of Revolution* and Fallon's *Milton Among the Philosophers* point this out. While I agree with the linking of spirit and matter in Rogers's and Fallon's accounts, I put that link to different use. Rogers uses Milton's monism not to focus on the subject's vulnerability to passion but to show his interest, if not his consistent faith, 'in a liberal political philosophy' derivable from an 'abstract logic of the equal allocation of power and responsibility to discrete and only loosely related elements' (111, 109). Fallon argues that Milton simply shifts freedom of the will from 'separable incorporeal substance' to 'the universal animation of matter' (246). I, by contrast, will emphasise how the inseparability of rational and material substance compromises individual autonomy.
32. Norbrook's reading of the fall extends from 480 to 491 of *Writing the English Republic*. The tradition in which Norbrook writes certainly pre-dates the inception of Habermasian early modern criticism. In terms of accounts written in the last half-century, lines of thinking similar to Norbrook's can be found, for example, in Lewis's *A Preface to Paradise Lost* (New York: Oxford University Press, 1961), 125–8; Northrop Frye's *The Return of Eden: Five Essays on Milton's Epic* (Toronto: University of Toronto Press, 1965), 63–9; Joan Bennett's *Reviving Liberty* (Cambridge, MA: Harvard University Press, 1989), 109–18; and Jordan's *Milton and Modernity*, 95–114.
33. See *Writing the English Republic*, 484, 488.
34. For Norbrook's own account of Satan and the fallen angels, see *Writing the English Republic*, 450–5.
35. For one example of how this works, see Achinstein's account of Milton's use of similes, how they 'perform a task of separating the reader from immediate experience of the events transpiring in hell' and 'call for readers to make interpretations, to be prompted to apply readerly skills and power'. *Milton and the Revolutionary Reader*, 217–18.

36. *Milton and the Revolutionary Reader*, 213. See Chapter 5, 'Milton and the Fit Reader: *Paradise Lost* and the Parliament of Hell', 177–223, for Achinstein's full argument.

37. See *Historicizing Milton: Spectacle, Power, and Poetry in Restoration England* (Athens, GA: University of Georgia Press, 1994), esp. Chapter 3, '*Paradise Lost* and the Politics of Joy', 67–95.

38. *Writing the English Republic*, 485, 486–7.

39. Another example of an episode that might be said to have positive affinities with Habermasian ideals is the debate between Satan and Abdiel in book 5. Carrol Cox has argued that this debate has less to do with such clashes than with the rise, in the seventeenth century, of a kind of abstract individuality that enables open, status-free discussion. I, by contrast, would argue that by being disagreeable, Satan, like a *parrhesiastes*, provokes Abdiel, who in turn emphasises the irreversible, closed nature of the game that ends in the expulsion from Heaven, and thereby (inadvertently) reveals that in God's kingdom, certain matters should not be open to debate, since to do so would be to reveal the split by which sovereign, heavenly discourse articulates its non-universal nature, its self-conscious interest in something other than common interest: its refusal, that is, of abstract individuality. See Cox's 'Citizen Angels: Civil Society and the Abstract Individual in *Paradise Lost*', *Milton Studies XXIII* (Pittsburgh, PA: University of Pittsburgh Press, 1987), 165–96.

40. *Writing the English Republic*, 487, 485.

41. For an account of the role of pleasure and persuasion in the fall that supplies an impressive and illuminating amount of contextual background, see James Grantham Turner's *One Flesh: Paradisal Marriage and Sexual Relations in the Age of Milton* (Oxford: Clarendon, 1987), esp. 291–309.

42. For a recent version of this argument, see Chapter 6 of Herman's *Destabilizing Milton*, 127–54.

43. In *Doctrine and Discipline of Divorce*, Milton mentions the 'rational burning' that marriage is to remedy, but in that tract, as well as *Tetrachordon* and *Colasterion*, he consistently emphasises that what we look for in marriage is 'sweet and gladsome society', 'conversing solace' that is 'fit and matchable', 'free and lightsome'. Indeed, a good marriage is conceived of as a break from the more strenuous conversations that might take place in public and that Milton here assumes to be excruciating. See *Complete Prose Works of John Milton*, vol. 2, 239, 251, 273, 739, 755, 597, 731, 733.

44. Wendy Wall has argued that in the seventeenth century, domestic space simply cannot be characterised in this way. See *Staging Domesticity: Household Work and English Identity in Early Modern Drama* (Cambridge: Cambridge University Press, 2002), 13.

45. *Writing the English Republic*, 485–9.

46. While I have shown how this is implicit in his reading of Adam and Eve, it is made more explicit in Norbrook's recuperation of Milton's advocacy in *Areopagitica* of *vita activa* – his revival of the classical republican notion that equates privacy with *privatus* (or privation) and his emphasis on the good life being the public one. See 'Milton's *Areopagitica*, Censorship, and the Early Modern Public Sphere', 3–33, in Richard Burt

(ed.), *The Administration of Aesthetics: Censorship, Political Criticism and the Public Sphere* (Minneapolis, MN: University of Minnesota Press, 1994). Part of this article can be found in 118–39 of *Writing the English Republic*.

47. See *Complete Prose Works*, vol. 2, 362–415. Cicero is recommended reading in the fields of ethics, politics and rhetoric.

48. Milton is rarely compared at length with Cicero, and when he is, it is usually with emphasis on the value of self-government and the sort of civic virtue that would foster it; often this entails a focus on elements of Ciceronian thinking that are compatible with Plato, and particularly with the Platonic advocacy of rational self-control set against the passions. See Martin Dzelzainis, 'Milton's Classical Republicanism', 3–24, in *Milton and Republicanism*; Dzelzainis, 'Milton and the Limits of Ciceronian Rhetoric', 203–26 in Neil Rhodes (ed.), *English Renaissance Prose: History, Language, and Politics* (Tempe, AZ: Medieval and Renaissance Texts and Studies, 1997); William Walker, 'Human Nature in Republican Tradition and *Paradise Lost*', *Early Modern Literary Studies* 10:1 (2004); and Todd Sammons, 'Ciceronian Inventio and Dispositio in Belial's Speech during the Debate in Hell', 14–21, in *Milton Quarterly* 25:1 (1991).

49. Plato, *Gorgias*, trans. Donald J. Zeyl (Indianapolis, IN: Hackett, 1987).

50. For a recent account of Stoicism and how scrupulous its management of the passions (as a form of false judgement) could be, see Martha Nussbaum, 'The Stoics on the Extirpation of the Passions', 359–401, in *The Therapy of Desire* (Princeton, NJ: Princeton University Press, 1994).

51. For his strongest statement against immoderation (one that is incompatible with the oratorical treatises), see his attack on Epicurean philosophy at the close of M. T. Griffin and E. M. Atkins (eds), *On Duties* (Cambridge: Cambridge University Press, 1991), 145–7, and in the first two books of Julia Annas (ed.), *On Moral Ends*, trans. Raphael Woolf (New York: Cambridge University Press, 2001). To appreciate fully the depth of differences (despite similarities) between public behaviour advocated by Cicero and by Diogenes, see the chapter on Diogenes, 22–83, in R. D. Hicks (ed.), 'Diogenes Laertius', *Lives of Eminent Philosophers*, vol. 2 (New York: G. P. Putnam's Son's, 1925); and 'The Sixth Discourse: Diogenes, Or On Tyranny', 249–84, in J. W. Cohoon (ed.), *Dio Chrysostom I* (New York: G. P. Putnam's Sons, 1932).

52. Unlike Diogenes, Cicero is opposed to actions 'strongly discordant with civilized behavior, such as singing in the forum', and even says that 'the reasoning of the Cynics must be entirely rejected' (*On Duties*, 56–7). And Cicero certainly subscribes to public/private divides in his emphases on decorum and seemliness (37–9, 49–50).

53. *De Oratore III*, in *De Oratore III, De Fato, Paradoxa Stoicorum, De Partitione Oratoria*, trans. H. Rackham (Cambridge, MA: Harvard University Press, 1982), 49.

54. *De Oratore II*, in *De Oratore I and II*, trans. E. W. Sutton (Cambridge, MA: Harvard University Press, 1948), 285. Indeed, Cicero goes so far as to claim that being won over is more often a matter of passion than of deliberation. 'Nothing in oratory', he writes, 'is more important than to win for the orator the favour of his hearer, and to have the latter so

affected as to be swayed by something resembling a mental impulse or emotion, rather than by judgement or deliberation.' See *On the Orator*, in *On the Good Life*, trans. Michael Grant (New York: Penguin, 1971), 255; and *De Oratore I and II*, 325.

55. *On the Orator*, 247.
56. *De Oratore III*, 83.
57. See *Orator* in *Brutus/Orator*, trans. G. L. Hendrickson and H. M. Hubbell (Cambridge, MA: Harvard University Press, 1939), 473, 477. The power of metaphor, for instance, derives from how it 'directly hits the senses' and 'give[s] people much more pleasure' than mere description. See *De Oratore III*, 125–9.
58. See *De Oratore III*, 149, 155, 157; *Orator* 441, 457, 479; and *De Oratore III*, 81.
59. *De Oratore I and II*, 223.
60. *On the Orator*, 246.
61. *De Oratore I and II*, 339, 333.
62. *De Oratore I and II*, 331; *On the Orator*, 246, 307.
63. *Complete Prose Works*, vol. 2, 523, 527.
64. See especially the subsection entitled 'Institutions of the Public Sphere', 31–43, in *The Structural Transformation of the Public Sphere*.
65. *A Preface to Paradise Lost*, 105.
66. See *Milton and the Revolutionary Reader*, esp. 205–13.
67. One example would be the moment in which the narrator distinguishes Love's revels in Paradise from less genuine ones; Love reigns 'not in the bought smile / Of harlots, loveless, joyless unendeared, / Casual fruitions, nor in court amours, / Mixed dance, or wanton masque, or midnight ball' (7.765–8).
68. See *The Major Works*, 310.
69. *Complete Prose Works*, vol. 2, 545.
70. Merritt Hughes (ed.), *Complete Prose Works*, vol. 3 (New Haven, CT: Yale University Press, 1962), 212.
71. *Milton and the Revolutionary Reader*, 213.
72. As Weinfield has shown, this advice is aligned with a certain tradition of enlightenment from Bacon to Voltaire, one that understands reason as that which calculates; this is a tradition that, in Weinfield's account, emphasises 'the necessity of working without speculating' (206).
73. *The Major Works*, 317.
74. French Fogle (ed.), *Complete Prose Works*, vol. 5, pt. 1 (New Haven, CT: Yale University Press, 1971), 37.
75. Don M. Wolfe (ed.), *Complete Prose Works of John Milton*, vol. 1 (New Haven, CT: Yale University Press, 1953), 364.
76. *On Duties*, 41, 6–7, 36.
77. *On Duties*, 36; *Brutus*, 215–17, 231.
78. *De Oratore III*, 41.
79. *Orator*, 361.
80. See *The Second Defence* in *The Major Works*, 320.
81. This quotation is drawn from *The Major Works*.
82. Though neither is interested in the coffeehouse for the same reasons as I am, some critics, such as Christopher Hill and Stephen Dobranski,

have made some tentative connections between Milton and this seventeenth-century space. See Hill's *Milton and the English Revolution* (Harmondsworth: Penguin, 1977), 98; and Dobranski's '"Where Men of Differing Judgments Croud": Milton and the Culture of the Coffee Houses', in *The Seventeenth Century* 9:1 (1994), 36.

83. See Habermas, *The Structural Transformation*, 32–3.

84. Aytoun Ellis, *The Penny Universities: A History of the Coffeehouse* (London: Secker & Warburg, 1956), 34.

85. For a dramatisation of the diverse range of personalities and topics of discourse and performance in the coffeehouse, see *The character of a Coffee-House* by 'eye and ear witness', 1665.

86. *A Character of Coffee and Coffee-Houses*, 1661.

87. According to the author of *A Character of Coffee and Coffee-Houses*, '[a] School it is without a Master' where people have a 'confused way of gabbling'.

88. *The Character of a Coffeehouse; with the symptoms of a town-wit*, 1673.

89. *A cup of coffee, or Coffee in its Colours*, 1663.

90. *The Character of a Coffeehouse; with the symptoms of a town-wit*. For another pamphlet that emphasises the devilry of coffee and the coffee-house, see *The Maidens complaint against coffee*, 1663.

91. *Coffeehouses Vindicated*, 1674.

92. For more on behaviour in coffeehouses, see Lawrence E. Klein, 'Coffeehouse Civility, 1660–1714: An Aspect of Post-Courtly Culture in England', in *Huntington Library Quarterly* 59:1 (1997), 36–7, 40. For more on Whig and Tory characterisations of the coffeehouse, see Lawrence E. Klein, *Shaftesbury and the Culture of Politeness: Moral Discourse and Cultural Politics in Early Eighteenth Century England* (Cambridge: Cambridge University Press, 1994), 97–8. Two recent studies, Markman Ellis's *The Coffee House: A Cultural History* (London: Weidenfeld & Nicolson, 2004), and especially Brian Cowan's *The Social Life of Coffee* (New Haven, CT: Yale University Press, 2005), have begun to describe the pleasures afforded by this early modern space, though without much attention to its connection with reason and argument.

93. *Milton and the Revolutionary Reader*, 25. See the introduction of Achinstein's book for her account of how the 'torrent of words' in Revolutionary England offered opportunities for the cultivation of critical discernment.

94. Many of the texts of these figures are covered in Chapter 1. See also Worden's four chapters on English republicanism in *Republicanism, Liberty, and Commercial Society, 1649–1776* (Stanford, CA: Stanford University Press, 1994), as well as his entry on English republicanism, 443–75, in the *Cambridge History of Political Thought, 1450–1700*, ed. J. H. Burns (Cambridge: Cambridge University Press, 1991).

95. Fink, the first modern critic to label Milton a classical republican, claims that Milton wanted to justify the popular will as part of a mixed state, but could only do so if the 'mad multitude' employed reason to restrain irrational passion. See *The Classical Republicans: An Essay in the Recovery of a Pattern of Thought in Seventeenth Century England* (Evanston, IL: Northwestern University Press, 1945), 116–18. For some

examples of reason set in opposition to passion, see Skinner, *Visions of Politics*, vol. 2 (New York: Cambridge University Press, 2002), 290, and 'Classical Liberty and the Coming of the English Civil War', 9–28, in vol. II of Martin Van Gelderen and Skinner (eds), *Republicanism: A Shared European Heritage*, vol. II: *The Values of Republicanism in Early Modern Europe* (New York: Cambridge University Press, 2002); Worden, *Republicanism, Liberty, and Commercial Society*, 46, 57; and 'Milton and the Tyranny of Heaven', in Gisela Bock, Skinner and Maurizio Viroli (eds), *Machiavelli and Republicanism* (Cambridge: Cambridge University Press, 1990), 229; Scott, *Commonwealth Principles*, 153, 171; and Perez Zagorin, *Milton: Aristocrat and Rebel: the Poet and his Politics* (New York: D. S. Brewer, 1992), 153–4.

96. See *The Political Works of James Harrington* (Cambridge: Cambridge University Press, 1977), 23.
97. See *The Commonwealth of Oceana and A System of Politics* (Cambridge: Cambridge University Press, 2001), 10, 19.
98. Just before he enumerates a few factors common to most republicans, Norbrook shows how English republicanism 'was not a fixed entity' (*Writing the English Republic*, 18).
99. Although he supplies a list of basic republican commitments, for instance, Worden writes that republicanism 'was never a self-contained or self-sufficient programme'. *Republicanism, Liberty, and Commercial Society*, 46, and 'Milton and the Tyranny of Heaven', 227.
100. *Writing the English Republic*, 18.
101. *The Political Works of James Harrington*, 15.
102. 'The republicanism of the 1650s', says Worden in a much-cited dictum, 'was a protest against the English republic, not a celebration of it.' *Republicanism, Liberty, and Commercial Society*, 48.
103. *The Major Works*, 335, 339.
104. 'Milton and the Tyranny of Heaven', 244.
105. Arendt, *The Human Condition* (Chicago: University of Chicago Press, 1958), 207.
106. In the commonplace book, for instance, Milton registers that 'The study of laws, by an edict very well known, being considered not as a liberal art but as a trade and a really mechanical art, [was] brought into the world to harass the human race' (*Complete Prose Works*, vol. 1), 468.
107. Discussing how republicans knew that 'action involved innovating, changing the world,' and that, because action produces change, it is necessarily deprived 'of the conditions which had legitimated it', Pocock argues that the fact of contingency – of the unstable, fleeting effects of all action – is never far from the foreground of republican thought. Thus 'the republic was most often invoked as a paradigm of extreme difficulty, bordering on impossibility, of achieving stability in the political world.' *The Political Writings of James Harrington*, 18, 17.
108. For more along these lines, see Wendy Brown, *Politics Out of History* (Princeton, NJ: Princeton University Press, 2001), esp. Chapter 5, 'Politics without Banisters: Genealogical Politics in Nietzsche and Foucault'.

Epilogue: The Futures of Open Subjects

In considering the history of selfhood, I have at points also considered how selves can and should go about shaping their futures. The last chapter, for instance, focused on how we can use critical discipline to alter the degree to which we are vulnerable – to others, to their words and to the structures of the world. An underlying question had to do with whether, in managing how structures affect us, we might enduringly affect them.

For Habermasian critics of Milton, the answer is yes. Rational conversation at its best leads to agreement about how the legislative sphere might bring about a definite, improved future for the bounded self. Indeed, the republican criticism with which I have taken issue in this book invests in boundedness not just as a practice of the self (of self-protection) but also as what legislation can help secure, more or less in perpetuity. I have shown how such investment is evident not just in Milton studies but in Richard Chamberlain's account of the boundary-respecting politics of friendship in *The Faerie Queene*; in Patterson's admiration of the Roman citizens' demands for free speech and for protection against Coriolanus; and in the high marks that she and Norbrook give to Maria Fairfax for her supposedly proto-liberal powers of self-possession. In these literary accounts as well as in many historical and political ones, the greatest value of our social practices – our friendships and our civic lives, our private conversations and our public arguments – rests in how they can guarantee personal boundaries, including and perhaps especially when the guarantee comes in lasting, legislative form.

From this perspective, attending too much to what does not last leads to trouble that never ends. Without question, this is the attitude expressed in Adam's lamentations after eating: 'O fleeting joys / Of Paradise, dear bought with lasting woes!' (10.741–2). Focus on what is fleeting, Adam suggests, makes us forget, to our peril, that some things last all too long – things that cannot be reversed once they are in place. But for Milton, as for most republicans, the transitory does not always lead to tragedy, and too much belief in immutability equals illusion. Work by Cicero through Nedham and beyond, Chapter 1 showed, assumes that for every subject and every republic there arrives an end, one that often comes earlier than we anticipate and that makes hopes of either's permanence appear misplaced. I have attended to how republican thought is, thus, as much about everyday practice, requiring daily renewal and existing only in moments – our attitudes and priorities, the virtues we privilege in a given instance – as it is about durable constitutions and lasting bodies of law. When we privilege courage, as republicans such as Cicero often do, we embrace vulnerability as virtue; and when vulnerability is virtue, the present bulks large. Our futures recede from view and become radically uncertain.

According to Cicero and English Renaissance republicans, this is not simply reason for despair, or for Stoic endurance. Embracing what does not last is not always sinister – for Milton, Marvell, Shakespeare and Spenser alike. I have described how this is so the night that Britomart and Amoret spend 'twixt themselves alone'; when Aufidius relates the dream in which he and Coriolanus undo each other; when Isabel Thwaites is taken in at the nunnery about to be dispossessed; and, in the last chapter, when the fallen angels have their brief triumph over the divine wrath that has enfeebled them. For my figures of focus, vulnerability can be as attractive as it is admirable.

The point, I think, bears emphasis. I thus want to end with a few words about Satan, the fallen angel who least appreciates being vulnerable, and contrast the future he imagines with the one that becomes imaginable when we instead hold vulnerability in high esteem.

Satan adopts an attitude akin to the one shared by Brutus and Sicinius in *Coriolanus*: the attitude of distance and calculating detachment. So often we find Satan looking downward, trying and failing to find delight in the destruction that is his ideal future, the future in which his rule, his brand of legislation, would supplant God's. Only when he gives up his maniacal desire to produce the fall, only when he can take his eyes off the horizon, does he experience the intensity of bliss, perhaps most notably when he beholds Eve:

Such pleasure took the serpent to behold
This flowery plot, the sweet recess of Eve
. . ..
That space the evil one abstracted stood
From his own evil and for the time remained stupidly good . . .

> But the hot hell that always in him burns,
> Though in mid-Heaven, soon ended his delight
>
> (9.453–70)

Satan is most pleased in such moments of transportation, when he is abstracted from himself, when his discipline is less than absolute – his self-perception less than exactly accurate and his future lost from view. Usually, for example, when he fabricates an account of himself for Gabriel, he can at best only describe the feeling. 'Who would not, finding way back, break loose from hell, / Though thither doomed?' he asks. Who would not 'hope to change / Torment with ease and soonest recompense / Dole with delight, which in this place I sought' (4.889–90, 892–4)? But for Satan change rarely takes place – he shifts from one pleasureless space to the next, so focused on his future as to exist almost as that imagined future, a bit of hell on earth all to himself. Time and again, 'like a devilish engine', Satan 'back recoils'

> Upon himself; horror and doubt distract
> His troubled thoughts and from the bottom stir
> The hell within him, for within him hell
> He brings, and round about him, nor from hell
> One step no more than from himself can fly
> By change of place.
>
> (4.17–23)

And so for Satan speech also reinforces his hell within, bringing any more therapeutic experience to an immediate end. When he watches Adam and Eve in Paradise, for example, he stands frozen in wonder, undone, but when he recovers his 'failed speech' it is only to reassume the self-hardening, distanced attitude that yields so little: 'should I at your harmless innocence / Melt, as I do, yet public reason just . . . / compels me now / To do what else, though damned, I should abhor' (4.357, 388–92). Unlike other fallen angels – and unlike, say, Britomart and Amoret – he cannot put giving an account of himself and his place in creation to pleasurable use. He cannot enjoy with others of the fallen the mere act of imagining an *Ausgang*; unable to access its escape, he explains to Jesus in *Paradise Regained*, he 'feel[s] by proof / That fellowship in pain divide not smart' (1.400–1).

Satan is inconsolable. He needs his world elsewhere to exist beyond the space and time of interaction; thus his speech proves him, as he puts it, 'only supreme / In misery' (4.91–2). His hell within is so intractable, so determinative of his self-conception, that he must lose the power of speech in order to partake of a curative akin to that of those who fell with him. Otherwise he cannot give himself what he does give them (whether or not he intends it), when so often his words enlighten their 'drooping cheer' (6.496–7).

He makes their 'unhappy mansion' (1.268) less miserable, as I have described, but not for himself. Instead he remains like those fallen angels who, after his departure, fail to entertain the irksome hours, those 'roving on / In confused march forlorn', 'the adventurous bands' who 'With shuddering horror pale and eyes aghast / Viewed first their lamentable lot and found / No rest' (2.614–19). Whatever shape he assumes, whichever perspective of distance he achieves in his unhappy adventures – in book 3 he finds a spot from which 'far and wide his eye commands,' 'a spot like which perhaps / Astronomer in the sun's lucent orb / Through his glazed optic tube yet never saw' (3.614, 588–90) – Satan remains, irreparably, what he is in God's eyes, a being who sees and who deserves to see 'undelighted all delight' (4.286).

Satan's aerial perspectives, mirrored in the critical distance that he seems to have on himself, cuts him off from the cheerful ways of men and fallen angels alike, cuts him off from pleasurable publics; his discipline and distance, his steadfast desire to legislate a durable future, afford him only the most excruciating self-knowledge, happiness permanently deferred. If Michael's instructions to Adam suggest the importance of developing futural discipline that would be impervious to emotional distraction, Milton's portrayal of Satan himself locates danger within that very discipline.

The great value of rational sociability in Pandemonium, by contrast, is defined by giving up Satanic distance. Like the world elsewhere that Coriolanus fleetingly brings into being, like the nunnery in 'Appleton House' that vanishes but reappears – like the friendship between vulnerable subjects that resurfaces time and again in *The Faerie Queene* – the fallen angels' pleasing sorcery occurs outside the sphere of legislation (in this case divine) that would give them a guarantee and that would aim to protect their form of life for good. But this outside is the only space that makes sense for them. Their sorcery can work only if they are vulnerable, only if the fallen angels are imperfectly protected against words, if their future – their damnation – can be made to seem uncertain. This means that the future of the vulnerable subject, like that of the Ciceronian republic, not only is but must be a precarious history of precarious life – the tenuous, contingent history of our tenuous, contingent existence, the none the less persistent history of lives embraced in all their precariousness.

Index